Visitor's Guide
Germany:
BAVARIA

VISITOR'S GUIDE

Germany:
BAVARIA

George Wood

MPC

Published by:
Moorland Publishing Co Ltd,
Moor Farm Road West, Ashbourne,
Derbyshire DE6 1HD England

ISBN 0 86190 372 2

1st edition 1987
2nd edition, fully revised and redesigned 1994

British Library Cataloguing in Publication Data:
A catalogue record for this book is available from the British Library.

Colour origination by: DP Graphics, Wiltshire

Printed in Hong Kong by: Wing King Tong Co Ltd

Cover photograph: *Königsee* (Hedley Alcock)
Rear Cover: *Statue of the Bavarian lion at Lindau* (MPC Picture Collection)
Title page: *Altes Rathaus, Lindau* (MPC Picture Collection)

Illustrations have been supplied by: H. Alcock: p82; MPC Picture Collection:
pp3, 22, 35, 43, 50, 58, 62, 63, 67 lower, 74, 95 top, 99 top, 135, 138 top;
U. Winter: p78; K. J. Wood: pp10 bottom, 71, 191; M. A. Wood: pp111 top;
all remaining illustrations are by the author.

Editorial & Design: John Robey
Cartography: Morag Eaton

CONTENTS

Key to Symbols used on the Maps

⋔	Church or Ecclesiastical Site	♣	Parkland
⌖	Museum or Art Gallery	⌖	Zoo or Animal Park
⊼	Archaeological Site	⌖	Skiing
⊞	Building of Interest	➤	Birdlife
⌖	Castle or Fortifications	⌖	Cave
⌔	Boating or Steamer Trips	✳	Other Places of Interest
⌖	Interesting Railway	⌖	Gardens
✐	Sports/Swimming Facilities	⌖	Walk

Key to Map Features

▬▬▬	Autobahn	———	National Border
▬▬▬	Other Roads	·—·—·—	Internal Border
▬▬▬	The Holiday Road	⬯	Lake and River
▪ ▪ ▪ ▪	The Romantic Road	- -•- -	S-bahn
▬▬▬	The Alpine Road	- - - -	Railway
▬▬▬	The Eastern Marches Road	⬟	Urban Areas
		●	Town or village

How To Use This Guide

This MPC Visitor's Guide has been designed to be as easy to use as possible. Each chapter covers a recommended route. MPC's distinctive **margin symbols**, **important places** printed in bold and a comprehensive **index**, enable the reader to find the most interesting places with ease. Each chapter has an **Additional Information** section giving addresses and opening times. The **Fact File** at the back of the book gives practical information and useful tips. The maps of each region show the main towns, villages and places of interest, but are not designed as route maps and a good road atlas will prove invaluable.

INTRODUCTION

Bavaria, or Bayern to give its German name, is the largest of the German states or *Länder*. The total land area is similar to that of Scotland, distances being roughly 370km from north to south and the same from east to west. In the south and south-east, Bavaria shares a border of some 400km with Austria, while on the eastern side is the Czech Republic. The northern and western borders are shared with the *Länder* of Thüringen, Hessen and Baden-Württemberg.

The political history of Bavaria is more complex than that of most other European countries. Inevitably it is necessary to refer to the political background but for the tourist and holidaymaker it will suffice, at this stage, to say that the former independent kingdom of Bavaria ceased to exist after World War I. It was absorbed into greater Germany at the end of March 1920, remaining after World War II in what became the Federal Republic. The last monarch was Ludwig III who does not appear to have been of particular significance. Several of his predecessors, however, had a profound influence on the development of their country, pride of place going, for the foreign visitor at least, to Ludwig II (ruled 1864–86).

Much of Bavaria is quite sparsely populated but there are several major centres of population of which München (Munich), the state capital, is the most important. The total population of Bavaria is around 10 million of whom well over half live in and around the principal cities and towns. The population of Bavaria is greater than that of Austria, Switzerland or Belgium. Whereas in Germany as a whole Catholics and Protestants are more or less evenly divided, in Bavaria some 71 per cent are Catholic. Thirty-five per cent of the land area is forest, the 'Bavarian Forest' with the adjoining 'Bohemian Forest' on the Czech side of the border constituting the largest afforested area in Europe. The Alps occupy some 15 per cent of the land leaving just 50 per cent for all other purposes, the most important of which is agriculture. Dairy-farming is important nearly everywhere and in the mountain regions there are traditional ceremonies associated with the movement of cows to the high pastures in the spring and their return in autumn.

The popular impression is that Bavarians are great beer drinkers and this is true in some areas, particularly München with its great breweries and the *Oktoberfest*. Nevertheless, beer certainly takes second place in the great Franconian wine-producing area with vineyards mostly along the River Main. In the south-west corner of Lower Bavaria (Niederbayern), in the district known as the Hallertau, is the largest hop-growing area in all Europe.

Germany's highest mountains are to be found in the Bavarian Alps along the border with Austria with such giants as the Zugspitze (2963m, 9718ft), the Hochblassen (2706m, 8875ft) and the Watzmann (2713m, 8898ft) to name just a few of the many peaks over 2,000m (6560ft). The rest of the state is by no means flat and there are some respectable summits along the Czech border with the Dreisessel (1332m, 4368ft), the Rachel (1453m, 4765ft) and the Arber (1457m, 4778ft) all providing a stiff challenge for the rambler.

Bavaria's waterways have long been important commercial arteries. From west to east the River Donau (Danube), which has its source in the Black Forest, flows for some 350 of its total 2850km length in Bavaria while in the opposite direction the Main (pronounced 'mine'), rising near Bayreuth, wends its tortuous way westwards for an almost identical distance to leave Bavaria only when it reaches the outskirts of Frankfurt. Not surprising that for centuries men have dreamed of linking these two great rivers to create a major east–west waterway. It was Kaiser Karl der Grosse (Charlemagne) who in the year 793 started the digging of a canal which would have achieved this object albeit on a fairly modest scale. King Ludwig I revived the idea in the 1820s and eventually a through route was established but only for vessels up to 120 tons and 32m (105ft) long. After World War II the project for a major link was once again revived and the new waterway which has been built provides through transit for vessels up to 110m (360ft) long and a load capacity of more than 1500 tons. So at last the dream has been realised. The Rhein-Main-Donau-Kanal between Bamberg on the Main and Kelheim on the Donau now enables large ships from northern France, the low countries, northern Germany and Switzerland to travel via an inland route to Austria and beyond to the Black Sea. Many other rivers criss-cross the land, some being navigable to a greater or lesser extent. Most of them drain into either the Donau or the Main.

There are many attractive lakes, some of which are described later. Since Bavaria has no coastline the lakes and rivers are popular for bathing and all kinds of water activities but as there are also dozens of attractive and well equipped swimming pools indoors and out there are always swimming possibilities near at hand.

The language of Bavaria is German and those with a knowledge of it are not likely to experience any difficulty. The *Bairisch* dialect — shared with Austria — has regional variations while the Regensburgers have their own distinctive speech. Then there is Swabian in the west — if anything even more of a puzzle than *Bairisch* — and Franconian in the north but all this need not worry the visitor unduly. English is widely understood; young Germans often learn English as their first foreign language and will be anxious to try out their knowledge on English-speaking visitors.

The inhabitants are not all alike, of course. A Bavarian can also call himself a Franconian or a Swabian for these areas have belonged to Bavaria since around 1800. The true Bavarian on the other hand, that is from Upper or Lower Bavaria or the Upper Palatinate, is a member of the same ancient race as the Austrians, though the latter are often reluctant to acknowledge this. The visitor who comes with a pre-conceived notion of a Bavarian as a beer-swilling, leather shorts-wearing yodeller will have to perform a rapid mental adjustment; and if his idea of a typical Bavarian house is a chalet with rocks on the roof he must be prepared for a lot of surprises.

Accommodation

Parts of Bavaria have long been popular tourist goals but since World War II the emphasis has been on Upper Bavaria with its mountains and winter sports facilities, made familiar by Olympic and other international events. Other areas have developed gradually over the years and there is now ample provision for holidaymakers everywhere with numerous camp sites and youth hostels, some of these in novel locations. In the chapters which follow it is not the intention to refer in detail to holiday accommodation. The reader may assume that in each place or the immediate vicinity there is a range of accommodation including hotels, inns, pensions, self-catering flats or bungalows and so on. Prices are generally modest but for the foreign visitor the 'value for money' depends largely on the international exchange rate prevailing at the time of the visit. Significant variations in the range in a particular place are mentioned. Needless to say, Germany's high accommodation standards prevail everywhere.

The Bavarian landscape varies from high mountains to quiet villages in wooded valleys. Missen (above) is ideal for walking in summer and skiing in winter; the Zugspitze, in winter (below)

Architecture

Architecture cannot fail to feature to some extent in the itinerary of every visitor. Bavaria is extremely rich in fine buildings both religious and secular and reference has been made to examples of the various styles as this fascinating country is explored. From a church architecture point of view, 1803 was a momentous year for this was when the so-called 'secularisation' took place and the Catholic religious foundations in particular were dissolved by the Bavarian state and stripped of their assets. Great harm was done to the Church and not only were Bavarian religious traditions overturned but there were enormous losses of cultural value.

There are virtually hundreds of castles or palaces and mention is made of some of the most important of these. Since nearly every one is to a greater of lesser extent a museum, and many museums are housed in historic buildings anyway, they have all been listed together in the 'Additional Information' sections at the end of each chapter. While many architectural styles are represented in Bavaria, it is the baroque and rococo which reign supreme:

Barock (baroque). The style of the seventeenth and eighteenth centuries with Italian origins. Free use of allegorical decorations in relief by means of stucco (pulverised marble and plaster) and adoption of relief effect by painting. Baroque is the outstanding art form of Upper Bavaria. Examples: the *Klosterkirche* in Fürstenfeldbruck and the *Rathaus* (town hall) in Landsberg.

Rokoko (rococo). Playful development of baroque adopted in the eighteenth century, principally between 1720 and 1780. Much gilding and decoration with a shell motif. The form reached its peak in Upper Bavarian churches where with the aid of stucco, relief and painting, the impression of space, height etc is no longer limited by the physical dimensions of the building. Examples: church at Wies and the Amalienburg (Nymphenburg) in München.

Kirche is the usual word for church and, as in the example above, is often incorporated with the name of the church as one word. A cathedral is *Dom* or occasionally *Münster*.

Festivals

Bavaria is a land of festivals and at almost any season there is some event which the traveller should endeavour to see or participate in. The mid-winter visitor will find much of interest with Christmas markets and numerous festivities from the beginning of December until Christmas Eve, Christmas itself and then New Year. The use of candles on Christmas trees is still common in Germany and adds a nice touch. New Year's Eve (*Sylvesterabend*) is a time for merry-making and every district has it own brand of activity with either a religious or a secular slant to the goings-on. Everywhere though, there is an atmosphere of expectation as midnight approaches and as soon as the clock strikes twelve the air is filled with noise as fire-crackers are let off, drums are beaten and voices are raised in excitement. All this is supposed to stem from ancient rites performed to drive away evil spirits at the opening of a new year. Nowadays it is largely a matter of having a traditional excuse for yet another evening of jollity, not that the fun-loving Bavarians really need any excuse.

In the New Year, 6 January is *Dreikönigstag*, Three Kings' Day (Epiphany) and some families wait until this day before adding the kings to the Christmas crib. By the ninth century the three kings, sometimes called the Magi, had acquired the names of Caspar or Kaspar, Melchior and Balthasar. The Christmas story of the visit of the kings to the baby Jesus is well known and prior to the Reformation many miracle plays were performed re-enacting the famous journey. In many Roman Catholic areas a modified form of the ceremonial has persisted in the form of *Sternsinger* (star singers) who don regal robes and go through the streets or from house to house collecting for charity. In the Bavarian Alps the group may be accompanied by others who form a procession and stop from time to time to sing carols appropriate to this time. Many superstitions are connected with Epiphany; to the visitor the most obvious is the chalk inscription often seen on the door lintel with the initials of the kings and the numerals of the year on either side written thus: 19C + M + B94. The chalk marks often endure throughout the following year. Pre-lenten jollifications take various forms and names, with *Fasching* in München of particular interest. The church calendar provides numerous reasons for a holiday or festival and every town and village has its own special events to celebrate as well. Mention is made of many of these later in the book.

Visitors may come across posters advertising a *Dult*. This word rarely appears in dictionaries; it is normally associated with a church anniversary, for example that of the consecration of the church. In Bavaria it is often widened to include annual fairs and markets, especially where there is no permanent market or market day. The *Dult* is then something of a cross between a street market, a flea-market (*Flohmarkt*) and a jumble sale, and no two are alike. Early May is a favourite time for these fairs which may be called *Auedult* (meadow market) or *Maidult* (May market). There is also a *Hofdult* (court market) in Altötting in May-June, a *Frauendult* (women's market) in Pfaffenhofen (August) and even a *Nikolausdult* in Schrobenhausen on 6 December. Lists of public holidays are given in the Fact File.

Touring and Travel

A glance at the map reveals that Bavaria begins in the west just about 20km from the centre of Frankfurt and since that city is a focal point for travellers by road, rail or air this seems to be the logical place to start touring. Visitors not taking their own car could hire a vehicle at Frankfurt for there is no doubt that with a car one can make much better use of the time available, even though Bavaria is remarkably well served by the Deutsche Bundesbahn — Federal Railway — and by some private lines and 'bus services.

Where distances are referred to the metric versions are used since these are found on signposts and maps, but for important distances the imperial equivalents are also given. In a few cases there are established English versions of place names as well as the German ones and both are given initially and thereafter the German form is used. Words which occur frequently such as *Rathaus* (town hall), *Kirche* (church), *Kloster* (monastery, nunnery, convent, etc), *Gasthof* (inn) etc have an English translation given the first time they arise and thereafter the German form is used as being more helpful to the visitor. The glossary in the 'Fact File' can be consulted in case of doubt. Reference has been made to some of the gastronomic specialities of the various regions, best sought out in the old family inns rather than in modern 'chain' establishments. It should be noted that most restaurants and inns close for one day a week for their *Ruhetag* (rest day). If the *Ruhetag* of an establishment mentioned is known, this has been stated in the text.

An endeavour has been made to divide Bavaria into areas which can be fitted into a logical touring pattern. Most of the areas are too big to be covered from a single base and this guide generally assumes that a progressive tour will be made.

The whole of Bavaria is very good rambling country and much has been done to encourage the walker to see the best of the countryside. Numerous long-distance paths have been identified and thousands of walks have been marked by local authorities or rambling organisations, with details obtainable at local tourist information offices. Nevertheless, it is prudent to obtain a fairly large-scale map of the area if only to avoid missing something of interest and it is, of course, essential if one intends to depart from the waymarked paths. Nor has

Feuchtwangen, on the Romantic Road, is one of Bavaria's many colourful small historic towns, where the visitor will find much of interest

The mayor takes a break with the spectators during Grafenau's summer festival

the cyclist been forgotten. Many parts are ideal for cycling and some hosts have bicycles available for the use of their guests. In any case, bicycles can be hired quite cheaply everywhere. (See 'Fact File'.)

The motorist will often wish to use his vehicle to reach the starting point of a walk and for his benefit many free *Wanderparkplätze* (walker's parking places) have been provided. These usually have a map showing the rambles in the vicinity with details of the waymarks, distances or time required for each walk. All such walks can be completed in one day, the majority being less than 10km. Some of these special car parks can be recognised by their distinctive blue 'P' sign with a pictogram of a couple of hikers. The motorist will also require a smaller scale map for his travels about the area and those available from filling stations are very suitable for this. For example, sheets 4, 5, 6 and 7 of the series issued by Aral cover the whole of Bavaria at a scale of 1:400,000. Their filling stations also carry a series specially designed for the touring holidaymaker at a scale of 1:200,000. For those with some knowledge of German there are many booklets obtainable locally giving detailed descriptions of walks. Walking is the single most popular activity and while a book of this size cannot contain a comprehensive catalogue of the rambling possibilities, most chapters will include details of walks which may be regarded as typical of the area.

Finally, a few tips for the travelling tourist. Plan the day's itinerary with care in order not to miss worthwhile sights which may not lie on the direct route. Don't attempt too much in one day — leave time for a leisurely meal, a quiet stroll, a swim or just a seat in the sun. Avoid the main tourist attractions at weekends and holidays. It is always quieter in spring or autumn; if visiting Bavaria in summer, plan your sightseeing if you can for mid-week and early in the morning or towards evening. Take care to be suitably clad for the weather. Especially in the mountains the weather can change very quickly so before setting out on a ramble or ski-tour check the weather prospects. The locals will usually know if the signs are favourable for their own district.

Wear sensible footwear for walking. Town shoes, sandals and high heels are of no use in the mountains. In hilly areas do not be tempted to leave a marked path for an attractive-looking short cut through meadows or woods.

When travelling from place to place without pre-booking, avoid big and crowded hotels and seek the more modest rural inns and *pensions*, many of which enjoy a local reputation for good food and regional specialities.

1
THE ROMANTIC ROAD & ALLGÄU

The Romantic Road

The Romantic Road (Romantische Strasse) is the oldest and one of the longest of Germany's many tourist routes and runs from Würzburg in the north to Füssen on the fringe of the Alps in the south, a distance of some 350km. Würzburg can be reached by road or rail from Frankfurt in less than $1\frac{1}{2}$ hours.

A good starting point for exploring **Würzburg** (population 130,000) is the Court Garden (Hofgarten) attached to the Residenz — the home of the former prince-bishops of Würzburg. The square on the town side of the palace provides plenty of parking space (2-hour time limit). Do not overlook the fantastic wrought-iron entrance gate at the eastern end of the building. A nearby statue shows the creator of this masterpiece, dressed in his working clothes.

Then this magnificent palace, the creation of Balthasar Neumann (1687–1753), the most significant architect of south German baroque, must be inspected. Napoleon enviously described it as Europe's stateliest parsonage. At 13 years Balthasar was apprenticed in the trade of casting cannons and bells and when he was 24 came to Würzburg to work in Kopp's foundry. A loan from his home town and the support of some well-wishers enabled him to give up manual work and study geometry, surveying and architecture. In 1714 he was accepted as an ensign in the prince's forces and between purely military duties worked with Greising on Kloster Ettal, visited Vienna and worked in Milan before he was promoted to engineer-captain and in 1719 built his first house in Würzburg. Such was his meteoric rise to fame that the following year he was entrusted with the building of the Residenz and in 1722 with the oversight of all civic building in the city so that even where he was not responsible for the design, something of his taste and aptitude came through. When Friedrich Carl von Schönborn became prince-bishop of Bamberg and Würzburg in 1729 the completion of the still unfinished Residenz was authorised — it took until 1744 — and the now Lieutenant-Colonel Neumann was appointed director of all military, church and civil architecture in both bishoprics.

The splendid emperor's hall in the high central pavilion of the Residenz has a ceiling painting (1751) by the famous artist G. B. Tiepolo. At performances during the annual Mozart festival in June this hall is lit by hundreds of candles and the walks in the garden are lined with hundreds of flickering coloured lights. Across the street from the main building are the Bavarian State Wine Cellars for this is the land of the esteemed Franconian wine with the greatest vineyards in all Bavaria. Wine-tastings (*Weinproben*) take place almost every day and visitors are cordially welcomed.

A route from the Residenz in the old town on the east side of the River Main to the Marienberg fortress on the west side can be devised to take in most of the important cultural sights of the city. The town scene is enhanced by the towers and cupolas of many churches; a little to the north through Theaterstrasse which opens off the Residenzplatz (*Platz* means square) is the Stift-Haug-Kirche which should be visited if only to see the monumental crucifixion (1585) by Jacopo Tintoretto. Back towards the town centre is the Augustiner-kirche and the baroque façade of the Neumünster before reaching the Domplatz. St Kilian's *Dom* was only re-consecrated in 1967 after war damage. It contains elements of building styles and works of art from 855 to the present day. The ceiling of the choir is very fine but the rebuilt main and side aisles are rather disappointing in comparison; the mixture of old and new is not to everybody's taste.

Several more churches in the immediate vicinity are worthy of inspection but if time is limited the visitor should now make his way down towards the river, past the Marktplatz (Market Place) to the Altes Rathaus (old town hall) and then on to the Alte Mainbrücke (old Main bridge) to enjoy what is undoubtedly the most photographed Würzburg view, that of the Marienberg fortress on the hill above vineyards and as foreground the baroque figures of bishops and early saints upon the bridge itself. The figures include that of St Johann Nepomuk. He is the patron saint of bridges and also of Bohemia where he lived in the fourteenth century and was chaplain to Queen Sophia. Her husband Wenceslas suspected Sophia of infidelity and wanted Nepomuk to disclose what she had said in the confessional. When the priest refused to do this the king had him bound and thrown into the river from the highest bridge in Prague.

*The garden front of
the Würzburg
Residenz*

*Statue of St Johann
Nepomuk, Würzburg*

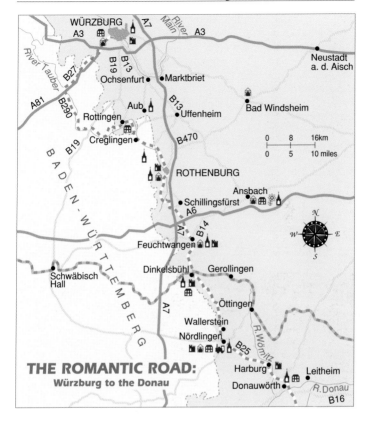

THE ROMANTIC ROAD:
Würzburg to the Donau

Nothing happened to prove the Queen's innocence nor did any divine intervention save Nepomuk's life but the onlookers saw a remarkable sight. When the drowning priest came to the surface for the third time he was wearing a glittering gold halo in which were five gleaming stars. As here in Würzburg Nepomuk is often easily recognised wearing his halo with the five stars as he stands watch on many bridges in central and western Europe. Another of the figures on the bridge is St Kilian after whom the cathedral is named.

Pedestrians may cross the bridge to reach the Marienberg fortress up fairly steep zig-zag paths. There is also parking space at the top. There is a *Gaststätte* (restaurant) up here, but the real goal is the splendid Mainfränkisches (Main-Franconian) Museum housed in the fortress. Galleries with various themes lead to the Riemenschneider Room. Tilman Riemenschneider (1440–1531) of Würzburg produced altarpieces, sepulchres, reliefs and statues for churches and dignitaries. He also helped to run the city, serving variously as councillor, judge, tax-collector, head of local defence and finally *Bürgermeister* (mayor), the highest civic post. In 1525 the Peasant's Revolt erupted across Germany; Riemenschneider refused to send troops to quell the uprising, but the revolt failed and he was imprisoned. Eventually released he died 6 years later aged 71. The museum houses many of his works, often brought back from locations far away to make this significant collection in his home town. The centrepiece is his sculpture *Eva*, considered to be his finest work. Without doubt the title 'Master Carver of the Middle Ages' is well deserved. There is a fine view over the city from the castle terrace.

Music plays an important part in the cultural life of Würzburg and in addition to the Mozart festival there is a 'baroque' festival in May as well as many occasional concerts, recitals and so on. There is a Kilian Folk Festival in July and the Wine-producer's Festival lasts for about ten days at the end of September. Würzburg is an excellent centre for touring and a booklet describing possible itineraries for day excursions is available from the information office near the *Hauptbahnhof* (main railway station). Würzburg is also a starting or calling point for various cruises up and down the River Main, mostly during the summer months.

The Romantic Road leaves Würzburg as Bundesstrasse (Federal Road) No 8 (such main roads will henceforth be identified only by the prefix 'B') and in the suburb of **Höchberg** watch for signs 'Romantische Strasse' and join B27 towards Tauberbischofsheim. However, this town, together with others such as Bad Mergentheim and Weikersheim on this part of the road actually lie outside the Bavarian border.

The traveller wishing to remain within Bavaria should leave Würzburg via Mergentheimer Strasse (B19) and head directly south for Röttingen (about 30km, 19 miles) to join the Romantische Strasse as it follows the pretty little River Tauber. **Röttingen** is little more than a substantial village. The baroque *Rathaus* presides over the small market place which presents a fairly unspoiled medieval scene. There is a small historical exhibition in the lobby. The old town wall has seven towers and the new bridge over the Tauber is once again under the eye of Nepomuk. There is an archaeological trail and also a rather surprising one with the theme of sundials which are found in considerable numbers in this area. For about five weeks in July-August there is a theatre festival here which attracts its audience from a wide area. About 10km north-east of Röttingen the parish church in the village of **Aub** has a crucifixion group by Riemen-schneider and the 1482 *Rathaus* overlooks a pleasant little square which has a notable baroque pillar surmounted by a gilded figure of the Virgin Mary.

In this valley there are signs — a bicycle above the words 'Liebliches Taubertal' (Lovely Tauber Valley) — which mark the line of a 100km (62 mile) cycle ramble between Wertheim where the Tauber enters the Main west of Würzburg and Rothenburg, a peace-ful route equally available to the walker. From Röttingen only a few minutes are needed to reach **Bieberehren**. Turn off the main road here and cross the river to the foot of the Kreuzberg, a modest hill surmounted by a chapel to which the approach — 274 steps — is flanked by the Stations of the Cross in a series of very detailed reliefs. From the chapel there is an extensive view eastwards over the valley.

Back on the Romantische Strasse pass through the village of **Klingen**, cross the Tauber again and leave Bavaria briefly to visit the attractive little town of **Creglingen** where one of Tilman Riemen-schneider's most famous masterpieces, the Marienalter, can be seen in the Herrgottskirche (Church of the Lord God).

Beyond Creglingen the named road re-enters Bavaria for the last time and after about 17km (11 miles) a brief halt should be made in the village of **Detwang** on the outskirts of Rothenburg to visit the little 1,000-year-old church of St Peter and St Paul. There is much of interest but the main attraction is another famous work by Riemenschneider, his Altar of the Holy Cross. It was originally made in 1508 for St Michael's Chapel in Rothenburg and was moved to Detwang in 1653.

Cross the river and climb steeply up to **Rothenburg ob der Tauber** (Rothenburg above the Tauber). The town walls are complete (total length 2.5km) and ample free car parks are available outside them. As one approaches Rothenburg today it must look much as it has done to travellers over the centuries for little has changed. So must the invading Swedish mercenaries of General Tilly have seen it in 1633; but they fully intended to ravage and destroy the town to take revenge upon the citizens for their stubborn defence. Tilly rode into the market place and, having lined up Bürgermeister Nusch and the town councillors before him, demanded wine before giving the soldiers leave to do their worst. He was handed a large silver cup and drank deeply; 'How much does this cup hold?' he demanded of Nusch. Upon learning that it held more than 3 litres he challenged the Bürgermeister to drain it in a single draught saying that if he did so, the city and the lives of the people would be spared. The cup was refilled and handed to the trembling Nusch who put it to his lips and

Rothenburg

drank steadily until it was drained. Tilly kept his word and Rothenburg was saved. The story is the subject of a folk-play each year at Whitsuntide; while every day at 11 o'clock crowds gather in the market place to see the drama re-enacted — albeit rather stiffly — by wooden busts of Tilly and Nusch in windows either side of the clock on the front of the Hall of Councillors.

More than 300 years later the town was again threatened with destruction when, during the closing stages of World War II, General Devers was planning an assault with his American troops. An American citizen working with the army knew and loved the city and persuaded Devers to spare it if a surrender could be arranged. The civilian worked out the terms and Rothenburg was declared an open city. Its beauties are enjoyed today because of this intervention by J. J. McCloy who was later to become the US High Commissioner in Germany and, fittingly, Honorary Patron of Rothenburg.

It cannot be denied that Rothenburg (population 12,500) is a perfect gem and in summer it is very crowded. The discerning traveller is advised to come at a quiet time of year to enjoy the many delights. Then he can stroll through the pleasant old streets, walk the walls or enjoy a leisurely meal in one of the excellent hostelries in the town. St Jakob's church (1311–1471) has many works of art including three Riemenschneider altars; there is a fine organ on which there are regular recitals in the summer. The medieval Kriminalmuseum has a gruesome collection of instruments of torture from all over Europe and traces the history of crime and punishment — not for the squeamish. The Puppen- und Spielzeug (doll and toy) Museum has dolls from 1780 to 1940 and many other toys. The tower of the *Rathaus* (thirteenth and sixteenth century) provides a wonderful bird's eye view of the town and surrounding countryside. The little Puppet Theatre has shows to appeal to various age groups. But above all, Rothenburg is a place for walking and looking.

From a base in or near Rothenburg many worthwhile excursions are possible. The motorist could reach the Main Valley towns of Ochsenfurt and Marktbreit comfortably in half an hour and Würzburg itself in less than an hour. **Uffenheim** is a pleasant town and has a highly superior camp/caravan site adjacent to the large, modern, heated outdoor swimming pool. To the north-east on the edge of the Naturpark Steigerwald, **Bad Windsheim** (population 12,000) is noted specially for the Fränkisches-Freiland open-air museum in which houses and farms have been re-erected to display the life-style and conditions of the Franconian countryside from the fourteenth century to the present. No dead museum this; the houses are assembled in three tiny villages and rural life carries on as in the past. Here also are the Ochsenhof-Museum, local history and art housed in a former grain store dating from 1537 and the Vorge-schichtsmuseum, a branch of the pre-history museum in München telling the geological and geographical history of this area.

East of Rothenburg on the southern fringe of the Naturpark Frankenhöhe is **Ansbach**, a delightful town with close on 50,000 inhabitants. The *Schloss* (palace) is the former Margrave's residence, started in 1713 on the site of an earlier palace. The great hall is two storeys high with a musicians' gallery along one side. The *Spiegel-kabinett* (mirror chamber) is remarkable with its many framed mirrors and valuable groups of porcelain figures and vases by many great European manufacturers. The present design of the *Hofgarten* was created in the first half of the eighteenth century and it has a 110m-long (360ft) orangery. The Margrave's museum is concerned particularly with the natural history of central Franconia from the earliest times until the end of the Roman period. The three prominent towers of the former collegiate church of St Gumbertus (thirteenth century) have now become the emblem of the town.

Schillingsfürst lies to the east of the Romantische Strasse some 12km (8 miles) south of Rothenburg. The small baroque-style *Schloss* occupies a good vantage point on a spur of the Franconian upland which falls quite sharply here to the south. The rooms in the *Schloss* are decorated with liberal stucco and contain fine furniture and porcelain. The unique oxen-treadmill in one of the outbuildings should not be missed.

Since Rothenburg the Romantic Road has been the B25 and the next stop is at **Feuchtwangen** some 40km (25 miles) away, a pleasant little town which suffers from the proximity of Rothenburg, but there is plenty to interest the visitor. Legend has it that Karl der Grosse (Charlemagne) founded the *Kloster* here after, arriving exhausted from the hunt, he was led by a dove to a spring which is now marked by the little dove fountain. A more substantial historical fact is that monks, probably from Hirsau in the Black Forest, founded a Christian establishment here in 817 from which developed the present collegiate church. This Romanesque building is of considerable interest to the historian but the casual visitor will be particularly attracted to the altar to St Mary created by Michael Wohlgemuth, the teacher of Albrecht Dürer. Both this church and the neighbouring St John's are now Protestant buildings. St John's is first documented as the parish church in 1257 but parts of it are much older.

Every corner of Feuchtwangen is steeped in history and the visitor will find his stay more interesting if he arms himself first with explanatory leaflets from the information office in the market place.

Roman-style architecture is at its best in the 800-year-old cloisters which become the location of the open-air theatre in the summer months. After the Old Town Festival at the beginning of June, the 'most beautiful little open-air stage in Germany' opens in the middle of that month and from then until the beginning of August the actors perform either a Shakespeare play or a local historic drama. The *Heimatmuseum* here is of outstanding interest and contains many examples of the varied and often amusing folk-culture of the district.

Only 13km separate Feuchtwangen from **Dinkelsbühl**, yet another charming medieval town. Free car parking is outside the old town walls and perhaps the first feature of note is the picturesque array of towers, many of them of unusual design. A little smaller than Rothenburg, Dinkelsbühl gives the impression of living much more in the present and is obviously a centre for the local population as well as a tourist resort, with old houses, fountains, churches, walls and towers. Do not allow modern shop-fronts to detract from the glories above them. In the market place note the Deutsches Haus Hotel (1440), considered to be one of the finest half-timbered houses in southern Germany. Visit the sixteenth-century *Ratstrinkstube*, the former councillors' taproom. Outstanding amongst the town's several churches is the Catholic parish church of St George. It is an important Gothic building erected between 1448–99, the finest example of a south German hall church. The three aisles have a common height of 22.5m (74ft), exactly the same as the width of the church which is 77m (252ft) long. Among several altars there is one presented by the shoe-makers' guild and dedicated to St Crispin, patron saint of cobblers the world over.

Dinkelsbühl has a remarkably lively programme of entertainments and activities for its guests. Musical and theatrical presentations are numerous and in the summer months there is a special programme of events for children and young teenagers. Various festivals also feature in the yearly round, the most famous being the Dinkelsbühl *Kinderzeche*, children's festival, another reminder of General Tilly and the Swedish hordes. In 1632 this town was besieged and, like Rothenburg the following year, held out stubbornly against the invaders until there were not enough able-bodied men left to man the battlements. Most mayors would have pleaded for clemency but instead a small boy marched out through the gates followed by all the town's children, each carrying flowers. As they marched solemnly towards the enemy camp General Tilly's heart softened and he spared the town. Every year since then, except in times of disaster, the *Kinderzeche* has been celebrated each July and is now a fine folk festival with music, dancing and a representation of the town's patron St George slaying the dragon. From a Dinkelsbühl base the visitor could explore some of the territory described in Chapter 7.

After Dinkelsbühl the Romantische Strasse leaves Franconia, enters Swabia and in 32km (20 miles) reaches **Nördlingen**, an exciting medieval town of some 20,000 inhabitants. Fifteen million years ago an enormous meteorite struck the earth and created the 25km-wide shallow crater of which Nördlingen is the central point. The geological puzzle about the origins of this 'crater' was partly solved as a spin-off of the training of NASA astronauts in the area. The full story is told in the Ries Museum. Of interest is the remarkably intact town wall of 1327, still in its original state with five gates and eleven towers. The complete circuit of the town on the wall is a modest stroll of 3.5km and is a useful introduction to the narrow streets and alleys which can then be explored at leisure.

Right in the centre is the town church of St George with its 94m-high (308ft) tower called Daniel. There are sufficient sights here to occupy the tourist for quite a long time including the fourteenth-century church of St Salvator, the Reichstadtmuseum which includes a fine art gallery and the 700-year-old *Rathaus* with its famous external staircase. Every third year (1996, 1999, etc) in September there is a historical festival in honour of the city walls. Cars are banished from the old town which is given over to merry-making. Regular events in Nördlingen include concerts and theatrical productions during the winter months, a medieval spring festival on the second Monday in May with a procession of school children, Nördlingen Fair in the fortnight after Whitsun, horse-racing in July and open-air theatre in July and August. Details and exact dates for all these events from the town information office. Nördlingen is served by rail and it may be mentioned here that all principal places now on the route south are readily accessible by public transport.

There is a railway museum in the old locomotive shed, with steam train excursions to either Feuchtwangen or Gunzenhausen on many Sundays between Easter and October.

From Nördlingen the route turns south-east and in about 17km (11 miles) reaches **Harburg**, the name of both the town (population 5,600) and of the impressive castle above. This is no ruin but the biggest surviving castle in south Germany. Building took place from the twelfth to the eighteenth centuries, some of it in the baroque style. Conducted tours of the complex include the church, ramparts, keep, etc. The museum contains works by Tilman Riemenschneider and a collection of tapestries as well as Norman ivory work. The stately *Rathaus* is one of a number of fine timbered buildings and the ancient

The Wörnitz Tower, Dinkelsbühl

stone bridge over the River Wörnitz is also not to be missed. If this attractive little town has become rather overshadowed by its bigger neighbours, this at least means that it is a more peaceful place to linger. Leisure hours can be spent in many different ways — fishing in or boating on the Wörnitz; swimming in the Ozon-Hallenbad with its sauna, tennis, bowling and above all, walking, for Harburg is at the centre of a network of well marked footpaths.

Eight kilometres north-east of Harburg, **Fünfenstetten** is the terminal of a steam railway to **Monheim**, 6km further east on the B2.

It is about 20km (12 miles) from Harburg to **Donauwörth** (population 20,000) where the Wörnitz feeds into the Donau. It is a very popular centre lying at the crossing of the Romantische Strasse with the east-west route along the famous river (described in a later chapter). As the cultural and economic capital of northern Swabia (Schwaben) there is a rich and varied choice of entertainment and activity for visitors. The essential sights to be seen include the parish church built 1444–61, the significant baroque Church of the Holy Cross, the treasures of which include a famous monstrance of 1716, the Fuggerhaus (1539) and the Hintermeierhaus (late fifteenth century), now the *Heimatmuseum*. The Reichstrasse is one of the most beautiful streetscapes in southern Germany. June and July are the months of festivity here, a folk festival, *Schwäbischwerder* children's day and the Reichstrasse festival all following in rather quick succession. Between May and October there are classical chamber music concerts by candlelight in the *Schloss* at nearby **Leitheim**; advance booking is essential. Dates and details of events from the town information office. Needless to say, the usual range of activities is available and the information office can provide suggestions for cycle touring. There is a large caravan park about 8km south of the town at **Mertingen** on the fringe of the Augsburg Nature Park.

From Donauwörth B2 becomes the Romantische Strasse and there is nothing of special interest in the 43km (27 miles) to Augsburg. The motorist could make a wide sweep to the west and explore some of the Augsburg Nature Park before heading for the city itself.

Augsburg is one of the biggest centres outside München. The name derives from its founder, the Roman Emperor Augustus. It has been a trade and travel focal point for the whole of its 2,000-year history. It is not a place to be dismissed in a few words. Its 250,000 inhabitants see to it that culture and progress go hand in hand as befits the place which produced such sons as Mozart, the Holbeins and Brecht. Here, early aviator Soloman Idler tried to fly in 1635, Rudolf Diesel invented and tested his revolutionary internal combustion engine at the end of the last century and Willy Messerschmidt had his aircraft factory, one of his machines having been the first to break the sound barrier in 1943. It was the home of Hans Holbein the Elder whose paintings are in the cathedral. Hans Fugger was a village weaver who arrived in the fourteenth century and never looked back. The family prospered and became international bankers, like the Rothschilds of a much later age. The Fuggers put their wealth to good use and charitable purposes including the Fuggerei, a little town within a town: 106 houses built in 1525 for citizens and workers 'of good repute' to let at a nominal rent.

As in Würzburg, all the main sights are within a very compact area in the city centre and visitors should explore on foot. The *Dom* makes a good starting point; the first cathedral was built in the tenth century on the site of the earliest Roman settlement. In 1047–63 it was rebuilt as a triple-naved Romanesque basilica and from 1320 was Gothicized and widened to five naves with the addition of five chapels at the east end. Apart from size, the sightseer may not find the exterior particularly exciting. Inside it is a different matter. Under the west choir is the old crypt from 1060 and from the same period are five windows containing reputedly the world's oldest stained glass. Supported by two lions, an early bishop's throne is thought to date from about 1100, a monumental piece of interior architecture. Of particular interest and value are the paintings of Hans Holbein the Elder (1465–1524) and one by G. Petel painted about 1630.

A short walk northwards from the cathedral is the birthplace of Leopold Mozart, father of Wolfgang Amadeus. The house is now a museum and memorial to this famous musical family. Returning past the *Dom* take the opportunity of seeing the former bishops' Residenz built and added to over the long period 1508–1773 and perhaps rest for a while in the pleasant *Hofgarten* laid out in 1739. The church of St Anna is outwardly insignificant but contains the family vault and chapel of the Fugger family built in the style of the Florentine and Venetian Renaissance. Restoration work was carried out under the direction of Elias Holl (1573–1646), the city architect who had such a great influence on many buildings still in existence today and, indeed, on the layout of the town itself. He was responsible for the magnificent *Rathaus* started at the beginning of the Thirty Years' War and topped out in 1618. With its seven storeys it was a veritable skyscraper for its day. The building was seriously damaged in World War II but has been fully restored and presents a fine picture across the square with twin onion-domes flanking a central gable. The nearby Zeughaus was originally an arsenal. Built in 1602–7 it is the earliest baroque façade in Germany. Almost next door is the Fuggerhaus (1512–15) with its courtyards and next again is the Schaezler-Palais (1765–7), the most beautiful rococo building in Augsburg with a grandiose banqueting hall.

At the south end of the old town — at the opposite pole to the *Dom*, so to speak — is St Ulrich's *Münster*, a Catholic late Gothic church, the foundation stone of which was laid by Emperor Maximilian I in 1500. The church contains a number of interesting relics associated with the history of Augsburg. Back towards the old town centre is the former Dominican church of St Magdalene housing the museum of pre-history and relics of the Roman occupation. Built 1513–15 as a double-naved church with a row of chapels along each side and decorated during the years 1716–24 in elegant rococo stucco, it makes a fine setting for the historical exhibits. Many of the towers which once formed part of the town fortifications are still standing. A little way east from the Roman museum and across the Stadtbach (town brook) is one of these, the Vogeltor, where a left turn leads into the Fuggerei, the unique little 'town within a town'.

Augsburg also has a wide variety of entertainment especially for music-lovers. From October to June, the Stadttheater presents opera, operetta, ballet, drama and orchestral music. The Comedy Theatre also functions during the same period but is probably more suited to the native taste. Everyone could enjoy the shows at the puppet theatre near the Rotes Tor — one of the towers — at the south end of the old town. Here too, is the open-air theatre where operas and operettas are performed in June and July when there is also the Augsburger Mozartsommer, a series of chamber music concerts held in the banqueting hall of the Schaezler-Palais. A modest walk south-east from the Rotes Tor through Prof-Steinbacher-Strasse leads to the excellent botanic garden and to the zoo.

Friedberg (population 26,500) is just a few kilometres along the B300 east of Augsburg; in spite of its charming townscape it is not as crowded as some of its better-known neighbours. Significantly one of the 'sights' here is the silhouette of Augsburg seen in the west from the town wall. The eighteenth-century pilgrimage church Unseres Herrn Ruhe, reached through a leafy walk at the east end of the town, is one of the most beautiful in the Bavarian baroque style, with a richly decorated interior. Little is left of the original thirteenth-century castle but later additions, a tower from 1552 and works from the middle of the seventeenth century, still overlook the town and house the excellent *Heimatmuseum*. The lovely *Rathaus* was built in 1670–80. A folk festival takes place here at the beginning of August.

Continue southwards, but avoid going into Augsburg city again by turning left after about 3km into the B2 (signed Fürstenfeldbruck and München) and follow this for 11km to **Mering**, there turn right

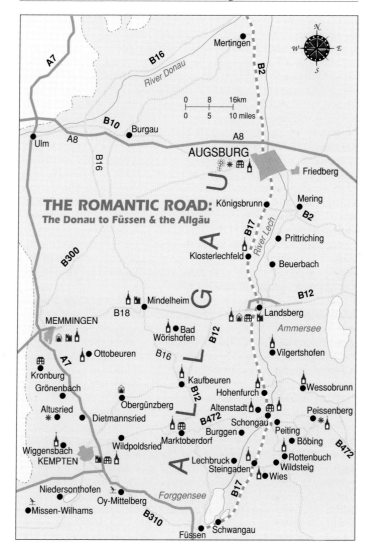

towards Königsbrunn (8km) to rejoin the Romantische Strasse (now B17) after crossing the River Lech. The Lech marks the eastern edge of the area known as Allgäu and a little of the country between the river and the western boundary of Bavaria is explored later in this chapter while the country east of the Lech is visited in Chapter 3. The 26km (16 miles) to Landsberg can be covered quickly for there is not too much of great interest except for **Klosterlechfeld** about midway which deserves a brief mention. The impressive pilgrimage and Klosterkirche Maria Hilf (1603), with its cylindrical form and cupola was based on the Pantheon in Rome. A main aisle was added later and the interior is decorated in the rococo style. Unless one intends to visit Klosterlechfeld, however, a more pleasant route from Mering is by the road on the east side of the river, reaching Landsberg via Prittriching and Beuerbach.

For a little while now the route has been in Upper Bavaria (Oberbayern). **Landsberg**, in a rather wild and romantic setting, is a town of 19,000 inhabitants, one of the main entrances being the Bayertor (Bavarian Gate), erected in the fifteenth century and considered to be one of the finest town gates in southern Germany. The beautiful *Marktplatz* is dominated by the *Rathaus* (1699–1702) which has first class external stucco and interior decoration by Dominikus Zimmermann who was *Bürgermeister* here from 1759 to 1764. There is a gallery containing the works of the Anglo-German artist Sir Hubert von Herkomer (1849–1914). In front of the *Rathaus* the elaborate fountain with a statue of Mary dates from 1783. The citadel here is where Adolf Hitler was imprisoned in 1924 and wrote *Mein Kampf*; ironically, Nazi war criminals were also incarcerated here awaiting trial in Nürnberg after World War II.

Outstanding amongst the churches of Landsberg is Mariae Himmelfahrt (Assumption of the Blessed Virgin), the parish church. This mighty fifteenth-century basilica replaced a thirteenth-century building on the same site. The baroque interior is of a rarely seen richness and the eye is drawn towards the vast high altar with its figures of Joseph and Joachim and the three archangels. Unusually, the windows flanking the altar are of stained glass and this seems to enhance rather than detract from the gilded reliefs. St Johanneskirche (1741) built to plans by D. Zimmermann, has a number of interesting features. The former Jesuit *Kloster* church of the Holy Cross was built in 1752–4. The rococo decoration of the present building includes work by several notable craftsmen, D. Zimmermann being responsible for the stucco in the sacristy. Many of the craftsmen worked in a comparatively small area: Riemenschneider worked almost exclusively in the Tauber valley and here in the Lech valley, Holl and Zimmermann had a significant influence.

Landsberg is one of many places with a traditional Christmas market; there is also a theatre and concerts are given in the *Rathaus* and in some of the churches. A visit to the town tourist office or to the area office nearby will reveal that, in the area soon to be reached, activities like walking, cycling and water sports are very popular. There is an annual guide to more than fifty *Hobbyferien*, that is, holiday packages with a particular theme. The term *Hobby* is interpreted rather freely. Cycling or rambling holidays can be *ohne Gepäck*, ie without luggage, which is forwarded to the next overnight stop. One package based on the Lech-Höhenweg long distance path has a mix of cycling and walking. Another provides tuition in sketching landscape and architecture as well as some touring.

In general, the touring holidays are not 'conducted'; the participants are provided with maps, accommodation vouchers, etc to make their own way from place to place. They are therefore specially suitable for couples or family groups but if one wishes to be included in a larger party this can be arranged sometimes.

The basic Lech-Höhenweg closely follows the river all the way from Landsberg to Füssen and good waymarking makes it unnecessary to give a detailed description of the route here but the content of the seven-day *ohne Gepäck* package may be of interest to those contemplating such a holiday:

Day 1: reception in Landsberg in the evening, descriptive slide show and distribution of maps, vouchers, etc. Day 2: guided tour of Landsberg and transport to a restaurant at Zollhaus 10km north of the town for lunch, returning on foot along the river bank. Day 3: continue southwards on east bank of river and cross to Hohenwart/ Römerkessel; 'bus excursion to Kloster Wessobrunn with guided tour of the monastery and to the pilgrimage church at Vilgertshofen (see Chapter 3). Day 4: on the east, and later the west, banks of the river to Schongau by which time the glorious spectacle of the Alps should be clearly visible ahead. Day 5: the route continues on the west bank past Burggen to the Litzauer Schleife, a spectacular horseshoe in the river and a natural monument; along the Lech 'lake' to Lechbruch. Day 6: from Lechbruch through Prem and between the two lakes Bannwaldsee and Forggensee to Füssen. Day 7: disperse after breakfast in Füssen. The price of this holiday includes bed and breakfast in good hotels or inns (rooms mostly with private facilities), luggage transport from place to place, the bus journeys, the guided tours and the lunch at Zollhaus.

The Romantische Strasse continues from Landsberg as the B17 and soon becomes a picturesque route with glimpses of the River Lech on the left. For some way the route passes through a charming area known as Pfaffenwinkel — very loosely translated as 'Priestly Corner'. The area concerned certainly had more than its fair share of religious establishments; it is roughly bounded on the west and east by the rivers Lech and Loisach and in the north and south by the Klöster Andechs on the Ammersee and Ettal near Oberammergau.

Leaving Landsberg, the jagged outline of the Alps will — weather permitting — be clearly visible on the southern skyline some 70km (45 miles) away. The giant Zugspitze (2,963m, 9,718ft) is almost directly ahead and the spectacular peaks extend east and west as far as the eye can see. There is no finer approach to the Alps than this, even Switzerland cannot quite equal the long-distance view that is obtained as one travels the closing stretches of the Romantische Strasse. Ever since the Donau was crossed far to the north the road has been climbing imperceptibly, each town lying just a little higher than the previous one. **Hohenfurch** (population 1,200), 22km (14 miles) from Landsberg, is already well into the foothills of the Alps at an altitude of 700m (2,296ft). This is an attractive rural holiday resort with its parish church noted for its stucco, and the late Gothic chapel of St Ursula.

In about 5km **Schongau** (population 10,600) is reached, an *Erholungsort* and a popular centre for the exploration of a beautiful area. A favourite pastime in Bavaria is *Eisstockschiessen*, a sort of curling on a smooth asphalt rink which is played in Schongau all year round. The old town wall is well preserved and there are a number of interesting and attractive buildings. The parish church was rebuilt in the eighteenth century and the interior includes fine stucco in the choir (1748). The so-called Ballenhaus in the Marienplatz was erected in 1515 to serve as a *Rathaus*. Both summer and winter visitors are catered for here; there is a ski-school and cross-country skiing trails.

An *Erholungsort* , as here in Schongau, is a general health resort, a place for recreation and recuperation; *Kurort* or *Luftkurort* refer to resorts where a *Kur* may be taken — a course of medical treatment, diet, etc. The latter are places where the air is considered specially beneficial for certain conditions. Spas are major health resorts with a wide range of medical treatment, often based on water therapy, and the names of such places are prefixed by the word *Bad* (bath). Many people prefer to stay in a health resort for the wide range of leisure facilities rather than for medical reasons. In Schongau, as well as the customary *Hallenbad* and heated *Freibad*, more informal bathing may be enjoyed at several places along the Schongauer See, an 8km-long fjord-like lake which also provides opportunities for sailing, canoeing and wind-surfing. Boats can be hired.

There are also many well marked footpaths and a fairy-tale wood with a deer enclosure. A pleasant 2km walk takes one to **Altenstadt** where the large Catholic parish church of St Michael is the only Romanesque vaulted basilica to have survived in Upper Bavaria and to have resisted the decorations of the baroque era. It was completed around 1200, much restored in 1826 and further renovated in 1961. In the south nave is one of the few remaining Romanesque decorated wooden crosses with its original paint, standing 3.2m (10.5ft) high and 3.2m (10.4ft) wide. The Grosser Gott von Altenstadt is depicted wearing a royal crown instead of the more usual crown of thorns.

From Schongau follow the Romantische Strasse (still B17) as it continues to **Peiting** but then make a detour eastwards (B472) towards Peissenberg. After 6km (4 miles) turn left into a picturesque road which skirts the hohe Peissenberg (988m, 3240ft), through **Sölder** and into Peissenberg in another 8km. The hohe Peissenberg boasts a pilgrimage church and a restaurant, together with outstanding views thought by some to equal those from alpine peaks three times as high. In **Peissenberg** the church Maria Aich and St George's Chapel are both worth visiting. Outdoor activities feature prominently in the romantic River Ammer valley with boat hire, angling and a 'wild water' school. There is a heated *Freibad* and informal bathing and sauna facilities at the Rigi-Rutsch'n leisure park.

From Peissenberg head south-west along a road with striking

Wies church has one of the finest rococo interiors in Bavaria

views. In about 10km (6 miles) the village of **Böbing** is another recognised *Erholungsort* with provision for summer and winter visitors. Continue to **Rottenbuch** (population 1,700), yet another health resort and visit the outstanding former Augustinian church Mariae Geburt (Birth of the Virgin). This Gothic creation of the eleventh and twelfth centuries is today internally pure baroque. In addition to the fine stucco, the choir stalls, the pulpit and side altars all require time to fully appreciate them. There are traditional folk evenings (*Heimatabende*) and the peasant theatre has productions from May to September. Also in September is the thoroughbred foal market, while on 6 November, St Leonhard's Day, the custom of the *Leonhardiritt* is observed; horses are ridden around the church and receive a traditional blessing.

Two or three kilometres south of Rottenbuch on the B23 is the Echelsbach bridge over the Ammer gorge. Park before crossing the bridge and after admiring the spectacular views take the nearby road westward through **Wildsteig** this attractive and peaceful village provides access to the ravine of the Ammer with its charming waterfalls and to areas where the visitor may find rare flora and fauna. Entertainments are similar to those in Rottenbuch, but for some odd reason the Leonhardiritt takes place in October rather than on the patron saint's day From the Echelsbach bridge to its destination in Füssen the Romantische Strasse shares the route with the Alpine Road (see Chapter 2). A few minutes after leaving Wildsteig turn left to visit the most famous of all the little Bavarian baroque churches. This is the so-called Wieskirche or, to be more precise, the *Wallfahrtskirche zum gegeisselten Heiland in der Wies*.

The origin of this church at **Wies** lies in an apparent miracle which occurred in 1730. One version relates how a farmer had in his meadow here a religious emblem in the form of the Saviour tied to the flogging post and he insisted that as he passed one day the figure suddenly shed tears. He took this as a sign and immediately built a little field chapel at the spot. The story spread quickly and in no time at all the chapel became a great place of pilgrimage. It became necessary to replace the chapel with a proper church and after the necessary permission had been obtained the foundation stone was laid in 1746. The church was consecrated in 1754 and the interior decoration was completed with the installation of the organ three years later. The pale yellow walls and red roof outside in no way prepare one for the splendour within. Every detail of the decoration is purest rococo and it comes as no surprise to find that the prime architect was none other than Dominikus Zimmermann. In this creation he reached the pinnacle of his life's work and, in fact, he died here in a nearby house in 1766. Dominikus was assisted by his elder brother Johann Baptist (1680–1758) and by many other famous artists of the period. Words just cannot convey any idea of the spectacle of 'Wies'. Take time to visit this church, preferably out of the main tourist season. If not, attendance at one or more of the concerts given each year in June-August with the theme *Festlicher Sommer in der Wies* (Festive Summer in Wies) would provide an opportunity for feasting ear and eye at the same time.

Back on the main road a left turn leads to Steingaden in about 4km. **Steingaden** (population 2,400) is another recognised *Erholungsort* catering for summer and winter visitors with a good range of facilities and entertainments. The so-called Welfenmünster, founded by Duke Welf VI in 1147 before his departure to the second crusade, has preserved in its façade an authentic reminder of that period. The interior has an assortment of decorations from different periods, indeed, somebody described it as an open book on the history of art.

The remaining 22km (14 miles) of the Romantische Strasse leaves Upper Bavaria and the Pfaffenwinkel and re-enters Swabia in the area known as Allgäu, passing through pretty countryside and a series of small resorts, then along the east shore of the Bannwaldsee with the 10km-long Forggensee sometimes visible behind. Much of the holiday activity here is naturally associated with these attractive lakes with their colourful summer camp sites. Approaching Schwangau two of the famous castles associated with King Ludwig II can be seen and this Romantic Road finally comes to an end in the town of **Füssen**, 350km (218 miles) from its northern tip in Würzburg.

Allgäu

Travel northwards now to explore that country lying between the River Lech and the western boundary of Bavaria; in other words, the Allgäu. This most beautiful area straddles the border between Bavaria and Baden-Württemberg and, for that matter, in terms of history and ethnic origins trespasses into the Austrian Bregenzerwald and into the near corner of Switzerland. However, no Allgäu border is marked on any map because it is, in the words of one authority, only 'a geographical idea' and certainly has nothing to do with today's administrative boundaries. This book is concerned only with Bavarian Allgäu.

In the height of the tourist season Allgäu is a very popular goal and the further south one goes the more people there seem to be. This is a very good reason for visiting the area 'out-of-season' if possible. There can be few more beautiful places than Allgäu in May when the fruit trees are in blossom and winter slowly withdraws to the high mountains, leaving the pastures to be covered with a lush green carpet which never dries out even in the hottest summer. The velvety brown cows emerge from their winter quarters and in some areas follow the receding snows up to the higher pastures. Not without reason does Allgäu claim to be the dairy of Germany with an enormous output of milk, butter and cheese. Look out in spring and early summer for *Tettigonia viridissima*, the great green grasshopper. The quiet days of autumn are also most pleasant, with the fruit being gathered, harvest festivals in swing and the cows ambling down to the lower pastures once again. The many excellent country inns are quiet after the hassle of the summer tourist season and the winter sports patrons have not yet arrived. In all seasons though, this is fine holiday country with many places of interest and beauty, as well as ample facilities for leisure activities.

Allgäu offers a number of gastronomic specialities and the visitor would be wise to try some of these when given the opportunity. The 'national' dish is *Allgäuer Kässpatzen* — noodles layered with fried onions and much cheese, most often *Emmentaler*, and melted butter poured over the whole. Various dumpling soups are popular especially on festive occasions. Freshwater fish from the many lakes in the Alpine foothills are very tasty and for the evening meal a lightly smoked country sausage called *Schübling* is often eaten. In general the menu will be weighted towards venison and similar dishes, frequently enriched with cheese.

Thirty kilometres (19 miles) west of Landsberg the attractive town of **Mindelheim** (population 12,200) is one of those pleasant medieval towns where little seems to have changed over the centuries. The parish church of St Stephan was built at the beginning of the eighteenth century and incorporates the bell-tower from an earlier building. As recently as 1933 the interior was improved by adding baroque items from other churches. The Jesuit church in Maximilian-strasse was completed in 1625–6. There is fine stucco work in the light and airy interior. The Liebfrauenkirche dates from 1455 and is home to a famous wood-carving *Die Mindelheimer Sippe* (1510–20). Parts of the town wall and three of the towers are preserved; one of these, the Obere Tor suffers the indignity of being dressed up in a grotesque costume each year at *Fasnacht*, the period of carnival which precedes Lent. On a hill just south of the town the Mindelburg — a castle dating from 1370 — provides a goal for a modest excursion with splendid views over the surrounding countryside.

Mindelheim

Ten kilometres (6 miles) along a pretty road south-east from Mindelheim is the famous spa resort of **Bad Wörishofen**. It was here that Sebastian Kneipp founded the first centre to practise his particular kind of physiotherapy. Kneipp was born in the little Allgäu village of Stephansried in 1821, the son of a weaver. Probably through working in the damp cellar, he contracted consumption and for a time it seemed that he might not live. Sebastian appears to have been convinced quite early in life of the healing properties of water and he took the radical step of bathing in November in an ice-cold river which seemed successful in ridding him of the disease. Against the wishes of his parents he became a priest and eventually monsignor and papal chamberlain. Despite opposition from the medical profession, he continued to develop his healing methods in Wörishofen. His success brought world renown and many famous personages were among his patients; members of royal and aristocratic families from all over Europe and Russia, the Rothschilds from Paris and Theodore Roosevelt, all made their way to Wörishofen. Sebastian Kneipp died in 1897 but his work lived on and there are now many Kneipp establishments in Allgäu combining modern medical centres with fashionable holiday resorts.

Having been awarded the honourable prefix, Bad Wörishofen today (population 13,600) is one of the outstanding spas of Germany. This is very much an all-year resort and especially attractive in the short days of autumn. The sixteenth-century former monastery church of the Capuchin monks is the present parish church (with stucco in the style of the Wessobrunn school) The early eighteenth-century church and *Kloster* of the Dominican order is noted for its rococo altars and stucco by Dominikus Zimmermann.

Memmingen, 27km (17 miles) west of Mindelheim is quite a different matter. A busy town of 38,000 inhabitants, it is steeped in history as the first glance at the medieval town centre will show. One of the finest market places in Swabia is surrounded by stately old patrician houses and the Renaissance *Rathaus* (1589) with its rococo ornamentation. The so-called Siebendächerhaus (House with Seven Roofs) really does have this number and is one of the most photographed buildings in Bavaria. The house was built in 1601 by tanners who would hang out the hides to dry under the overhanging roofs which were provided for just this purpose. A former patrician palace of 1766 decorated in the rococo style now houses the town museum and art gallery. The Frauenkirche, built in the fifteenth century, is famed for its beautiful frescos. They had been covered over and only came to light again during restoration work in 1891. There are also many good examples of upper Swabian art of the late Gothic period on all the walls of the church.

Memmingen makes two contributions to jollity in July, firstly with a traditional children's festival and on the following Saturday with the famous Memmingen *Fischerstecken*. This is the occasion on which the town chooses its fisher-king for the following year. At eight in the morning spectators line the banks of the town stream and the fishermen spring into the water with their nets to fish out trout. In short, at the end of the day he who has landed the heaviest fish becomes 'king' but it is not, of course, quite as simple as that. Under the cheers and jeers of the townsfolk the fishers go about their task. Should they not get sufficiently wet during this hectic activity, the onlookers come equipped with buckets and pails to empty yet more water on to the hapless victims in the stream. The battle over, the fish are weighed in front of the *Rathaus*, the old 'king' is chased from the throne and the new one installed in his place. Needless to say, the associated festivities go on deep into the night. More conventional entertainment is provided in the town theatre and in the *Stadthalle*, a concert and exhibition hall and not to be confused with the *Rathaus*.

Ottobeuren, 10km to the south-east, is a *Kneippkurort* with 7,000 inhabitants. Much of what was written about Bad Wörishofen applies equally to Ottobeuren but a significantly different history lies in Ottobeuren's close connection with the famous Benedictine abbey as it has developed. Although the establishment was founded in 764, buildings of the eleventh, twelfth, thirteenth and sixteenth centuries were the victims of fire and in the end the present complex was begun at the beginning of the eighteenth century using the most celebrated craftsmen of the day. The *Klosterkirche* is one of the most impressive baroque churches as well as being one of the largest. The two towers reach up to 82m (269ft) and the interior is 89m (292ft) long with a world famous organ by Karl Riepp. This is the church in which Sebastian Kneipp was baptised on 17 May 1821. Nearby **Stephansried** was his birthplace and there is a memorial where his father's house once stood.

In this north-western corner of Allgäu there is a group of little resorts which deserve brief mention. The area is bisected by the north-south motorway A7, west of which is **Kronburg**, a little summer resort near the gorge of the River Iller with Schloss Kronburg and the Allgäu farm museum in nearby **Illerbeuren**. **Grönenbach** is a *Kneippkurort* (population 4,200) with all the usual trimmings; the pilgrimage church of Maria Steinbach; the parish church of St Philipp and St Jakob (1479) which was given the baroque treatment in the seventeenth century and renovated in neo-Gothic in the nineteenth and, of course, the inevitable ancient castle. Other resorts include **Altusried** (population 7,500) an *Erholungsort* noted for spectacular performances in the open-air theatre (July-August); **Dietmannsried** (population 6,000), an unsophisticated scattered community close to the motorway with many footpaths, skiing trails and cycle routes and, finally, **Wiggensbach** (population 3,200), a good family resort with plenty of interest — grass skiing on the slopes of the Blender (1,072m, 3,516ft), fine baroque church (1770-1).

Obergünzburg (population 5,200), an *Erholungsort* at the junction of several picturesque roads on the River Günz, has a charming *Marktplatz* graced by the late Gothic St Martin's church and several other fine buildings. The *Heimatmuseum* has a specialised collection from the former German South Seas colonies.

Kaufbeuren is a former free imperial city on the River Wertach. Today it has some 43,000 inhabitants. The medieval old town has some fine baroque houses, especially in the Kaiser-Max-Strasse. St Blasius' church, the oldest parts of which date from 1319, contains a famed carved altar by Jörg Lederer (1518) and many other items of historic interest. Several other old churches invite inspection including St Martin (1438–43) and the sixteenth-century Trinity and St Dominicus. Kaufbeuren was the birthplace of the author Ludwig Ganghofer (1855–1920), a successful German writer. There is a memorial tablet on his house in Kirchplatz and the *Heimatmuseum* has a collection of mementoes associated with him, as well as a remarkable collection of crucifixes.

Every year on the third Sunday in July there is the *Tänzelfest*, the oldest historical children's festival in Bavaria. Some 1,600 children in authentic costumes present the ancient history of the town. This festival is popularly believed to have been instituted by Emperor Maximilian I in 1497 after he had seen a boys' shooting festival and decreed that it should become an annual event. It was soon complemented by processions of drummers, pipers and flag-throwers. 'Emperor Maximilian' still plays a central role in the festival with a triumphal entry into the town. The main feature today is a procession in which the history of the town is depicted by groups representing the various periods, the wars, the trades, happy times and sad times. There is an evening torchlight tattoo outside the *Rathaus* and a firework display.

Marktoberdorf is an *Erholungsort* of 15,500 inhabitants. A pleasant well kept town in glorious countryside, it is especially favoured by those who prefer a fairly active holiday for which every facility is at hand. The parish church of St Martin was started in 1732 to plans by the Füssen architect J. G. Fischer who was born here in 1673. The building incorporates a tower from 1680 although this was given an

additional storey and an onion-dome. Close by the church is the
Jagdschloss (1722–5), the former hunting lodge of the bishops of
Augsburg. This was also the design of J. G. Fischer but the building
was enlarged to its present size only 40 years later. Marktoberdorf is
in the centre of a network of cycle routes, most of which are designed
to be on traffic-free roads. It also serves the walker well with many
well kept footpaths and is at one end of the long-distance path called
Prälatenweg (Prelates' Way) which runs eastwards from here to
Kochel in Upper Bavaria. Thus, starting in Allgäu, it crosses the Lech-
Höhenweg already mentioned, crosses the Romantic Road and
penetrates into the lake country described in Chapter 3. Space does
not permit a detailed description of the whole route but the western
section is varied and interesting and could make a good 15km walk
in its own right.

The starting point is at the *Schloss* in Marktoberdorf where an inn,
the Sailerkeller, supplies refreshments. Look out for the distinctive
waymark of two bishop's crooks and start through the kilometre-
long Lindenallee towards **Bertoldshofen**, 4km from the *Schloss*.
Here, go past the church and the Königswirt inn (*Ruhetag* Monday),
over the Geltnach bridge to the last house and follow a grassy track
with a barrier, through a clearing with seats and into the under-

The Allgäu, like the rest of Bavaria, is well known for its beer

growth above the valley. Continuing uphill on the Schlossberg note a cross erected for Pfarrer (priest) Josef Izlinger who was killed here in 1481. The path leads into pastureland with a broad view to the peaks of the Allgäu and Ammergau Alps. Reaching the hamlet of **Burk**, continue past the church, pass or call at Café Brugger (*Ruhetag* Tuesday) and leave via Stöttener Strasse, eventually coming down to a stream by a row of trees. Straight on past a parking place and in 700m at **Geldloch** go to the right over the bridge and up into the meadows, with a hill on the left and a small lake down on the right. Continue to climb and upon reaching a little road turn left into **Echt** (altitude 842m, 2,761ft and 4.5km from Bertoldshofen) where drinks may be obtained from house No 2. Past the wooden chapel, fork right down into a wooded ravine, cross the stream and resume climbing to **Settele** 500m from Echt. Now there is a view of the Auerberg (1,055m, 3,460ft) which is the immediate goal.

Follow the waymarks generally uphill, keep the Weidensee (lake) on the right and past it turn right, away from the surfaced road down into the valley of a little stream then climb again to the hamlet of **Buchen**. Before the sign 'Geisenhofen', turn right down past the little church and into the *Landschaftschutzgebiet* (protected countryside). Before going further, look back for a rewarding view. Now the path goes steeply up into fenced pasture — heavy going here after rain. A second opening points the direction and soon turn left on the road leading to the Auerberg with its *Gasthof* and church, 6.5km from Echt. The inn has been in the possession of the Stechele family since 1601; thirteen beds are available. Intending overnight guest should book in advance (☎ 08860-235). From mid-September until March, Thursday is *Ruhetag*. An alternative route back to Marktoberdorf (doubling the distance) can be readily found or there is a bus from nearby Bernbeuren — check on the service before setting out.

Lechbruck is an *Erholungsort* with 2,200 inhabitants and was originally a *Flösserdorf* — engaged in the trade of floating timber down the river as huge rafts, replicas of which are sometimes made today as a tourist attraction. Lechbruck has all the usual amenities of a holiday resort in this area and claims that it is a *familienfreundlich* place. Families are welcomed and there is a lot of accommodation suitable for them at the lower end of the price range.

Half a dozen or so villages cluster around the A7 south of Kempten. Given the blanket name of **Oy-Mittelberg** this is a *Kneipp-* and *Luftkurort* of nearly 4,000 inhabitants. It lies between 900m (2,952ft) and 1100m (3,608ft) above sea level and the big mountains are very close. There are thirty ski-lifts and other mountain 'railways' within 15km and winter activities here are no less important than summer ones. In Oy the Zollhaus (1448), a customs house formerly connected with the international salt trade, is of interest while in **Petersthal**, a few kilometres from the centre, the rococo parish church should be seen.

Kempten (population 60,000) is the capital of Bavarian Allgäu and is one of the oldest towns in Germany. Many fine historic buildings remain and each Saturday from May to October there is a free conducted tour to the most important of them. Music, theatre and folklore are offered regularly but particularly during the Allgäu Festival weeks during the second half of August. This was once a Roman town (*Cambodunum*) and there are still remains of walls etc of that period, but the principal relics are to be found in the Roman collection in the Zumsteinhaus. The collegiate church of St Lorenz (1651–3) was the first large German church built after the Thirty Years' War; the style is Italian baroque with a richly ornamented interior. The old town church of St Mary (1427) nearby is a late Gothic brick building which was given the rococo treatment in 1767–8. The Gothic *Rathaus* with its onion-dome and double stairway graces the *Marktplatz*. The bronze Rathausbrunnen (fountain) of 1601 is considered to be one of the finest Renaissance fountains in Germany. The Residenz (1651–74) was the former seat of the prince-abbots. The Fürstensaal (Princes' Hall) on the first floor has rich ornamentation in stucco, as do a number of other rooms which were transformed with south German rococo between 1734 and 1742.

South-west from Kempten, **Niedersonthofen** with its large lake is popular with campers and water-sports enthusiasts but is otherwise not noteworthy. Another twin village is **Missen-Wilhams**, a little to the south and less than 3km apart at the foot of the Hauchenberg (1,242m, 4,073ft). Summer and winter activities include skiing tuition, with a special course for children who are provided with a midday meal. The caravan park is open all year and the *Ferienwohnpark* 'Oberallgäu' has many apartments with hundreds of beds for visitors. This is splendid walking country. The Hauchenberg is a long, lean mountain running roughly north-east to south-west and a walk along the ridge provides spectacular views.

A moderately strenuous ramble of 12-14km starts from the car park in Missen to climb fairly steeply north-east (waymark 1) for about 600m, partly beside the main road, to the settlement of **Berg** where route 1 turns sharply back to the left. From the turning, fork right almost immediately up the minor road serving the few houses of Berg and after passing the last of these, continue climbing steadily through meadows and trees until the crest is reached about 1.5km from the main road. Route 2 from Wilhams comes in on the left here.

Those starting the ramble in Wilhams may park near the church and take path 2 to the west of it to go towards Missen. After 650m turn left, noting that waymark 2 applies both ways and climb steeply, mostly through open pastureland for rather more than 1km to join route 1.

The worst of the climb is now over and the path continues in a north-easterly direction on the ridge with a variety of woodland and pasture. Route 1 continues straight ahead — ignore Nos 14, 19 and 13 coming up the ridge from the left, right and left respectively — and about 3km reaches the highest point of the walk at 1,242m (4,073ft). Now begin the gentle descent, still keeping to the ridge. Pass path 3 on the right from Diepholz and about 2km later are the Stations of the Cross which lead to the Lohweg-Kapelle, a remote chapel set among steep craggy rocks where care is needed in the confined space. Return to the path and soon turn right into No 6 to shortly reach the main road at **Freundpolz**. A little before this, however, path No 4 to the right runs parallel with the road back as far as **Diepholz**, about 2km. From Diepholz follow the road — not a very busy one — for rather less than 4km back to the turning at Berg. Those returning to Wilhams go in here but then fork left to join path 2 back to their starting point. Stout footwear is desirable for this walk.

The *Wanderkarte Erholungsgebiet Grosser Alpsee* is a local map and guide published in Immenstadt. Although the text of the guide is in German, the clear summaries of the fifty-three numbered routes in this area should be useful and the map itself (1:20,000) is extremely clear and has the legend in French and English as well as German.

The route has now reached the quite narrow corridor through which Bavarian Allgäu reaches its meagre section of the shoreline of the Bodensee. The Deutsche Alpenstrasse (German Alpine Road) passes through here and provides the theme for the next chapter.

Additional Information

Places to Visit
Ansbach
Residenz with Hofgarten and Orangerie
Open: Tuesday to Sunday, April to September 9am-12noon, 2-5pm, October to March 10am-12noon, 2-4pm. Closed 1 January, Shrove Tuesday, 1 November, 24, 25, 31 December. Restaurant.

Markgrafenmuseum
Schaitbergerstrasse 14
91522 Ansbach
☎ 0981-51296
Open: Tuesday to Sunday 10am-12noon, 2-5pm.

Bad Windsheim
Fränkisches Freilandmuseum
91438 Bad Windsheim
☎ 09841-3055

Open: Tuesday to Sunday, mid-March to mid-October 9am-6pm, mid-October to mid-December 10am-4pm. Open Easter and Whit Mondays and on Mondays in July and August.

Harburg
Schloss (Museum)
86655 Harburg
☎ 09003-1211 or 1268
Guided tours mid-March to end October, Tuesday to Sunday 9-11.30am, 1.30-5.30pm (4.30pm in October).

Rothenburg
Kriminalmuseum
Burggasse 3
91541 Rothenburg
☎ 09861-5359
Open: Easter to October 9.30am-6pm, November, January and February 2-4pm, December and March 10am-4pm.

Puppen- und Spielzeugmuseum
Hofbronnengasse 13
91541 Rothenburg
☎ 09861-7330
Open: daily March to December 9.30am-6pm, January and February 11am-5pm.

Schillingsfürst
Schloss
Open: Easter to 31 May and 1-31 October, Saturday, Sunday and holidays and June to September daily 9-11.30am, 2-5.30pm.

Würzburg
Residenz
Open: Tuesday to Sunday, April to September 9am-5pm, October to March 10am-4pm. Closed 1 January, Shrove Tuesday, 1 November, 24, 25, 31 December. Restaurant.

Mainfränkisches Museum
Festung Marienberg
97082 Würzburg
☎ 0931-43016
Open: daily 10am-5pm (4pm November to March). Restaurant.

Local Events and Festivals

Dinkelsbühl
Kinderzeche — 1 week mid-July

Donauwörth
Schwäbischwerder Children's Day — 1st Sunday in July

Feuchtwangen
Altstadtfest — 3rd Sunday July
Open-air Theatre — 7 weeks from mid-June

Kaufbeuren
Tänzelfest — weekend of 2nd Sunday in July

Memmingen
Fischertag and Kinderfest — 3 days to 3rd Saturday in July

Nördlingen
Stabenfest (Spring festival) — 2nd Monday in May
Pfingstmesse (Whitsun fair) — 9 days in mid-June

Rothenburg
Der Meistertrunk — Whit-weekend and various dates until early October.

Long Distance Paths
Liebliches Taubertal — 100km (62 miles) Rothenburg to Wertheim on River Main through Tauber Valley following the Romantic Road. Also suitable as a cycle tour avoiding main roads.

*Lech-Höhenweg** — 120km (75 miles) Zollhaus north of Landsberg through Lech Valley to Füssen

*Prälatenweg** — 140km (87 miles)
Marktoberdorf through the
Pfaffenwinkel to Kochel am See in
Upper Bavaria

* = *Wandern ohne Gepäck* (Hiking
without luggage) holidays
available.

Steam and Other Tourist Railways

Fünfstetten-Monheim
Bayerisches Eisenbahnmuseum eV
Postfach 1316, 86720 Nördlingen
☎ 089-915462 or 09081-9808 during
museum open hours (see below).
Three or four trains hauled by
historic steam loco *Ries*, on selected
dates May, June and July

Nördlingen-Dinkelsbühl-Feuchtwangen
Address etc as above
3 or 4 steam or historic diesel trains
one or two Sundays per month
Easter to October. Refreshments
and cycle transport on all trains

Nördlingen-Wassertrüdingen-Gunzenhausen
Address etc as above
Historic steam-hauled trains
usually one Sunday per month
May to October. Refreshments on
trains

Eisenbahnmuseum Nördlingen
Address etc as above
Open: May to October, Sunday
12noon-4pm. Also some 'steam'
weekends. Groups by arrangement

Tourist Information Centres
The Romantic Road
Städtisches Verkehrsamt
Stadthaus
91508 Ansbach
☎ 0981-51243
Town information.

Kreisverkehrsamt
91506 Ansbach
☎ 0981-468161 or 2
Area information.

Fremdenverkehrsverband
Pfaffenwinkel
Postfach 1247
86956 Schongau
☎ 08861-7713 or 211117

For local detail, accommodation
lists, etc write to 'Tourist Information' giving postcode and name of
town:

86150 Augsburg
91430 Bad Windsheim
91550 Dinkelsbühl
86607 Donauwörth
91555 Feuchtwangen
86313 Friedberg
86655 Harburg
89896 Landsberg
86715 Nördlingen
86971 Peiting
97285 Röttingen
91541 Rothenburg
91583 Schillingsfürst
86956 Schongau
86989 Steingaden
97070 Würzburg

Allgäu
Fremdenverkehrsverband Allgäu
Fuggerstrasse 9
86150 Augsburg
☎ 0821-33335
For general information about
Allgäu and Bavarian Swabia.

86825 Bad Wörishofen
87600 Kaufbeuren
87435 Kempten
87616 Marktoberdorf
87700 Memmingen
87719 Mindelheim
87634 Obergünzburg
87724 Ottobeuren
87466 Oy-Mittelberg

2
THE ALPINE ROAD

The German Alpine Road (Deutsche Alpenstrasse) runs between the extreme south-western and south-eastern corners of Bavaria, from Lindau on the Bodensee (Lake Constance) to the Austrian border on the outskirts of Salzburg. The straight line distance is about 260km (162 miles), but the Alpine Road stretches some 350km (219 miles). This must surely be one of Europe's longest routes of continuous scenic interest, with almost the whole road in, or very close to, the often snow-capped mountains.

The Bodensee is some 60km long and up to 15km wide but Bavaria can only claim about 12km of the shore line. It is a warm and sunny area with vineyards and orchards. The main Bavarian resort is **Lindau**, a town of 24,000 inhabitants with a delightful atmosphere reminiscent of more southerly lands. The historic centre is mainly a pedestrian zone and access for vehicles is severely restricted. There is a good reason for this for Lindau is, in fact, an island connected to the mainland only by road and railway bridges. There is a splendid traffic-free harbour promenade where visitors and locals gather to watch the coming and going of the lake steamers. A quite restful time may be had by using the frequent services to visit and explore the various towns around the lake in Germany, Austria or Switzerland.

The old *Rathaus* built 1422–36 in the Gothic style has been rebuilt and restored many times over the years. Cavazzen, built in 1729, has been described as the most beautiful citizen's house on the lake and today houses the town museum and a valuable art collection. The historic lighthouse at the harbour entrance dates from the thirteenth century. The oldest church on the island is that of St Peter (built about 1000) in which the remarkable fresco, the Lindau Passion by Hans Holbein the Elder was only uncovered in 1967.

Lindau has belonged to Bavaria only since 1805. Before that, as a

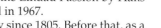

Lindau: harbour (above); painted façade of the Altes Rathaus (below)

'free' imperial city, it was tossed to and fro repeatedly as first the Austrians then the French took possession of it. Some of this history comes out in Geissler's delightful story of *Der Liebe Augustin*, that charming but entirely fictional philanderer born in Mittenwald in 1777 who made his home in Lindau. Those who have enjoyed the story and want to discover the haunts described in the book will not be disappointed, for Lindau has preserved the myth for visitors. The locals point out Dammgasse No 4 where Augustin lived and visitors can climb the narrow stair to see the famous four-poster bed which featured in some of his exploits. All this is pure fantasy, but many come just to revel in a little harmless make-believe.

West of Lindau are the resorts of **Bad Schachen**, a pleasant lake-side spa, **Wasserburg** and **Nonnenhorn**, both of which enjoy the designation *Luftkurort* and are essentially summer places with much activity on the waterfront. Nonnenhorn is noted for its cherries and the enterprising local wine *Elbling*, drunk young and most refreshing. Note the *Weintorkel*, an enormous old grape press dating from 1591. A short walk from the village centre following signs 'St Anton' leads up through vineyards and orchards to the tiny village of that name. The way up to the chapel, also called St Anton, can be seen and here at 460m (1,508ft) (although only about 65m [213ft] above the lake level) there is a grand panoramic view southwards over the lake to the Swiss Alps and eastwards towards the Austrian and Allgäu Alps and the Bavarian hinterland. There are several alternative routes back to the starting point. Lindau and the places on the lakeside can all be reached by train, making this an ideal area for the visitor without his own transport.

The Alpenstrasse leaves Lindau as B308 and runs northwards for a few kilometres before turning east to continue right across this southern fringe of Bavaria. After 20km (12 miles) the *Heilklimatische-* and *Kneippkurort* of **Scheidegg** (population 4,000) is reached. The new resort designation refers to the benevolent climate, and a wide variety of medical treatments is available. Children and young people have special pastimes and activities arranged for them in the resort. Summer and winter visitors are welcomed and there are some good value packages outside the high season. The resort includes the village of **Scheffau** about 5km to the south. Both places are within 3km of crossing points on the Austrian border, providing an opportunity for a round tour through the famous Bregenzerwald (Forest of Bregenz). In this remote corner of the state, one is much nearer to northern Italy than to the Bavarian capital!

Lindenberg (population 11,000) just a few kilometres along, a *Hohenluftkurort* since 1923, is in the centre of the west Allgäu Alpine foothills and enjoys an ideal climate with freedom from fog — good for those with any respiratory problem. The main attraction is the little lake called Waldsee where there is angling and bathing although there is also a *Hallenbad* with sauna. There is a good and varied entertainments programme and an excellent range of facilities for other leisure pursuits. Many footpaths attract summer ramblers and in the winter there is a ski-school and a ski-lift. Many of the tracks are kept clear for cross-country skiing or winter walking. The town has a history of straw and felt hat-making and there is an unusual museum devoted to the subject. The new 'baroque' parish church (1912–14) with its twin towers is the emblem of the town.

Weiler-Simmerberg with **Ellhofen** are three neighbouring villages which constitute a *Luftkurort* with 4,600 inhabitants and a mineral spring. Several different medical treatments are available here and the waters are said to be beneficial to rheumatism sufferers. In Weiler the parish church dates from 1745 and the pretty *Rathaus* from 1681. The west Allgäu *Heimatmuseum* is to be found here and is well thought of. All the places mentioned can be reached by public transport, train to Röthenbach and then by bus.

From the Alpenstrasse some of the majestic peaks of the Allgäu Alps can be seen ahead. The most prominent summits include Buralpkopf (1,772m, 5,812ft), Rindalphorn (1,822m, 5,976ft) and Hochgrat (1,832m, 6,008ft). In about 12km (7 miles) **Oberstaufen** is reached. This *Kurort* of 6,800 inhabitants is a delightful town in every way. Up to date in a refined sort of way and with every possible means of entertaining the visitor, Oberstaufen, home town of the female Olympic champions Heidi Biebl and Christl Cranz-Borchers, is ideal for an extended stay in the area. Many people visit Oberstaufen in order to take a *Schrothkur*. The name comes from the Bohemian Johann Schroth who discovered that controlled fasting could be helpful in the treatment of certain ailments. Fasting may come hard in an area with so many fine hostelries but the *Kur* is a fairly light-hearted affair with some emphasis on *Glühwein* (mulled wine) which 'improves the circulation and encourages regularity in the normal bodily functions'! If for a few days the pangs of hunger assail, there are many ways of forgetting this — perhaps a visit to a cheese factory or a walk to the little churches in Zell or Genhofen; or just to sit and contemplate the mountain scenery. Thursday is 'big drink day' for those taking the *Kur*. Breakfast is an eighth of a litre of *Glühwein* or herb tea, at midday there is vegetable soup, semolina and raspberry juice. At three o'clock another eighth of *Glühwein* is permitted and between then and midnight up to a litre of wine may be consumed. The evening meal is of home baking specialities liberally garnished with parsley and chives. Some people certainly find the treatment beneficial and *Schrothkur* establishments have a good reputation. New centres are still being opened to provide for the traditional inclination of Germans to take a *Kur*.

From Oberstaufen many excursions into the mountains are possible and maps and guides are readily available. One which can be recommended requires the use of car or bus to the lower station of the *Kabinenseilbahn* (cable railway with four-seat cabins). From here, given sufficient time, the very fit could climb the steep path about 4km to the summit cross on the Hochgrat (1,832m, 6008ft). More pleasant, especially for a family excursion, is to take the cable-car to the upper station (refreshments available) and walk the remaining short distance to the summit in about 20 minutes. If this lovely vantage point is chosen for a picnic, look out for the antics of the alpine choughs, cheekily demanding a share of the food.

The journey back to the valley can be accomplished on foot following the clear path which zig-zags to and fro across the cable-car route. A hut part way down provides much-needed refreshment, for even downhill the walk is quite a strenuous one. Do not be misled by the short distance; at least 2 hours should be allowed for the descent and good boots are really essential, even in dry weather. Experienced mountain walkers could follow the splendid, easily identified and gradually descending high-level walk of 14-16km eastwards from the summit towards Immenstadt. This takes in the summits Rindalphorn (1,822m, 5,976ft), Buralpkopf (1,772m, 5,812ft) and Stuiben (1,749m, 5,736ft). From the latter, the path, now waymarked 41, continues to descend until, about 2km short of the town, the upper station of a chair-lift is reached (1,451m, 4,759ft) which will take one down to the town if required. From Immenstadt the train may be used for the return to Oberstaufen. This is a magnificent walk in good weather with wonderful views on every side. Walking boots are essential and waterproofs, warm clothing and some rations should be carried. Not suitable for small children.

Eastwards from Oberstaufen, road and railway follow the valley of the Konstanzer Ach, a little river. **Thalkirchdorf,** about 6km away, is in a rather narrow valley. It is a good walking centre and a popular winter resort with several ski-lifts nearby. In this area, look out in the summer months for notices announcing a *Bergmesse*. This is a simple religious service conducted on a hill top with an improvised altar — a moving experience with the mountains all round. After the service, secular activities take over and a band arrives. Beer and other beverages are on sale and a huge vat of sausages is heated for the mid-day snack. The oom-pah music echoes over the hills and some-

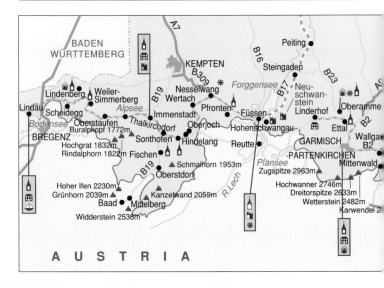

The ridge path from the Hochgrat to Immenstadt

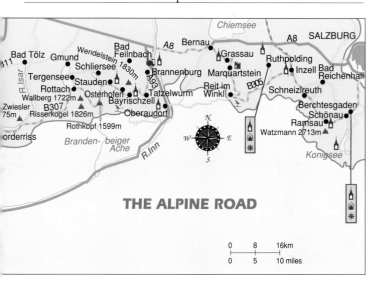

THE ALPINE ROAD

| 0 | 8 | 16km |
| 0 | 5 | 10 miles |

times there is dancing and singing as well. An unusual experience, but one which should not be missed if the opportunity arises.

After Thalkirchdorf, road and railway pass either side of the Grosser Alpsee, re-uniting in **Bühl** to continue together into Immenstadt. This lake, 3km long and 1km wide, is very popular for water activities and is in surroundings of great beauty in the centre of the area covered by the *Wanderkarte Erholungsgebiet Grosser Alpsee*. Bühl, the only resort on the lake is a popular walking and skiing centre, the nearby Gschwender Horn (1,450m, 4,756ft) having two ski-lifts.

Immenstadt (population 14,000) has some interesting historic buildings; the late baroque church of St Nikolaus (1707), the *Rathaus* (seventeenth century), the ruined castle Laubenberg just north of the town and Schloss Königsegg (1620) in the Marienplatz. Once again this is a place for active holidays the year round and there are well marked paths, cross-country ski-routes and downhill skiing.

The Alpenstrasse turns south-east to **Sonthofen**, reached in 7km (4 miles) a *Luftkurort* of 21,000 inhabitants. It is a popular holiday centre summer and winter as well as being an important business town. Guests are catered for with all the usual amenities and there are some attractions not found elsewhere. For example, the second Sunday in December sees the start of the 'Nikolaus' balloon race. There could hardly be a better centre for those wishing to explore the mountains, with more than a hundred mountain railways, ski-lifts and chair-lifts within a short distance. The camp site is open all year.

Seven kilometres (4 miles) south of Sonthofen on the often busy B19, **Fischen im Allgäu** is a delightful resort, which has retained much of its traditional charm. Should there be cool days in summer, the visitor may still lounge comfortably on the terrace of the heated swimming pool enjoying the artificial sunshine of infra-red lamps. After a summer visit many people like to return in winter. Indeed, it seems that summer merges almost imperceptibly into winter for it is said that one can bathe in the open air on the nearby Sonnenalp until well into December. The pool contains water heated in the depths of the earth and on cool days the rising steam presents an eery vision. So popular is this resort that it is as busy in November as other places are in the high season. Fischen has 3,300 inhabitants and many different entertainments for visitors when they are not skiing or climbing mountains. Of interest is the early baroque Liebfrauen-kirche in the cemetery with its high eight-sided domed tower.

Four or five kilometres further on is **Oberstdorf** at the foot of the 2,224m (7,294ft) Nebelhorn which can be ascended by one of the three mountain railways: there are also nineteen ski-lifts in the immediate vicinity for Oberstdorf (population 12,000), Germany's most southerly market town, is the most important winter sports centre in Allgäu. Nevertheless, it is equally a summer resort and visitors are offered a great variety of things to do all year round.

Before leaving Oberstdorf a rewarding walk of about 4km starts at the Gasthaus Breitachklamm where there is a good car park. The Breitachklamm (ravine) was made accessible to the public in 1905 and has become one of the tourist highlights of the area. Over 1.5km long, the ravine is also one of the most spectacular in all the Alpine regions, especially after rain. The gorge starts innocently enough but a short climb reveals the power of the water, rushing and plunging through the 100m-high (328ft) rocky walls which constantly drip and steam and create miniature waterfalls on all sides. The well defined tourist track needs no map-reading but time should be allowed to admire the little river as it tosses itself from rock to rock. At the end of the ravine proper, past a picture postcard hut, keep to the left and climb steeply to the Walserschanz (991m, 3,250ft) where the B19 crosses the frontier into Austria. There is a *Gasthof* here. Turn left along the road towards Oberstdorf for about 200m then left again following the signs down to the Zwingsteg (bridge) which takes one across the ravine at a dizzy height of about 80m (262ft). To complete the round walk continue up the opposite slope on a zig-zag path and stroll northwards through little woods, across fields and eventually down through a wood to the start.

Oberstaufen and all the places mentioned since then are accessible by train but Oberstdorf is the end of the line.

The crossing of the B19 into Austria at Walserschanz is about 4km from Oberstdorf and an excursion into the Kleinwalsertal, which is now entered, is something of a novelty. The road and the River Breitach are hemmed in by imposing mountains such as the Hoher Ifen (2,230m, 7,314ft) and Grünhorn (2,039m, 6,687ft) to the west and the Kanzelwand (2,059m, 6,753ft) and Widderstein (2,536m, 8,318ft) to the east. The picturesque route leads through the resorts of **Riezlern**, **Hirschegg** and **Mittelberg** to come to an abrupt stop at **Baad**, 19km from Oberstdorf, with the mountains barring further progress except on foot. There is ample parking here and good tracks for a few kilometres leading to fine mountain views. Given the time and the necessary stamina an all-day mountain walk of about 13km to the summit of the Widderstein can start from here.

Walk south from Baad across the River Breitach; after about 15 minutes enter the solitude of the Bärgundtal. Note the many wild flowers in the fields through which the Bärgundbach (stream) flows down the valley. All the time, the Dolomite-like summit of the Grosse Widderstein is seen ahead as the path is followed through the valley to the Unteren Bärgundalp, reached in about 45 minutes from Baad. A little later the real climb begins and before a noticeably steep incline the path goes upwards to the right to the Oberen Hochalphütte (1,889m, 6,195ft) 2 hours from Baad. From here, keeping to the left and going roughly due east, the south slope of the Seekopf is crossed and the main track is then allowed to go away left while the walker takes the smaller path past the lonely Hochalpsee (a little lake) up to the beginning of the gorge-like gulley on the south side of the Widderstein. Go up the gulley, first over scree and then over short rocky steps, and up to the left to the ridge over which the cross on the Grosse Widderstein (2,533m, 8,308ft) is reached in about $4\frac{1}{4}$ hours from Baad.

Retracing steps down the gulley but keeping left, reach the Obere Widdersteinalp (2,010m, 6,593ft) and descend slightly to the Gemstelpass (1,971m, 6,465ft) in about $1\frac{1}{4}$ hours from the summit. From here climb north-east through the Hochtal and in half an hour down to the Obere Gemstelalp (1,692m, 5,549ft); in another 10 minutes the Gsprengten Weg leads down over the ravine of the foaming Gemstelbach. After that, a long left and then a right hand curve brings the route to a good track at the Untere Gemstelalp, which leads due north to reach the settlement of **Bödmen** in 20 minutes. Here turn left into the good small road to reach Baad in half an hour, a total of $3\frac{1}{2}$ hours from the summit. Refreshments may be available at the huts at the

The Breitachklamm near Obersdorf

several 'alps' mentioned and overnight accommodation is possible at the Obere Widdersteinalp. Check on this before setting out from Baad but, in any case, remember emergency rations, warm clothing and stout boots. The map for this route is the 1:50,000 *Allgäuer Alpen*. Do not be misled by the modest distance; it is the total climb of 1,300m (4,264ft) which counts on this walk.

Splendid mountain scenery, rushing streams, wild flowers and perhaps animals, all this the Kleinwalsertal has in common with many other Alpine valleys. The novelty lies in its peculiar political and geographical situation. It is Austrian without doubt but there is access to it only from Bavaria. An agreement made in 1891 allies it economically with Germany but politically with Austria. This creates many anomalies; for example, mail must be franked with Austrian stamps paid for in German Marks!

Back on the Alpenstrasse (B308) **Hindelang** is reached (population 5,000) about 8km after leaving Sonthofen. It is well known because of its winter sports but is a splendid centre for every season of the year and especially fine in the late autumn just before the snow arrives. When the snow does come, Hindelang is invaded by skiers from near and far. At any season there are two things to attract the visitor regardless of weather. Both are to be found in the tiny church of **Bad Oberdorf** just 1km away. The first is a remarkably fine altar by Jörg Lederer and the other is the famous Holbein Madonna, more correctly the 500-year-old painting *Picture of the Mother of God* by Hans Holbein the Elder. The *Rathaus* is a former hunting lodge (1660) of the prince-bishops of Augsburg. Continuing eastwards climb steadily along a section said to be the most twisty road in Germany. Motorists should exercise the greatest caution.

In 7km **Oberjoch**, at an altitude of about 1,130m (3,706ft), is reached. The B308 goes ahead to cross the border and becomes Austrian road 199 leading to the heart of Tirol. B310 becomes the Alpine Road for a while, going north first to **Wertach** (population 2,300), a *Luftkurort* only 10km south of Oy-Mittelberg visited in the previous chapter. Just before reaching Wertach a road on the right signed 'Jungholz' may be noticed. This is another Austrian enclave which can only be reached from the Bavarian side of the mountains. It is much smaller but otherwise, conditions are similar to those found in the Kleinwalsertal. In Wertach, as in all the other places mentioned in the last few pages, the autumn movement of cattle from the high pastures takes place around the third week in September, a factor to bear in mind, not only for the spectacle but also possible congestion on the roads. Wertach is a resort for summer and winter with reliable snow conditions for several months. Water activities are centred on the nearby Grüntensee, a small lake, along the south shore of which runs the Alpenstrasse, now turned eastwards again to pass through **Nesselwang** (population 3,000) with its many excellent facilities including the Alpspitz-Bade-Center, a swimming pool complex. After Sonthofen the public transport user has to use buses from either Sonthofen or Oy-Mittelberg to reach the resorts, but at Nesselwang the main line railway is again at hand.

Pfronten is one of the foremost resorts in Allgäu and claims nearly 7,000 inhabitants but this includes a dozen outlying villages. The town itself is not actually on the Alpine Road but on a loop to the south which crosses the frontier into Austria at the foot of the Breitenberg (1,821m, 5,973ft) and then continues through the Tyrolean resort of Vils to return to Bavaria after about 8km just outside Füssen. Similarly, the railway which has reached Pfronten from Kempten takes the more southerly route and only gets back into Bavaria at the foot of the Zugspitze before running into Garmisch-Partenkirchen. The skiing area served by Pfronten covers an altitude of 900 to 1,730m (2,952 to 5,674ft) so that good snow conditions are virtually guaranteed for a very long season. The parish church of St Nikolaus in Pfronten-Berg has baroque frescos and tower. Entertainments are laid on in the summer and winter seasons and there are ski-lifts, chair-lifts and *Kabinenbergbahnen* (cabin cable cars).

On the Bavarian side of the border the Alpenstrasse now continues past the pretty Weissensee into **Füssen**, an important centre of 13,000 inhabitants. (This is is also the finishing point of the Romantische Strasse route described in Chapter 1.)

Füssen is a *Kneippkurort* but it is by no means a place dedicated solely to those coming for medical treatment and its claim is to cater for every taste. It has an art gallery, archaeological collection, historic buildings, steamer excursions on the Forggensee and, within walking distance, the first of the famous Königsschlösser, the fantastic castles of King Ludwig II. The Forggensee is an artificial lake nearly 10km long. It was formed by building a dam 323m (1,059ft) long and 41m (134ft) high across the valley of the Lech, the work being completed in 1955 to provide a head of water for the hydro-electric power station (open to visitors) at Rosshaupten at the north end. The lake takes its name from the village of Forggen which now lies beneath the water. There are 180km of footpaths including many in the fairly easy terrain around the many small lakes and along the River Lech which tumbles out of Austria just south of the town. The spray at the Lech Falls can create delightful rainbows and here, in the rocky wall, is a bust of Maximilian II, the father of Ludwig.

The nearby church marks the start of a modest but rather interesting walk of about 8km. From the main road, path 17, yellow way-mark, climbs steadily through the woods and soon comes to the first of the 'Stations of the Cross'. These take various forms as the path climbs, some found in a small chapel. By the time the last Station is passed, the summit (953m, 3,126ft) is in view with three wooden crosses on the skyline, for this is the Kalvarienberg (Hill of Calvary), one of several so named in Bavaria. The crosses are on a platform from which there is an extensive panoramic view of the countryside with the large Forggensee prominently below. Beneath the summit crosses there is a cavern containing a tomb with a stone figure representing Christ.

The path continues in an easterly direction until it joins a small road. Turn left here for a very short distance and then take path 14 to the right. This turning is about 1.5km from the start of the walk but something like 150m (492ft) has been climbed in this short distance. Path 14 continues in a left-hand curve above, but fairly close to, the south shore of the little Schwan-See (Swan Lake). After passing the lake, several paths continue in a generally easterly direction, keep towards the right and there are soon charming views down through the trees to the much larger Alpsee. The dominating Schloss Hohen-schwangau is passed as the path drops down to the village of the same name. This is an opportunity to visit the castle from which there is a fine view of the newer Schloss Neuschwanstein across the valley as well as the steep mountains towards the Austrian border to the south. To return to Füssen, leave Hohenschwangau along the main road but soon fork to the left to follow a track away from the traffic for the level walk back to the starting point, about 3.5km.

A pleasant ramble of 8-10km is westwards from Füssen through the suburb of **Bad Faulenbach** and along the straight and virtually traffic-free minor road (path 24) to the Alat-See, an idyllic little lake amongst the trees reached in just over 4km. The hotel here is open all year and is a delightful spot for the afternoon *Kaffeepause* or a more substantial meal. Boats can be hired or walks can be taken right round the lake (about 1.5km). A slightly more strenuous route begins by turning right in Bad Faulenbach and continues via the Neuer-Kobel-Weg (path 25) through the woods. The distance is about the same. For the return to Füssen take either of the routes already mentioned (they merge about 600m, 650yd, from the lake) or take a track (27) from the north shore over the ridge to the Weissensee, turning right on reaching path 26 along the south shore and back to the town. This adds about 2km. Or one can take path 28 from the south shore of the Alat-See and cross the border into Austria imme-diately after leaving the lake. Then, almost immediately, turn left

Outdoor chess at Weissensee, near Füssen

Füssen

through fields to a farm called Ländehof, about 1.5km from the border. From here path 21 follows the River Lech directly towards Füssen. In another 1.5km just before crossing back into Bavaria there is a fork where path 21 goes to the right and 22 to the left. Path 21 closely follows the river to pass the Lech Falls while 22 takes a slightly more direct route away from the river. The route back via Austria adds about 1km to the total distance.

There are many notable buildings in Füssen. The former Benedictine *Kloster* church of St Mang (1701) shows a strong Venetian influence, due to the fact that the architect studied in Venice. The *Kloster* building itself was the work of the same architect and today houses the *Heimatmuseum*. The little baroque Spitalkirche (1748–9) has a completely painted façade and is a beautiful example of Bavarian outdoor painting. A thirteenth- to fourteenth-century castle was converted in 1490–1503 into a residential *Schloss*, the north wing of which now houses part of the Bavarian art collection.

Much written about Füssen is equally applicable to **Hohenschwangau** for both resorts share many of the same sights and

Schloss Neuschwanstein

surroundings. The difference is that life here is dominated more by the two famous castles than by the excellent facilities. The 'old' castle is Hohenschwangau, standing on the site of a thirteenth-century building, the ruins of which were cleared to enable the present palace to be built, in the English Tudor style, in 1832 as summer seat for Crown Prince Maximilian of Bavaria, later King Maximilian II. The salons and drawing rooms have large murals depicting old German sagas and knightly exploits. These include scenes from some of the legends later used by Wagner in his music-dramas. Wagner was a frequent visitor here as guest of Maximilian's son Ludwig who was his great admirer. Wagner's piano is still here in working order.

There are splendid views from the terraces around the castle but the eye is drawn as by a magnet, to the imposing outline of the best known and most photographed German castle, Schloss Neuschwanstein. King Ludwig II laid the foundation stone of his palace in 1869. Neuschwanstein was conceived as a coherent whole inspired by the opera world of Richard Wagner but the king adapted it to his own ideas. For example, the paintings from *Tannhäuser* and *Lohengrin* were not as Wagner had described the scenes for his operas but portrayed the old sagas on which the operas were based.

There have been many Bavarian idols over the years but none is dearer to the hearts of the people than Ludwig II. His great grandfather was the first king of Bavaria, Maximilian I, who died in 1825 and was succeeded by his eldest son, Ludwig I. His son in turn later became Maximilian II to whom a son was also born in 1845 and was given, naturally, the name of Ludwig, especially as he was born on 25 August, St Ludwig's Day. Ludwig I stood down in 1848 following the 'scandal' of his affair with the dancer Lola Montez. Maximilian II came to the throne and when he died on 10 March 1864 young Ludwig was not yet nineteen. Europe was in turmoil; Austria and Prussia were at loggerheads, the latest Polish rising against the Russians was being put down, the French had occupied Rome and Garibaldi was trying to dislodge them. This then was the world of the young king, handsome, mysterious and already a trifle sad. It is said that he loved his cousin Elisabeth who had married the Austrian emperor and that Ludwig was never able to forget her.

In 1871 Europe entered a period of peace which lasted almost half a century until 1914. Ludwig II spent the next 15 years in flight from reality; he created the world of Louis XIV in Schloss Herrenchiemsee and in Schloss Linderhof. The private productions of theatrical works from the courts of Louis XIV and XV were as numerous as those of the Wagner operas. The world of *Tannhäuser* and *Lohengrin* he built at Neuschwanstein; in Hundings Hütte near Linderhof he imagined himself as Siegmund; in the Moorish kiosk, an Arabian sultan and in the Wintergarden Residence in Munich, an Indian mogul. He had plans drawn up for a Byzantine castle and a Chinese summer palace. Neuschwanstein was an anti-Bavarian demonstration on his part. The Bavarian lion was banished from the decorations to be replaced by the peacock and the swan. When he discovered the blue and white diamond of Bavaria in the pattern for a carpet he went into a frenzy. In the end, Ludwig shunned the light of day and would only travel by night in a splendid coach accompanied by faithful servants and torch-bearing outriders.

Finally, the most mysterious episode of all: his drowning in the Starnberger See on 13 June 1886. The only witness was his physician Von Gudden who died with him, and the deaths have never been satisfactorily explained. No doubt the disappearance of Ludwig was something of a relief to the government and the possibility of foul play cannot be ruled out. A hundred years on there is in Bavaria a Ludwig II Federation which keeps his memory alive. Whatever the government of the day thought about it, Bavarians today have much to be grateful to Ludwig for, as has the foreign visitor. No single individual has had a greater influence on the development of Bavarian tourism in the twentieth century than Ludwig. Millions visit his famous palaces every year, while music-lovers throng to Bayreuth every summer for the annual Wagner Festival.

Neuschwanstein alone attracts over a million visitors each year so visit outside the main tourist season if possible. Tours of the castle are conducted in many languages. In addition to the rooms provided as living quarters for the king and his court, the throne room and the music hall with its minstrel gallery are particularly worth seeing. Amateur photographers may be disappointed to discover that they cannot find a location from which to reproduce the spectacular picture of the castle which appears in so many books and on numerous posters. All the same, there are many good shots to be had, probably the best general view is that from the dizzy heights of the Marienbrücke, a footbridge over the gorge of the River Pöllat.

Before leaving the area visit the pilgrimage church of St Koloman (1673), about 3km north of Hohenschwangau close to the main road. Koloman appears to have been involved in political intrigue and he was hanged in Austria as a spy. Many typically Bavarian festivals take place in the district, including the *Wurmfeiertag* on 26 May. It has its origins in a plague of cockchafers which played havoc with farming in 1754. The farmers made a pilgrimage to St Koloman, promising that if their prayers for relief were answered they would make an annual pilgrimage, a promise which has been kept to this day.

Now there is a short break in the Alpenstrasse: it starts again at **Linderhof** 16km due east of Hohenschwangau but the way is barred by mountains such as the Hochblasse (1,988m, 6,520ft), the Scheinberg (1,926m 6317ft) and the Klammspitz (1,925m, 6,314ft). The motorist must, therefore, make a detour either to north or south. The north route involves returning along the Romantic Road as far as Steingaden, there to turn east and then south to Oberammergau, turning west to reach Linderhof. A shorter and quicker route goes south from Füssen to join the Austrian road 314 towards Reutte in Tirol. Before reaching Reutte a modern dual carriageway starts near Unterletzen and after about 6km connects with a road going east past the Plansee and back across the border at Ammersattel, a pass at 1,118m (3,667ft). The picturesque road now enters the German nature conservation area Ammergebirge and in about 7km arrives from the west at Linderhof and the re-start of the Alpenstrasse.

Ludwig II had Schloss Linderhof built to re-create the world of Louis XIV (Ludwig is the German form of Louis) and the rococo palace was built in 1874–8. Highlights of the interior are the first floor rooms containing pictures of French celebrities of the reigns of Louis XIV and XV. In particular, the gold-covered bedroom, although relatively small, is quite breathtaking in its splendour. Behind the *Schloss* is a grandiosely laid-out park with many places of interest including a grotto with a tiny lake and a Moorish kiosk. The waterfalls lead to a Neptune fountain which can send a 32m-high (104ft) spout of water into the air. The fountains play daily each hour from 9am until 5pm in the summer months.

Leaving Swabia and entering Upper Bavaria continue eastwards along the Alpenstrasse, flanked on either side by high peaks. After about 10km (6 miles) is **Oberammergau** (population 5,000), a charming large village 850m (2,788ft) above sea level. Here, there is a wide variety of leisure activities for the visitor's year-round enjoyment. In addition to many ski-lifts there are a chair-lift and a *Kabinenseilbahn*.

In 1632 the dreaded plague was brought to this valley by the Swedish mercenaries. In many parishes whole populations died or fled to safety. Oberammergau sealed itself off and forbade anyone to enter or leave. A man from the village was working meanwhile in nearby Eschenlohe and he took the risk of stealing into Oberammergau to see his family; he brought the Black Death with him and his own and many families were completely wiped out. In despair, the village council made a vow: if God stopped the plague they and their descendants would present a 'Passion of Our Lord' play every 10 years for all time. From that moment, it is recorded, no further deaths occurred and in 1634 the Passion Play was performed for the first

Schloss Linderhof

The painted façade of the Hansel and Gretel House in Oberammergau

time. It was repeated in 1640 and since then the 10-year cycle has been broken only by twentieth-century wars. In 1984 an additional performance celebrated the 350th anniversary of the first production.

Each play year the performance is repeated many times between mid-May and the end of September. All the performers are village residents, the allocation of roles taking place at public auditions. Children leave school at the appropriate time to take part in the crowd scenes when there can be up to 700 players on the stage at one time. The stage is in the open air but in the present theatre, built in 1930, the audience is under cover. The play goes on regardless of the weather and a duplicate set of costumes is kept so that one day's performance in the rain does not interfere with the following one.

The play is by no means a commercial venture and it is not staged for the enjoyment of the audience but to the glory of God in accordance with the ancient promise. Nevertheless, the 10-yearly influx of visitors is of immense value to the economy of the village. Most people coming from a distance buy tickets which include accommodation locally for the nights before and after the play which starts at about 8.15am and finishes in the late afternoon with a couple of hours' break at lunchtime. The play is in German, but translations of the full text are available in almost every language so it is easy to follow the action.

Many of the 1,400 or so people involved in every performance start the day with prayer in the Catholic church which was built 1736–42, another example of the work of the Wessobrunn school. This pretty little church is well worth visiting, as is the *Heimatmuseum* with its examples of fourteenth- to eighteenth-century folk art and local wood-carving. Oberammergau is the home of the Bavarian School of Wood-carving and there are many souvenirs in the shops displaying the work of local craftsmen. A walk through the village reveals many houses with painted façades. Two of the best are the Geroldhaus and the Pilatushaus, painted at the end of the eighteenth century.

Oberammergau is one of many destinations in a programme of excursions by Deutsche Bundesbahn (Federal Railway) designed to allow residents of München and visitors to walk in the mountains without using their own transport. Upon arriving at Oberammergau walkers are met by the leader — usually a member of the local Alpine club — who takes them for a $4\frac{1}{2}$ hour ramble to Linderhof from where they return by bus to Oberammergau.

Five kilometres south of Oberammergau is **Ettal** (population 1,000) which is an attractive village in its own right but is principally of interest because of Kloster Ettal, one of the best-known monasteries in southern Germany. The first religious institution was founded here in 1320 and after the installation of a Madonna brought from Italy, it quickly became an important centre of pilgrimage. In 1370 the monastery church was completed as a twelve-sided Gothic building based on the Church of the Holy Sepulchre in Jerusalem. In 1710 it was remodelled in the baroque style, retaining the twelve-sided design, while in 1745–52 a baroque dome was added following fire damage. The lavishly decorated façade and another choir were added in the eighteenth century. The twelve-sided section is more than 25m (82ft) across and is dominated by a gigantic dome fresco.

The picturesque B23 from Oberammergau continues another 5km to **Oberau**, a small resort in the Loisachtal, where the B2 is joined for the 8km south to Garmisch-Partenkirchen.

Garmisch-Partenkirchen (population 27,000), another example of the double name of which the Germans are rather fond, is one of the major Alpine resorts and has many dramatic and musical traditions; the composer Richard Strauss lived here in the street named after him until his death in 1949. In Garmisch the sights include the old church of St Martin although little remains of the original building of about 1280. When the church was extended in 1446, a spire and fine net vaulting in the nave were added. The Gothic wall paintings include a larger-than-life St Christopher (thirteenth century) and scenes from the Passion (fifteenth century). The new parish church of St Martin was built in 1730–4. King Ludwig II spent time here too and his Schachen hunting lodge just to the north was built as a picturesque retreat and now houses a museum of local history. The Moorish room is specially notable. The Werdenfels Museum at 47 Ludwigstrasse was founded in 1895 to demonstrate the work of the technical school of wood-carvers and cabinet-makers. The exhibits include folk culture, costume, ceramics and sixteenth- to eighteenth-century sculpture. At 45 Ludwigstrasse is the Gasthof Zum Rasen where folk dramas are performed by the Peasant Theatre between mid-July and mid-September.

In Partenkirchen the pilgrimage church of St Anton (1705–39) has an older octagonal part and a more recent section. Unremarkable externally, the two parts merge harmoniously within. The most striking feature is the ceiling painting of 1739.

There is a great deal to do in Garmisch-Partenkirchen but the outstanding excursion is to the summit of the Zugspitze, Germany's highest mountain at 2,963m (9,718ft). The modern cog-wheel train which goes the greater part of the journey starts from beside the main station and climbs steadily for about half an hour when it calls at Eibsee, a dark mountain lake surrounded by trees. One can change here and go direct to the summit by cable car, a massive altitude change of about 2,000m (6,560ft) in 10 minutes or so. By staying in the train, the Schneefernerhaus Hotel, at an altitude of 2,650m (8,692ft), is reached in another $\frac{3}{4}$ hour. The actual summit is then reached by means of a cable car in just 4 minutes. Here at the top is a permanent glacier skiing area with a series of ski-lifts having a total capacity of over 3,000 persons per hour. It is possible to do the round trip from Eibsee, one way by train and the other way by cable car, and descent from the summit into Austria is another option. The Schneeferner-haus is a modern hotel built right into the side of the mountain and it looks out over a fantastic range of snow-covered peaks as far as the eye can see. A night here — albeit a rather expensive one — is a memorable experience especially if there is a sunset or sunrise.

As well as the Zugspitze excursion there are no less than eight other cable railways and numerous ski-lifts. High in the mountains, Schloss Schachen, the hunting lodge of Ludwig II, is accessible only on foot from either Garmisch-Partenkirchen or Elmau. Stout foot-wear is essential for the summit is at 1,872m (6,144ft).

The Alpenstrasse B2 continues eastwards out of Partenkirchen with the peaks of the Wettersteingebirge prominent on the right, marking the border with Austria — Hochwanner (2,764m, 9,065ft), Dreitorspitze (2,633m, 8,636ft) and Wettersteinwand (2,482m, 8,140ft). After about 12km fork right in Klais leaving the Alpen-strasse for a little while, to visit nearby **Mittenwald**. A town of 8,300 inhabitants tightly squeezed in between the mountains, this is an-other of the outstanding Alpine resorts of Bavaria and the supposed birthplace in 1777 of that fictional character Augustin Sumser en-countered at the beginning of this chapter.

Towering over the town to the east is the sheer wall of the Karwendel with its west summit (2,385m, 7,822ft) sitting astride the border and today easily reached in 10 minutes from the lower station beside the River Isar by the Karwendelbahn cable car. This is the latest and most spectacular addition at Mittenwald and makes it possible for tourists to enjoy views previously only seen by energetic climbers who spent many hours on the ascent from the valley. A deservedly popular summer resort but with plenty of winter facili-ties also. There are many kilometres of well kept and marked footpaths radiating from the town for walks of every length and degree of difficulty. Many of the paths are kept clear in winter so walking does not have to be regarded as a purely summer activity.

For a moderately strenuous walk of 18 or 24km (11 or 15 miles) start from the *Kurpark* near the lower station of the Kranzberg chair-lift and take the easy nature trail (*Naturlehrpfad*) following the little River Lainbach until the Lautersee is reached at 1,010m (3,312ft).

There is a café here and a pleasant natural bathing place. The nature trail goes along the east lake shore and crosses a minor road. Turn right here and continue to the end of this road at Ferchensee (1,059m, 3,473ft — café) and continue straight ahead on an easy path along the north bank of the Ferchenbach — a stream fed by the lake just passed — eventually crossing the stream and following the other bank for a short distance, then crossing back and dropping down to Schloss Elmau, now a hotel. Turn east here, choosing the minor road beyond the *Schloss* or the rather more difficult hill path off to the right just before reaching it. After about 4km the two routes cross so there is an opportunity for a change of mind. The path soon crosses the Kreidenbach and the road does so a little later near Schloss Kranzbach. They combine again shortly before the hamlet of Klais about 8km from Elmau where it is possible to get a bus or train back to Mittenwald.

There are several possible walking routes back, none of them very direct, if one wishes to avoid the main road traffic. Easy walking is possible by following the Rossgraben (a little river) south from Klais to the Wildensee (1,136m, 3,726ft — café) then dropping down past the Korbinianhütte (café) to the starting point. The last 2km could be avoided by using the Kranzberg chair-lift from near the Wildensee. The distance from Klais to Mittenwald is around 6km. This walk has

The summit buildings on the Zugspitze in winter

the advantage of getting away from the crowds in and around Mittenwald, especially at summer weekends. Choose a quieter time for sight-seeing there.

The parish church of St Peter and St Paul was built 1738–40 and incorporates the Gothic choir of an earlier building. The decoration is unique, the vaults and friezes are covered in tendrils and blossoms, some of the finest stucco work in Germany. Mittenwald is famous as a centre of violin-making and credit for this is given to one Matthias Klotz (1653–1743) who probably studied under Amati in Cremona. There is a memorial to him outside the church. The history of violin-making here is graphically portrayed in the Geigenbau-Museum (Violin-making Museum) and there are collections of other instruments as well as a section devoted to peasant culture.

The carving skills of the inhabitants are nowhere better seen than in the fantastic wooden masks they make for men to wear at the time of the pre-Lenten celebrations called *Fasching* or *Fastnacht*. The colourful activities come to a climax on the Thursday before Lent and the opportunity is taken, not only to prepare for the period of fasting, but to drive out winter and welcome spring. There are processions which are accompanied by much bell-ringing as a mountaineer arrives dressed in the traditional *Lederhosen* (leather shorts) and a decorated belt to which sixteen bells are attached and he leads a group of similarly equipped bell-ringers. The wooden masks are donned by many of the male participants before the procession and there is a great deal of jollity and leg-pulling as the groups go from hostelry to hostelry. The masks are not removed, even for drinking, until the day comes to an end. Later on there is dancing and by tradition no woman may refuse a masked man's invitation to dance.

Mittenwald has a fine modern swimming pool in which the *Hallenbad* is connected by a channel to the outdoor pond, so that one can swim freely between the two, even in the coldest weather.

On leaving Mittenwald return to the Alpenstrasse and in 10km (6 miles) reach the pleasant resort of **Wallgau**. The route follows the Rivar Isar eastwards along a picturesque private toll-road — it cannot officially be called the Alpenstrasse — for about 12km to **Vorderriss** where the road becomes the B307 and can re-assume the name. For another 11km the route continues to follow the river, sweeping across the beautiful Sylvenstein-Stausee on a modern viaduct, but at the foot of the Hoher Zwiesler (1,375m, 4,510ft) it divides and the left fork (B13) follows the Isar north to Bad Tölz, while the B307 continues to the Achen Pass (941m, 3,086ft) and follows the Grosser Weissach river down to the Tegernsee at **Rottach-Egern**.

Continue on the B307 past Tegernsee (see Chapter 3) and turn right at Gmund to follow a secondary road 8km (5 miles) to **Hausham** to rejoin the B307 past Schliersee until a road goes off left to both **Stauden** and **Fischbachau** about 3km away. Benedictine monks founded a cell at Fischbachau in the eleventh century but they did not remain long. The farming community inherited a fine church which was consecrated in 1110, long after the monks had disappeared. The Romanesque building owed something to the spirit of Hirsau in the Black Forest where the monks originated but was considerably altered in the seventeenth and eighteenth centuries when abundant stucco was introduced. The frescos in the nave show scenes from the life of St Martin to whom the church is dedicated and date from 1737–8. However, Fischbachau has an even older church, used before the monks descended upon them, and known as the Alte Pfarrkirche (Old Parish Church). Externally the main building is still pure Romanesque but the interior was given stucco treatment around 1630. Of particular interest is the charming rococo organ of 1750.

Back on the B307, the cable railway up the west side of the Wendelstein (1,838m, 6,028ft) can soon be seen. A strenuous 13km walk taking in the Wendelstein summit starts at the **Osterhofen** station of the cable railway (5 minutes from the DB station) where there is parking space. Set off in an easterly direction on a gently rising track to the settlement of **Hochkreut**. At the second farmhouse from there — house No 16 — join the Wendelsteinweg from Bayrischzell and follow its red markings through the wooded west slopes of the Legerwaldgraben. In $\frac{3}{4}$ hour the little Siegel-Alm (1,325m, 4,346ft) is reached and in another $\frac{1}{4}$ hour arrive at the basin of the Wendelstein *Almen* (Alpine meadows). Now walk up to the right for half an hour to the gap between the Kesselwand and the Wendelstein and then to the left to reach the saddle at the foot of the Wendelstein summit in about $2\frac{1}{2}$ hours from Osterhofen. (Save time by using the cable car for the ascent.) Up to the left is the little Wendelstein church, the highest place of worship in Germany, while to the right there is the upper terminus of the cog-wheel railway up from Brannenburg. It takes about 20 minutes more to reach the summit at 1,830m (6,002ft) and there is a small fee to use the good path, for the actual summit is private property. The stupendous view makes it money well spent. To the east, below the highest point, are the domes of the sun observatory and the mast of Bavarian Radio.

With cable car and railway to bring the tourists it is not surprising to find a hotel up here as well. From the hotel terrace go down stone steps and then follow the curves through scree beneath the cableway and follow the sign 'Breitenstein, Feilbach'. After $\frac{1}{4}$ hour fork left

(Breitenstein) to reach an *Alm* hut (Quellbrunnentrog) in about the same time. Just before the hut keep left at the sign for Geitau and Breitenstein. Parts of the path (red waymarks) across the *Alm* basin are narrow but in an hour from the summit a climb up to a broad meadow saddle reveals splendid views to the south. A waymark points to the Koth-Alm. Turn half-right after 10 minutes and then at a wooden cross, turn right down to the Koth-Alm at 1,448m (4,750ft). A track leads to the Kesselalm (refreshments) and later down a zig-zag path to reach the first houses of **Birkenstein** after half an hour. Go right here to a surfaced road; 100m to the right is the Gasthaus Oberwirt. The route now turns south to the end of the surfaced road at a cattle grid. About 150m further at a second cattle grid follow the sign for Geitau and the clear path straight ahead; shortly before reaching the railway at **Geitau** join a surfaced road until, in front of

Statue of Matthias Klotz who made Mittenwald a centre for violin making

a house near the embankment, a sign to the left indicates 'Bayri-schzell' (there is a *Gasthaus* 50m to the right, *Ruhetag* Thursday) and this eastbound path between a wood and the railway reaches the start at **Osterhofen** in $\frac{1}{4}$ hour. The whole circuit takes about $5\frac{1}{2}$ hours or about 3 hours if the ascent is made by cable car. There is overnight accommodation at the Wendelstein Hotel and at the Koth-Alm.

Five kilometres on from Osterhofen, **Bayrischzell** (population 1,600) is where the Benedictine monks first came in the eleventh century to found a short-lived cell, and the *–zell* in the name has survived. This is the ideal Alpine village and it is indeed a place for superlatives. Upper Bavaria is certainly not short of attractive villages but Bayrischzell stands supreme. For most of its existence it lay off the beaten track and was little visited, for the railway south from Schliersee only reached here in 1911. Today a fast train comes from München in 90 minutes. The late Gothic tower of the church stands out from quite a distance and it is surprising to find on closer investigation that the main part of the building is eighteenth century and was decorated in 1736 with stucco and frescos. This is one of the few places where Sunday church-going is still an occasion for wearing the attractive traditional costumes of the district.

After Bayrischzell, the Alpenstrasse gives access to a wonderful

A colourful corner of Neubeuern, near Brannenburg

rambling and skiing area going up to 1,450m (4,756ft). This final curvaceous section of the B307 is a spectacular route between the mountains so take time to enjoy the views. The resort of **Sudelfeld** is reached after about 7km (4 miles). The road ends at **Tatzelwurm** and further progress is only possible on a private toll road unless one takes a right fork to Oberaudorf and Austria. A short distance from the junction is the popular Berggasthof Feuriger (fiery) Tatzelwurm (closed 5 November-15 December and Tuesdays January-May). It takes its name from a mythical fantasy-dragon which hoaxers persuaded some newspapers to 'reveal' to the world in the 1930s. Needless to say, it has never been seen, but it is good for the tourist trade — a sort of Bavarian Loch Ness monster!

To the left the private road leads to **Flintsbach** (population 2,500) and **Brannenburg** (population 5,000) both of which are health resorts in the *Luftkurort* category. They, together with **Degerndorf**, are within a stone's throw of each other. This is the Inn Valley shared by the river, the railway, the motorway A93 and several other roads. Brannenburg is the lower terminal of the cog-wheel railway which goes up to the Wendelstein (upper station 1,723m, 5,650ft) in 55 minutes. Brannenburg's late Gothic church Mariae Himmelfahrt was rebuilt in the rococo style at the end of the eighteenth century while Degerndorf's St Aegidias has a nave which is still Romanesque, a late Gothic tower and baroque ornamentation of 1741.

There are many worthwhile short excursions to be made in this area — the *Klosterkirche* at **Reisach**, and **Oberaudorf** with its colourfully painted houses and a church noted for its rococo decoration and a late Gothic Madonna. At **Bad Feilnbach**, about 8km northwest of Brannenburg, is one of the largest camp sites in Upper Bavaria and many self-catering apartments.

From Flintsbach the road resumes the Alpenstrasse designation. Leaving Brannenburg cross the *Autobahn*, join B15 and continue through Rieschenhart and Raubling until in about 6km the junction with the München-Salzburg motorway A8 is reached. This now becomes the Alpenstrasse for 19km (12 miles), travelling east to **Bernau** (population 5,000), a *Luftkurort* near the south-west corner of the Chiemsee (explored in Chapter 5) at the north foot of the Kampenwand (1669m, 5475ft). The finest house is the Gasthof zum Alten Wirt which was erected in 1697 although its origins go back as far as 1477. Today it is noted for the comfort of its accommodation. Leaving Bernau follow the B305 to **Rottau** and **Grassau** which comprise a *Luftkurort* with a population of 5,300. The church in Grassau (8km, 5 miles, from Bernau) dates from 1491, it was extended in 1696 and its Romanesque tower was capped with an onion-dome in 1737. Inside, a fresco from the fifteenth century has been restored. Even more noteworthy, over the entrance door is a detailed portrayal of a Corpus Christi procession dating from 1700.

Three kilometres on, **Marquartstein** (population 2,900), a *Luft-kurort* at the foot of the Hochgern (1,743m, 5,717ft) on the River Tiroler Ache, is an attractive village overlooked by a medieval fortress which was restored in the last century. Music lovers may be interested to know that Richard Strauss was very fond of this village and it was here that he composed his *Salome* at the beginning of this century. Families will enjoy the *Märchen- und Wildpark* (fairy tale and deer park) with its many attractions, including summer bob-bahn, miniature railway, etc. Much of the 17km (11 miles) from Marquart-stein to Reit im Winkl is in a narrow gorge with sheer cliffs rising on either side of the road. In between are the villages of **Unterwössen** and **Oberwössen**, the latter of interest for the three little lakes accessible from here. Two of them, the Eglsee and Wössener See are quite near but the Taubensee is high above at an altitude of 1,138m (3,732ft) and demands a long and strenuous walk to reach it. The Austrian border actually passes through the centre of the lake.

Reit im Winkl (population 2,800) is an entrancing Alpine village where the houses are outstandingly decorated with colour and flowers. It has grown from a tiny frontier hamlet into a popular resort and yet has retained its rural charm. Admittedly, it is even more charming outside the main tourist season but that is something it shares with most other places in these Bavarian mountains. There are two chair-lifts and twenty-one ski-lifts. For the walker there are rambles of all grades starting from the village centre. A modest stroll starts from the church and follows the road to the end of the village and then climbs gently to the Grünbühel where the ditches are the remains of earthworks dug during the Tirolean war of liberation in 1809. Although this little climb takes only a few minutes, the whole valley lies below and, to the south-west, are wonderful views to the 'Emperor' mountains including the so-called Zahmer (peaceable) Kaiser and the Wilder (ferocious) Kaiser, all in Austria and with the highest peaks well over 2,000m (6,560ft).

The path continues to climb fairly gently (10 minutes) to the war memorial chapel (1924) visible on the Pankrazhügel, with a fine view in every direction. Behind the chapel the path climbs rather steeply in a northerly direction towards the Hausberg and after many twists and turns reaches the Hausbach waterfall at 835m (2,738ft) in an-other 10 minutes. A path now leads directly — and rather steeply — back down to the village. The whole walk takes about an hour.

Once more between mountains and through a fairly sparsely

populated but remarkably pretty countryside, the B305 passes a string of lovely little lakes — Weitsee, Mittersee, Lodensee and Forchensee. Several villages offer refreshment or unsophisticated accommodation but there is no holiday resort as such until, just after passing Weich, the road goes northwards to reach **Ruhpolding** (population 6,800) about 30km (19 miles) from Reit im Winkl. Ruhpolding has both a very large *Freibad* and a *Wellenhallenbad* — an indoor pool with artificial waves. The village itself is not too hemmed in by high mountains for four Alpine valleys converge here making it an open, airy place. There is a cable railway to the Rauschberg (1,645m, 5,395ft), three chair-lifts and ski-lifts, so once again there is ready access to the slopes in summer and winter. If Ruhpolding can be visited when it is not thronged with tourists so much the better.

The parish church of St Georg is reckoned to be one of the finest village churches in Upper Bavaria. Its size is the first surprise for it is no less than 40m long (130ft) with a width of 14m (46ft) and a height of 19m (62ft). Built between 1738 and 1757, this is a fine church. There is a richly decorated pulpit, beautiful choir stalls and several interesting altars. The baroque decoration is a veritable feast for the eye. But the artistic highlight of the church is the Romanesque Madonna, only re-discovered in 1955 and which now graces the right side-altar. Despite its age, this carving with its out-of-proportion baby Jesus in his mother's lap could well have been the work of a modern artist. It is something not to be missed. The *Heimatmuseum* is highly ac-

Detail from Marquartstein's maypole

claimed and is housed in a former hunting lodge dating from 1587. The Museum für Bäuerliche und Sakrale Kunst (rural and religious art) is also very fine and complements the *Heimatmuseum*.

A popular walk of about 13km is to the pilgrimage church of Maria Eck. Leave the village at the north end and, past the hospital, turn left and take the right hand of two roads to **Obergschwendt**. By the first house on the right (bear in mind possible new building) take the fairly level path to the right, mostly in the wood. It runs roughly parallel with the road and the last part before Eisenärzt climbs continuously — not recommended after rain. The road is rejoined and just before entering the village a little road goes off to the left; an alternative good track goes up between the station and the church. Both routes climb steadily to reach Maria Eck (823m, 2,700ft) in about 40 minutes.

In addition to the church itself there is a Minorite *Kloster* and a *Gasthaus*. There are splendid views to the high mountain ranges, to the Chiemsee and even to the Bayerischer Wald far to the north, given good visibility. From Maria Eck go south-westwards past the *Gasthaus* to the Scheichenberg (1,256m, 4,120ft) in about 3km, a steady climb. Keep right here and drop down to the Hocherbalm and then to the Steinberger Alm (refreshments) and continue downhill following a little stream until Ruhpolding is reached.

Children will like to visit the Ruhpolding Märchenfamilienpark (Fairy-tale Park) with its many models of fairy-tale characters — Snow White and the Seven Dwarfs, Hansel and Gretel, the Sleeping Beauty and many more as well as a miniature railway, adventure playground, mini-dodgem-cars and a café.

Back to the Alpenstrasse and in less than 8km (5 miles) reach **Inzell**, the third of these charming Upper Bavarian villages which, with Reit im Winkl and Ruhpolding make up the so-called Chiemgauer Feriendreieck (Chiemgau Holiday Triangle). Inzell with 3,500 inhabitants has many holiday flats. The Gasthof Zur Post dates from the first half of the sixteenth century and its artistic corner towers and courtyard entrance beautify the village centre. Opposite, the parish church of St Michael (1727) has a double onion-domed tower; it is not overloaded with decoration within, the principal sight being the cross at the triumphal arch.

At Inzell, the Deutsche Ferienstrasse, nearly at the end of its long journey from the Baltic, loses its separate identity and joins the Alpenstrasse. On the left, just after Inzell, is the tiny Zwingsee and the end of the valley of the same name, a relic of a glacial gorge from the Ice Age. At **Weissbach** the rocky walls and cliffs climb steeply up out of the valley to over 1,000m (3,280ft). The small village of

Schneizlreuth (population 650) is a good centre for exploring many little lakes and two typical Alpine gorges, the Aschauerklamm and the Weissbachschlucht. For a more sophisticated resort the prosperous spa town of **Bad Reichenhall** (population 20,000) is less than 8km to the east and has every diversion for the holidaymaker.

The Alpenstrasse drops down into the Saalachtal and after Unterjettenberg where the main road to Bad Reichenhall goes off, climbs to the Schwarzbachwachtsattel Pass at 868m (2,847ft). Now there is a view down into the Ramsau valley, one of the most delightful in the Berchtesgaden area which is by no means short of fine views. The pilgrimage church of St Fabian and St Sebastian is one of the most photographed churches in Upper Bavaria because of its beautiful setting. The church was founded in the early sixteenth century and the seventeenth-century groined vault, the baroque high reliefs and medieval wood-carvings ensure a continuing pilgrimage, now of art lovers rather than the pious.

A pleasant short ramble of less than 8km goes through the Zauberwald (Magic Forest) to the Hintersee. Take the Hintersee road west from Ramsau and after about 2km, at the Gasthof Datzmann, go right at a sign marking the entrance to the Zauberwald. Walk downhill to start with, then over a stream, after which turn to the left and a little later to the right over a bridge into the wilderness of the forest. Follow the rushing stream, the Ramsauer Ache, and arrive at a well made track through this near-primeval landscape. Huge rocks overgrown with moss are scattered through the wood, witnesses of a time when these great mountains were less stable than they are today. Twenty minutes from the main road is the point where the boggy bank of the Hintersee reaches almost to the side of the track. Turn right along the lake (note the reflections of the mountains) and after a good 10 minutes reach the old Hinterseestrasse. Now walk up to the right on this little road, then downhill again. Mountains dominate the scene ahead with a distant view of the permanent snowfield of the Blaueisgletscher (Blue Ice Glacier) up to the right. After a bridge, turn right into the dark pines of the Zauberwald and see on the left a miniature cable railway and other Alpine scenarios operated by a waterwheel. At the next fork go left and reach the Gasthof Datzmann again after a short climb.The total time for the circuit is about 1½ hours. Return along the road to Ramsau or wait for the occasional post-bus. This is also suitable as a winter walk.

The Alpenstrasse now enters an outstanding mountain holiday area, the so-called Berchtesgadener Land. This mountain-ringed area comprises the almost adjoining resorts of **Berchtesgaden**, **Bischofswiesen** and **Schönau** together with the surrounding countryside and settlements along the B305 from Ramsau to Marktschellenberg close to the Austrian border on the outskirts of Salzburg. The total population is around 20,000 but is, of course, well scattered. Two mountain railways, two chair-lifts and over two dozen ski-lifts are here to serve the visitor as well as all the more usual leisure facilities. Berchtesgaden even boasts a golf course, a rather rare thing in Bavaria. But as with all the other resorts along the Alpine Road, it is the scenery which stands supreme and in this furthest corner of Bavaria there are delights on every side.

To the south-west, the mighty Watzmann (2,713m, 8,898ft) towers over the land, second only to the Zugspitze in height. To the south, the village of **Königssee** stands at the north end of the tranquil lake of the same name which nestles between the peaks. One of the most beautiful lakes in Bavaria, it is a favourite excursion and somewhat overburdened with tourists during the peak summer holiday season. From the northern tip — the lake is 8km long, 2km wide and up to 188m (616ft) deep — one can see the tiny church of St Bartholomä across the water. Built in 1700 in the shape of a clover leaf with attractive cupolas, the church, occupying space between the lake and the east wall of the Watzmann, can only be reached by motor-boat from the pier at the north end. At St Bartholomä one can disembark to enjoy the peace. This excursion is one which no visitor should forego. The quietness is occasionally enhanced rather than broken by the demonstration of the remarkable seven-fold echo when a trumpet call is flung back and forth from the Falkenstein precipice. Motorboat trips operate throughout the year except when the lake is frozen.

The Alpenpark is an area of about 460sq km surrounding the resorts. The southern part of the area is given over to the Nationalpark Berchtesgaden, a conservation area. The last native bear was killed in 1835 but there is no lack of wildlife here including chamois, deer, ibex and — above 1,200m (3,936ft) — marmots. A climb through the nature reserve south of the Königssee to the Funtensee (1,601m, 5,251ft) provides a good chance of seeing some of these creatures in their natural habitats. The picturesque autumn ceremony of bringing the cattle down from the high pastures is always of interest but has a particular attraction here for the animals have to be ferried across the Königssee. The possibilities for climbing, walking, motoring or cycling excursions are endless. Mountain weather being what it is, there is always the chance of a wet day when the natural attractions are less than enticing. This need not be an unmitigated disaster for there are many ways of putting the day to good use.

In **Berchtesgaden** the *Heimatmuseum* can be recommended; its exhibits are largely from the College of Wood-carving and include

400 hand-carved coats of arms. The former Augustinian canonry church of St Peter and St Johannes is on a site first dedicated to these saints in 1122. In the thirteenth century the second building (from which the west part and the cloisters have survived) was erected. Prior Johannes added the slender early Gothic choir in 1283–1303 and around 1470 the Romanesque nave was pulled down and replaced by a pillared hall. The choir slopes upwards at the end of the nave, a unique example of early Gothic in Bavaria. The residential building of the canonry later became the Residenz. The building has been much altered over the years but the Romanesque cloisters are among the best of their kind. The Residenz now houses the Schlossmuseum, mainly concerned with an excellent art collection which includes works by famous names.

The Salzmuseum is a specialist museum dealing with salt-mining and the lives of salt miners. It works in cooperation with the Berchtesgaden salt mines opened in 1517 and still operating today. In earlier years only members of royal families, church dignitaries and the like were allowed to visit the mines but today they are open to all as a major tourist attraction with about half a million visitors each year. Today's thousands, like the distinguished visitors of the past, must don the clothing worn by the miners of old and start the tour horseback fashion by riding astride the old mining train through a

The tiny church of St Bartholomä at Königsee

600m-long (1,968ft) tunnel to the Emperor Franz pit, an enormous cavern with an area of 3,000sq m. At a lower level is a grotto, bright with many-coloured salt rocks, reached by a sedate walk downstairs or, more excitingly, down a 34m-long (111ft) chute polished over the years by the seats of miners' (and tourists') trousers. Here there are a film theatre and displays of the various equipment and activities associated with the mine. A second chute takes one down to the illuminated underground salt lake crossed on a raft. After passing through another sparkling grotto, an inclined elevator returns the visitor to a higher level to rejoin the 'train' for an exhilarating dash back to the open air. The visit, including time for changing clothes, takes approximately $1\frac{1}{2}$ hours.

Other wet weather sights include the Frauenkirche am Anger (sixteenth century), the much-photographed pilgrimage church of Maria Gern (1709) north of Berchtesgaden and the pilgrimage church of Kunterweg (1731–3) west of the town. The baroque market place is amongst the finest in Upper Bavaria but the fountain crowned by the Bavarian heraldic lion was only installed in 1860 to celebrate the fiftieth anniversary of Berchtesgaden's allegiance to the blue and white kingdom. During Advent the houses round the square are illuminated and the fountain carries an enormous wreath. Winter visitors can enjoy the added attractions of the various festivities which go to make up the Advent-Christmas-New Year seasons. A nice custom here in Berchtesgaden on Christmas Eve is the placing of a lighted candle on every grave in the cemetery.

For many people the area is synonymous with the dark days before World War II and Neville Chamberlain's abortive visits to Bavaria to secure 'peace in our time'. When Adolf Hitler was released from Landsberg prison in 1925, he rented (and later bought) a fine country house high above Berchtesgaden. With its completely encircling balcony and a roof of shingles secured by heavy stones as seen so often in Alpine regions, it had a marvellous view of the mountains. Hitler's later additions were destroyed shortly before the end of the war but the Teehaus, the so-called Adlerhorst (eagle's nest) at 1,834m (6,015ft), survived and today (as the Kehlsteinhaus) is run by the Alpine Club as a mountain *Gaststätte*.

Fifteen kilometres north of Berchtesgaden the Alpenstrasse crosses into Austria and the city of Mozart, Salzburg. The music-lover could easily enjoy the world-famous Salzburg Festival from a base on the Bavarian side of the border. Salzburg and Berchtesgaden together with Bad Reichenhall, although separated by the present national boundary, have a common political and economic history and today form the Austro-Bavarian Holiday Triangle.

Additional Information

Places to Visit

Berchtesgaden
Salzbergwerk and Salzmuseum
83471 Berchtesgaden
☎ 08652-600260
Open: May to mid-October daily
8.30am-5pm, mid-October to April
Monday to Friday 12.30-3.30pm.

Garmisch-Partenkirchen
Jagdschloss Schachen
Open: daily April to September
8am-1pm, 2-6pm. Guided tours
11am, 2pm. Restaurant.

Linderhof
Schloss, Grotto and Moorish Kiosk
Open: daily April to September
9am-12.15pm, 12.45-5.30pm: open
daily except Friday October to
March (Schloss only) 10am-
12.15pm, 12.45-4pm. Restaurant
and café. Park.

Marquartstein
Märchen-Und Wildpark
83250 Marquartstein
☎ 08641-7269
Open: daily Easter to October 9am-
6pm. Restaurant.

Mittenwald
Geigenbau-Museum
Ballenhausgasse 3
82481 Mittenwald
☎ 08823-8418 or 8561
Open: Monday to Friday 10-
11.45am, 2-4.45pm Saturday,
Sunday and holidays 10-11.45am.

Ruhpolding
Märchen-Familienpark
83324 Ruhpolding
☎ 08863-1413 or 08641-7269
3km SW of Ruhpolding. Open 9am
from about Easter to end-October.
Refreshments.

Schwangau
Burg Hohenschwangau
Open: daily, summer 8.30am-
5.30pm, winter 10am-4pm.
Restaurant nearby.

Schloss Neuschwanstein
Open: daily April to September
8.30am-5.30pm, October to March
10am-4pm. Closed 1 Jan-uary,
Shrove Tuesday, 1 November, 24-5,
31 December. Guided tours only.
Inn nearby.

Local Events and Festivals

Mittenwald
Fasching or Fastnacht (Pre-Lenten
   festivities)
Climax Thursday before Lent.
Similar in other places.

Oberammergau
Passion Play — Mid-May to
September every 10 years (2000
etc). About 70 performances.

Long Distance Path
Über Den Grat — 60km (37 miles)
High level route (1,522-2,615m,
4,992-8,577ft) linking peaks of
Allgäu Alps, Oberstdorf to
Hindelang. Accommodation in
mountain huts. Not for beginners.

Mountain Railways
K = cabin cableway
Z = cog-wheel railway

Aschau
Kampenwandbahn (K)
Journey time 14 min.
Daily 9am–5pm (4.30pm in winter).

Bad Reichenhall
Predigtstuhlbahn (K)
Journey time 10 min.
Daily 9am–4pm.

Bayrischzell
Wendelstein-Seilbahn (K)
Journey time 6 min.
Daily 9am–4pm.

Berchtesgaden
Jennerbahn (K)
Obersalzburgbahn (K)
Journey time 20 min.
Daily 9am–4.30pm.
(4pm in December and January)

Bergen
Hochfelln-Seilbahn (K)
Section 1 — Journey time 7 min.
Section 2 — Journey time 4 min.
Daily 9am–11.30am, 12.30–4.30pm.

Brannenburg
Wendelstein-Zahnradbahn (Z)
Journey time 55 min.
Hourly 9am–3pm, upper station
hourly 10am–5pm. May vary.

Füssen
Tegelbergbahn Schwangau (K)
Journey time 6-10 min.
Daily 8.30am–4.30pm.

Garmisch-Partenkirchen
Zugspitzbahn (Garmisch to
   Schneefernerhaus) (Z)
Journey time 80 min.
Daily. Leaves Garmisch hourly
7.35am–3.35pm and S'fernerhaus
hourly 9am–5pm.

Seilbahn (S'fernerhaus to summit) (K)
Journey time 4 min.
Daily 8.45am–4.45-pm (3.45pm in
winter).

Seilbahn (Eibsee to summit) (K)
Journey time 10 min.
Daily 8.30am–5.30pm (4.30pm in
winter).

Tiroler Zugspitzbahn (from
   Ehrwald in Austria) (K)
Section 1 — journey time 6 min.
Section 2 — journey time 6 min.
Section 3 — journey time 2 min.
Daily. Approx hourly 9.15am–
4.15pm.

Osterfelderbahn (K)
Journey time 9 min.
Daily 8.30am–5pm (4pm in winter).

Hochalmbahn (K)
Journey time 4 min.
Daily. At least hourly during
operation of Osterfelderbahn

Kreuzeckbahn (K)
Journey time 8 min.
Daily 8.14am–5pm (4.30pm in
December and January).

Wankbahn (K)
Journey time 14min.

Eckbauerbahn (K)
Journey time 14min.

Hausbergbahn (K)
Journey time 5min.
All daily 8.30am–5pm.

Grainbach
Hochriesbahnen (K)
Journey time 5 min.
Daily 9am–4pm.

Lenggries
Brauneck-Bergbahn (K)
Journey time 17min.
Daily 8.15am–4.30pm.

Mittenwald
Karwendelbahn (K)
Journey time 10 min.
Daily 9am–5pm.

Oberammergau
Laber-Bergbahn (K)
Journey time 12 min.
Daily 9am–5pm (4pm November-
April).

Oberstaufen
Hochgratbahn (K)
Journey time 15 min.
Daily 9am–5pm.

Oberstdorf
Fellhornbahn (K)
Sections 1 & 2 — journey time 13 min.
Daily 8.15am–5pm

Kanzelwandbahn (K)
Journey time 12 min.

Walmendingershornbahn (K)
Journey time 5 min.
Both daily 8.15am–4.45pm.

Nebelhornbahn (K)
Journey time 12 min.
Daily 8am–12noon, 1.20pm–5pm.

Pfronten-Steinach
Breitenbergbahn (K)
Journey time 11 min.
Daily 8.30am–12noon, 1–5pm.

Ruhpolding
Rauschbergbahn (K)
Journey time 4 min.
Daily 9am–5pm.

Schliersee
Schliersbergbahn (K)
Daily 9am–5pm.

Taubensteinbahn (K)
Journey time 15 min.
Daily 8.45am–4.15pm.

Tegernsee
Wallbergbahn (K)
Journey time 12 min.
Daily 8.30am–4.30pm.

Tourist Information Centres
Fremdenverkehrsverband
Sonnenstrasse 10
80331 München
☎ 089-597347
General information about Upper Bavaria.

For local detail, accommodation lists, etc write to 'Tourist Information' giving postcode and name of town:

83435 Bad Reichenhall
83735 Bayrischzell
83471 Berchtesgaden
83233 Bernau am Chiemsee
82488 Ettal
87629 Füssen
87435 Kempten
88131 Lindau
82481 Mittenwald
82487 Oberammergau
87534 Oberstaufen
87561 Oberstdorf
82467 Garmisch-Partenkirchen
83224 Grassau
87509 Immenstadt
83334 Inzell
83242 Reit im Winkl
83700 Rottach-Egern
83324 Ruhpolding
87527 Sonthofen

3
THE LAKES

A n area of some 900sq km south-west of München has been
named Fünf-Seen-Land — Five Lakes District — although
there are really many more lakes than that. Five of them, however,
are readily accessible from München using the excellent suburban
railway system (S-bahn) and it is better to explore these first before
going further afield to visit others right up to the Alpenstrasse. From
the city centre the S-bahn journey takes 30–50 minutes according to
destination. Trains are at least every 40 minutes, often more frequent.
For the tourist wishing to use the S-bahn the very economical 24-
hour tickets are to be recommended. The cost for an adult is little
more than the price of an ordinary single journey ticket from
München to, say, Starnberg and the 24-hour ticket can be used for the
return journey and for any other journey on the MVV (Münchner
Verkehrs- und Tarifverband) whether by S-bahn, U-bahn (underground), bus or tram within 24 hours. Children pay one-third of the
adult price.

The whole of the 'Five Lakes' area is excellent for walking and
cycling and there are many package arrangements for exploring the
countryside without carrying luggage. Rewarding day walks can be
started from any of the S-bahn stations or from any other point round
the lakes. The Starnberger See is the biggest Bavarian lake after
Chiemsee and its northern tip is only 20km (12 miles) from the centre
of München. The lake is about 20km north to south and up to 5km
wide. It is served by S-bahn line 6 and four stations are adjacent to the
lake; Starnberg is at the north end and Possenhofen, Feldafing and
Tutzing are on the western shore.

The MVV and other organisations have waymarked a comprehensive network of footpaths, and a map showing those in the vicinity
can be found at each station. The 48km (30 miles) of the route right

round the Starnberger See are more than could be accomplished in one day, but there are plenty of places for overnight stops. For the rambler there is a special map, *Wanderkarte-Fünfseenland* (1:50,000), and an accompanying pocket guide giving a description of ten selected one-day walks. These publications are also useful for the cyclist planning his own route. Cycles may be hired at railway stations and elsewhere — see 'Fact File' for details.

From around the end of March until the end of September there are regular steamer services on the Starnberger See. There are also dance cruises on Saturday evenings from July to September. **Starnberg** with its surrounding villages has some 18,000 inhabitants and is a busy and attractive small town right on the lake shore. The excellent transport facilities between here and München have made it a popular residential town for city workers as well as an excellent holiday centre. Water activities feature strongly, of course, with much boating, wind-surfing, diving, etc. The old parish church of St Josef (1764–6) is regarded as Starnberg's trade mark. It is a rococo building and the high altar is considered a fine example of the period. The picture gallery in the *Heimatmuseum* has works by several artists who were active here.

Starnberg is the base of the organisation LEO Aktiv Reisen which provides three/ten-day cycle tours, mainly in the Fünf-Seen-Land and Pfaffenwinkel. All the principal sights and resorts mentioned in the next few pages are included in these tours. The 'packages' include hire of suitable cycles, pre-booked accommodation, maps and literature, transfer of luggage, etc.

The north-east corner of the lake provides for an easy walk of 11km with fine views across the water. Start on the Seepromenade near the landing stage opposite Starnberg station and go eastwards following waymarks '1'. Still following the shore turn into Nepomukweg and pass the Hallenbad and then the lake bathing area to reach the recreation area of **Kempfenhausen** in about 2km. Now turn south, continue to follow the shore through some wooded plots and past numerous attractive houses until **Berg** is reached in another 2km. The *Schloss* here has less to offer the visitor than its rather fine park. Ludwig II spent happy youthful days here and it was here that he met his death. A cross in the reeds at the water's edge marks the spot where his body was found on the morning of 13 July 1886. A chapel was built here in 1900 in neo-Romanesque style in memory of the unhappy monarch.

From Berg, Ludwig could look across the lake to Possenhofen, the home of his cousin Elisabeth (Sissy) who was later to become empress of Austria. She had her summer seat at nearby Feldafing on

the west shore for 24 years and thought that the views to the east and
south across the lake were the finest in the world.

The walk continues through the Berg Schlosspark past the memorial chapel, more or less following the shore line. There is a good viewpoint at a Bismarck monument (1899) before reaching **Ammerland** where, during the summer months, there is the opportunity of crossing the lake by steamer to Tutzing for the train back to Starnberg or München. The walk from Berg represents the first section of the long-distance path called the König-Ludwig-Weg which was opened in 1977 and can be walked as a *Wandern ohne Gepäck* (walking without luggage) holiday which includes six overnight stops. The route is designed to embrace as many places of interest as possible, amongst them Kloster Andechs, the Ammersee (steamer crossing), Wessobrunn, Hohenpeissenberg, Rottenbuch, Wies, Neuschwanstein, Hohenschwangau and Füssen. Those participating in the 'package' are provided with all necessary maps and guide books, or they are available locally for those making their own arrangements. A guide in English is *King Ludwig Way* by Fleur and Colin Speakman.

If there are children in the party an alternative to the lake crossing after arriving at Ammerland is to visit the beautiful Märchenwald Fairy-tale Park in **Wolfratshausen** about 7km to the east. First walk about 2km to **Münsing** where there is a 'bus service to Wolfratshausen. Here, all the favourite fairy tales characters are brought to life with the press of a button. There are also a large play area, a miniature railway and old-timer cars to travel in and a racing track with miniature cars and motor-cycles for budding juvenile drivers. There is a bus service back to Starnberg or S-bahn direct to München from Wolfratshausen.

At the southern tip of the lake **Seeshaupt** is another important resort but as it is beyond reach of the S-bahn it is less likely to get completely overrun at summer weekends. This is the starting point for an excursion into the Osterseen, a group of no less than twenty-one tiny lakes (so much for five lakes!) the origins of which go back to the Ice Age and there is much to interest geologists here. The largest of these lakes is called Ostara after the heathen goddess. This is a landscape conservation area and there is plenty here for the nature-lover who is prepared to park and walk.

Continuing round the Starnberger See, the route leads to **Bernried** where a splendid Nationalpark with many fine old trees was the gift in 1913 of the appropriately named German-American Mrs Busch-Woods. The parish church was originally a Romanesque building but was given decorative treatment in the early baroque period. The tower, which stands on original foundations, was the work of Caspar

THE LAKES

Feichtmayr who came from this area and was a successful architect.

Johannes Brahms lived in **Tutzing** in 1873 and there is a memorial to him on the Brahmspromenade. The sixteenth-century *Schloss* has been, since 1957, the home of a protestant academy. Already mentioned for its views **Feldafing** has a golf course and a well known Kalvarienberg. In the park of the rather pricey Kaiserin Elisabeth Hotel there is a statue of the one-time empress. This is the embarkation point for the very short trip to the Roseninsel with its *Schloss* and the Teehaus Maximilian II. The former home of Elisabeth in **Possenhofen** has been in private ownership since 1950. In 1958 the city of München purchased land on the shore here which is now the popular bathing place, Paradies, which can accommodate 10,000 bathers.

The other big lake is the Ammersee lying a little to the west of Starnberg. The road between the two goes past Kloster Andechs where the visitor should stop for one of the most rewarding views in this area. Heiliger Berg (Holy Mountain), is the local name for the 711m-high (2,332ft) hill on which the *Kloster* and its church stand; at a slightly lower level is the beer hall where the famous Andechs brew is dispensed. A castle here was the seat of the counts of Diessen-Andechs but in 1209 it was destroyed by the Wittelsbachs and the last count died in exile in 1248. To prevent the treasures of the castle chapel falling into enemy hands, these were buried under the chapel together with three consecrated communion wafers and the building was razed to the ground. The treasures were rediscovered in 1388 and the hill became a place of pilgrimage and led, at the beginning of the fifteenth century to the building of the present church.

In the middle of the eighteenth century the building was converted to a baroque masterpiece. Time is needed to absorb every aspect of the church which, in truth, is neither Gothic nor quite baroque but a harmonious blend of styles. The Klostergasthof (*Ruhetag* Thursday) dates from the fifteenth century but was tastefully modernised in 1969 to make it a most pleasant and well cared for hostelry. In the spacious Bräustüberl (open daily), or on its terrace with a fine view towards the Alps, you collect your beer and food — including famous Andechs *Kloster* cheese — from the counter and sit at one of the bare wooden tables.

Down on the east shore of the Ammersee, **Herrsching** is an

Wessobrunn, the birthplace of Bavarian baroque

attractive resort of about 6,000 inhabitants. It is the terminal of line 5 from München, the only S-bahn station on the lake. Steamers (April–October) are timed to fit in with the trains. Herrsching claims to have the longest lakeside promenade in Germany — 10km without a break. Here again, recreational activity tends to centre on the lake but there is a variety of entertainments and leisure pursuits for all tastes.

In the south-west corner of the lake, **Diessen** is of similar size and is served by the Federal Railway. The outstanding sight in this popular resort is the church of St Maria, formerly a collegiate church of Augustinian canons. The present building was begun in 1720 and the shell was almost complete when it was torn down and started afresh; it is now one of the most important baroque buildings in Bavaria. The outstanding feature is the high altar up a flight of steps. Behind the altarpiece is a platform which can be fitted with different pictures to suit the various holy days. The church of St Georgen at the west of the town is also worth seeing. Originally a fifteenth-century building, it was enlarged in 1750 when many famous craftsmen were involved. Diessen provides for a comprehensive range of water sports and other activities. A regular annual event is the south German *Töpfermarkt* (pot market) which takes place on Ascension Day. The König-Ludwig-Weg passes through and there is a huge network of marked paths for which a *Wanderkarte* is available.

Four kilometres to the south at **Raisting** is the Deutsche Bundespost (Post Office) satellite tracking station. This tiny idyllic village hosts part of the modern intercontinental telecommunications service. Huge parabolic antennae are directed to the skies and automatically follow the paths of the satellites. For most people the astonishing view of the installation is sufficient but those with a technical interest may be allowed to visit it. The enormous 'dishes' tend to overshadow the historic environment but the parish church of St Remigius (1692–6) with a rococo interior is worth a pause. Two kilometres to the south, the former pilgrimage church of St John the Baptist is actually adjacent to the tracking station and it is possible to take rather bizarre photographs of 'ancient' and 'modern'.

A modest motor tour (35–40km) from Diessen covers two more important churches. Due west via Dettenschwang and Issing is the pilgrimage church of **Vilgertshofen**, which has stucco in the Wessobrunn style. One of the artists was also responsible for three unusual ceiling paintings in the nearby inn which show biblical characters in the garb of Lech valley farmers.

South-eastwards from Vilgertshofen a pretty road soon reaches **Wessobrunn**, a village mentioned before. It is hard to understand today, how this village could have been the eighteenth-century cradle of so many fine craftsmen. Whole families were involved: the Schmuzers, the Zimmermanns, the Feuchtmayrs and others. In those days, Wessobrunn was the hallmark of good workmanship, artistic genius and even fantasy. These workers had been encouraged by the Benedictine monks in the nearby abbey, the place where in the ninth century a monk wrote the *Wessobrunn Prayer*, the oldest text in the German language. The original manuscript is now in the State Library in München. Secularisation brought an end to the *Kloster* and only the Fürstenbau (1580) remains of that building, but it has some excellent Wessobrun workmanship. Nearby the parish church of St Johannes (1757-9) also has fine interior decoration by members of the Wessobrunn school. A valuable relic is the wooden crucifix from about 1250 which had been in the earlier Romanesque church, only the tower of which remains. Behind the old *Kloster* walls is a reputedly 700-year-old lime tree with a circumference of 13m (42ft).

Before passing on to some of the smaller lakes in this first group, here are details of a pleasant walk of about 17km linking Starnberger See and the Ammersee. This is a good outing for the München-based visitor who should take the S-bahn train to Starnberg.

After leaving Starnberg station turn right on the promenade and following waymark '3' cross back under the railway at the first subway to go more or less ahead into Söckinger Strasse and shortly turn left into a street called Maisinger Schlucht. This leads into the actual *Schlucht* (glen) but care is needed not to miss the signs. Once in the glen it is only a matter of going forward on the shady path (notice the picturesque caves) until **Maising** is reached in about 4.5km. Walk on almost to the end of the village street and shortly before the road makes a pronounced turn to the right, keep left and go along a beautiful path to the Gasthaus Seehof (*Ruhetag* Monday) on the Maisinger See. There are several paths here and the route goes up on to the embankment to continue in a south-west direction with the lake on the right through a *Naturschutzgebiet* (nature reserve) to **Aschering**. About 50m past the 'bus stop in this village the route bears to the left and there is a sign for Andechs. Following this woodland path the tiny Ess-see with the renowned Max-Planck-Institut is shortly passed on the left and soon after this the main road just before **Rothenfeld** has to be crossed. Pass through the car park opposite and take the small path on through the wood; emerging from this a few minutes later Kloster Andechs is seen on its hill ahead. Follow the path with the Stations of the Cross up to the *Kloster*. From here, clear footpaths go down either side of the little River Kienbach to **Herrsching** and the stream is followed through the town to the S–bahn station for the return train to München if desired.

A short distance north of Herrsching is the Pilsensee with the S–bahn station of Seefeld-Hechendorf at its north end. **Seefeld** has its *Schloss* and *Schlosspark*, Burg Seefeld, which is privately owned. **Widdersberg,** a short distance to the south-east of the lake, was already settled in Roman times and there is a Roman gravestone from the second century. A mere stone's throw to the north is the Wörthsee (S-bahn station Steinebach, line 5).

Wanderweg No 4 starts at the station and makes a complete circuit of the lake, almost exclusively on the water's edge. The 13km route is so obvious that no description of it is needed here. The lake is 3.5km long and 1.7km wide and takes its name from the tiny island near the west shore, known to the locals as Mausinsel (Mouse Island). **Steinebach** was once a sleepy farming village but is now a popular bathing place, busy at weekends. The old church of St Martin was re-organised in 1735; worth seeing are the frescos dating from 1738 which were only uncovered after World War II. Neither Pilsensee nor Wörthsee are big enough to have a steamer service but both have boats for hire and plenty of space for water activities.

Finally in this area, the miniscule Wesslinger See — only 600m by 500m — is fine for a refreshing dip and this is regarded as one of the 'Five Lakes'; it is the nearest one to München (S-bahn station Wessling, line 5). For a small place **Wessling** appears to be over-provided with churches — there are no less than five. The church of Christ König is near the station. The new parish church of St Georg was consecrated in 1939 and has a spectacular high onion-dome with a built-in clock. Older relics have been installed within, including a larger-than-life Christ figure (sixteenth century), a statue of St Georg (seventeenth century) and a fifteenth-century Madonna.

South-west from, and within 20km (12 miles) of the south end of the Starnberger See, are two lakes close together, the Riegsee and the Staffelsee with the resort of **Murnau** between them. Staffelsee is the larger, some 4km from north to south and east to west but they share the same very picturesque countryside and have access to similar facilities. Both lakes have camp sites and good natural bathing places. The Riegsee is one of the warmest lakes in Upper Bavaria. The Staffelsee has motor-boat trips in summer. There is a DB station at Murnau but the S-bahn is beyond reach. This is a *Luftkurort* with a population of 10,500 and a good range of visitor facilities. The Alpenhof Motel Murnau has been awarded a coveted Michelin star for its local specialities such as *Grillierter Staffelsee-Hecht*, grilled pike from the Staffelsee. There is good walking here but cyclists will notice that it is steeper than around the 'Five Lakes'. Murnau itself is at an altitude of 700m (2,296ft).

One of the traditional Bavarian farmhouses re-erected at the Glentleiten open-air museum near Grossweil

Walchensee

There is an annual spectacle on the Staffelsee the second Thursday after Whitsun when Fronleichnam (Corpus Christi) is celebrated at the village of **Seehausen** with a procession of about a hundred boats and barges all colourfully decorated following a vessel carrying the Monstrance, making stops at the lake islands of St Jacob and Wörth. In Murnau the parish church of St Nikolaus was built 1717–27 on the site of a former twelfth-century building. The powerful vault fresco in the dome was a nineteenth-century addition. There is good stucco and the high altar has excellent sculpture. It was first erected in the monastery at Ettal in 1730 and brought to Murnau in 1771.

Ten kilometres south of Murnau is **Eschenlohe** where the unfortunate Schisler was working before he returned to Oberammergau, taking the plague with him. About the same distance east is another of Bavaria's beautiful lakes, the Kochelsee. Before Kochelsee, however, visit the outstanding Freilichtmuseum (open-air museum) von Glentleiten on the slopes above **Grossweil**. Typical old farmhouses from all over Upper Bavaria have been carefully dismantled and re-erected here to provide a unique historical record of rural life. Some forty buildings from the sixteenth century onwards, but mostly from the eighteenth century, are here. There are regular displays of traditional craftsmanship and other special events such as the erection of the *Maibaum* (maypole) on 1 May, a children's week in August (advance booking advisable) and a *Christkindlmarkt* at the end of November.

Roughly the same size as the Staffelsee, the Kochelsee lies at an altitude of 600m (1,968ft). Its north end leads out to a flattish moorland — a protected area — but if one looks south the spectacular backdrop of the Alps gives the lake a gloriously romantic appearance. This is one of the most pleasant bathing places in Upper Bavaria and is also a popular camping area. The resort of **Kochel** (population 4,700) is at the north-east corner of the lake and provides well for summer and winter visitors. Kochel is at the east end of the long-distance path, the Prälatenweg from Marktoberdorf mentioned in Chapter 1. The main road south (B11) starts to climb as soon as it leaves the Kochelsee and ascends by a series of somewhat alarming hairpin bends to the Kesselberg (858m, 2,814ft) before dropping to the north end of the Walchensee at 802m (2,630ft). With an area of 16.4sq km this is by far Germany's biggest mountain lake; it has a depth of 196m (642ft) and is well stocked with fish but the water is on the cool side for bathing. **Walchensee** is the starting point for an excursion to the Herzogstand (1600m, 5250ft). A chair-lift takes just 11 minutes to reach it with outstanding views of the lakes and mountains.

Two more major lakes should be visited, the Tegernsee and the Schliersee, mentioned briefly in Chapter 2. From Walchensee the motorist must go round the south end of the lake, the road round the north end being barred to motor vehicles. The route is a very pretty one and follows the valley of the little River Jachen between a series of imposing peaks with the Benediktenwand (1,801m, 5,907ft) on the left and the Zweiterköpfl (1,432m, 4,697ft) on the right with the higher Alpine summits of the Karwendelgebirge behind.

This is a toll road running more or less parallel with the Alpenstrasse route already described and some 12km (7 miles) from the B11 gives the oportunity for a stop in the scattered village of **Jachenau** to see the church, not only because of its stunning situation — a bonus for photographers — but because its history goes back to 1291. It was renovated in the eighteenth century when stucco decoration of the Wessobrunn school was introduced.

The Rivers Isar and Jachen join near **Hohenburg** with its medieval castle (1718), now a boarding school. The nearby chapel of 1722 has a copy of the Altötting *Gnadenbild*, the so-called Black Madonna (see Chapter 5).

Continuing northwards through the Isar valley, the resort of **Lenggries** (population 10,000) is a *Luftkurort*; the wide range of facilities for guests includes the Brauneck (1,530m, 5,018ft) cable car and two chair-lifts. In winter these are supplemented by no less than eighteen ski-tows. From the lower station of the Brauneck cable-way a splendid mountain walk to the summit starts with an immediate stiffish climb keeping to the right (north) of, and at first, roughly parallel with the cables. The route continues westwards climbing all the time and in about $1\frac{1}{2}$ hours the Reiseralm (refreshments) is reached at 900m (2,952ft). More than half of the climb is now over and the clearly defined route soon turns south-west towards the upper cable car station. For the moment the path continues in the wood but coming out into the Garland basin the goal is clearly visible. Across the basin there is a stiff climb to a small saddle a few metres before the station and in another 10 minutes the summit cross is reached at 1,555m (5,100ft). A little below the summit at the Brauneck-Hütte (refreshments and overnight lodgings) there is a first-rate viewing platform. On a clear day the greater part of the Alpine chain can be seen, far to the south perhaps a glimpse of the sparkling glaciers in the central Alps and to the north-west, the Upper Bavarian lakes.

The descent is on the south side of the cables and soon after passing the station near two *Alm* huts there is a sign 'Kot-Alm'. In fact, from here the Kot-Alm hut (refreshments) can be seen below but it takes another 20 minutes or so to reach it across an area which is sometimes boggy. At the east end of this *Alm* basin a little road is reached and the descent is continued until shortly after the lower edge of the woods the path goes left, leaving the road. Close the cattle gate here and continue down along a meadow track along a fence, through a short, rather overgrown cleft to reach a much more obvious track going roughly due north. Pass a quarry on the left and the hamlet **Gildenhöfe** can be seen ahead. Go through this, climb briefly and pass — or call at — the Café Bergbahn and in a few minutes arrive back at the starting point. This walk entails a total climb of 900m (2,952ft) and good stout footwear is essential. A total of 5 hours should be allowed for the whole circuit but the time can be halved by using the cable railway for the outward leg. The *Wanderkarte* sheet L8334 Bad Tölz (1:50,000) is useful.

The Isar follows the route for another 10km to the spa of **Bad Tölz**. With some 13,000 inhabitants this is the most important centre in this area and a wide range of medical treatment is available here but there is plenty for the fit and healthy to do. The Blombergbahn chair-lift takes one from the valley to a height of 1,237m (4,057ft) in two stages which can be used separately for access to some excellent mountain walking. A golf course is at hand but summer and winter seasons are equally popular here. The original settlement owed its existence to a crossing place of one of the old salt roads over the Isar. It became the home of boatmen and fishermen and developed slowly over the centuries. In 1846 an iodine spring was discovered and led to the founding of a health resort. Out of the main holiday season one may stroll in a leisurely fashion through the old town — as distinct from the more modern spa area — and enjoy the colourful façades of the old gabled houses.

The town parish church Maria Himmelfahrt was developed from a late Gothic building damaged in a fifteenth-century fire and altered many times since. The tower was only added about 100 years ago and seems to stand a little uncomfortably beside the rest of the building. Belonging to this church too, is the Winzererkapelle of 1513, named after a distinguished citizen Kaspar Winzerer to whom there is also a memorial in front of the former *Rathaus*, now the *Heimatmuseum*. Another significant religious house is the pilgrimage church Maria-hilf built in 1735–7. Matthias Günther painted the frescos of the Tölz plague procession of 1634.

A modern procession is the *Tölzer Leonhardifahrt* which takes place annually on 6 November. St Leonhard is the patron saint of animals (he shares the honour with St Martin) and in many Bavarian towns and villages it is the custom for horses to be ridden round the church and blessed in the *Leonhardiritt* (Leonhard Ride) on the saint's day

The monastery church at Benediktbeuern

Interior of the church at Benediktbeuern

(*Leonharditag*). In Bad Tölz the ride has developed into a full-scale folk festival with a procession of decorated carts accompanied by whip-cracking and other festive noises. The church associated with the event is the unusual Leonhardikapelle which occupies a fine vantage point on the Kalvarienberg (708m, 2,322ft) north of the town. After the traditional procession there is a display of whip-cracking in the Marktstrasse using old-time coachmen's whips.

If **Benediktbeuern** was not visited from Kochel it is a rewarding excursion to make from Bad Tölz. It lies about 14km westwards along the B472. The Benedictine *Kloster* was founded in the middle of the eighth century, was destroyed by the invading Hungarians in 955 and re-established in the eleventh century. The monks here were much occupied with cultural activities including painting and literature. This is where, in the thirteenth century, the *Carmina Burana* was written, well known today through the exciting musical setting of the work by Carl Orff. The *Kloster* was burned down in the fifteenth century, and rebuilt only to be dismembered in the 1803 secularisation. For a time, the buildings became a glassworks and research establishment until in 1930 they were taken over the Salesians of Don Bosco as a centre for youth work, with religious instruction, science and culture.

The buildings are haunted by the spirit of baroque but it is the church of St Benedikt which stands out as the remarkable architectural achievement. Constructed in 1680-6, this is surely one of the most spectacular of the Bavarian baroque churches. The Italian influence is obvious and the Asam family, father and two sons, was responsible for much of the stucco and painting.

The cultural and secular history of the *Kloster* buildings is recorded in a museum in which the old glassworks with its ovens has been reincarnated and is a reminder that while the Fraunhofer firm had the premises they developed optical instruments and lenses of exceptional quality. Their name continues to be associated with glass technology and in 1986, York Glazier's Trust, who are responsible for the medieval glass in England's famous York Minster, collaborated with the Fraunhofer Institute in experiments designed to protect valuable old glass throughout Europe from the effects of 'acid rain'.

Before going on to the remaining two lakes call at **Dietramzell** 14km (9 miles) north-east of Bad Tölz, a modest resort in a picturesque location and the churches are a good reason for coming here. Pride of place goes to the former collegiate church of the Augustinian canons built 1729–41. The architect is unknown and the exterior gives no hint of the visual feast within. The interior includes fine stucco work and pastel-coloured frescos together with a painting of the Assumption of the Virgin Mary which is the centrepiece of the massive high altar. This splendid church came within a hair's breadth of destruction in the 1803 secularisation purge. Adjoining the collegiate church is the parish church of St Martin consecrated in 1722. The stucco and paintings, seriously damaged after 1803, were restored in 1966. There are two pilgrimage churches nearby; south of the *Kloster* is Maria Im Elend (1690) with an onion-dome, interior fitments from 1791 and a rich assortment of memorial tablets.

North, on the road towards Munich, is the rococo building consecrated in 1774 and dedicated to St Leonhard. It is finely decorated and has a dome fresco dating from 1769. This church is another to which pilgrims and horses come for blessing, although in this case on the third Saturday in July.

South now to the Tegernsee and the four main resorts on its shore, Gmund (population 4,000) at the north end, Bad Wiessee (population 5,000) on the west bank, Tegernsee (population 4,700) on the east bank and Rottach-Egern (population 6,500) in the south-east corner. The lake is 7.5km north to south and 2.5km east to west. The most popular resort is **Bad Wiessee**. Originally a farming village, Wiessee climbed quickly to spa status with the discovery of iodine and sulphur springs in the first decades of the twentieth century. One can still find reminders of its rural origin but it is as a health and holiday centre that it is known today, with a range of activities including conducted rambles in the valley or mountains according to season, coach or sleigh rides and there is a golf course. Five ski-tows are available for the winter visitor and concerts and theatrical productions take place from time to time throughout the year.

Gmund shares in the visitor facilities of the larger places. St Aegidius parish church is one of the most significant buildings on the lake. The present structure was consecrated in 1693, the work of an Italian architect, which helped to put the stamp of Italian baroque on Upper Bavarian church building. The high altar is from the Tegernsee *Kloster* church.

It was about 746 that Benedictine monks from St Gallen in Switzerland founded a *Kloster* in **Tegernsee**. At the height of its fame it was one of the most important cultural centres in Europe; the illumination of manuscripts and calligraphy reached its peak here. The area has always attracted artists and writers and the *Heimatmuseum* housed in Schloss Tegernsee recalls those who stayed here. Incidentally, many of the historic rooms of the *Schloss* are included in the museum. The former *Kloster* church, now the parish church of St Quirin, was rebuilt in 1684–9. It is a fine building, especially the Quirinus and Benediktus side-chapels with their ornate rococo decoration although, unfortunately, only a few of the altars in the three-aisled basilica have survived. As a resort, Tegernsee has plenty of visitor facilities and a historic steam railway between Tegernsee and Schaftlach for railway enthusiasts.

The parish church of St Laurentius at Egern is often overlooked. It dates from 1466 and was stuccoed in 1671–2. From the fifteenth century until secularisation this was a goal of pilgrims coming to revere a Madonna known as the *Egerner Gnadenbild*. Egern is part of the health resort called **Rottach-Egern**; all the usual facilities are on offer and there is access to the mountains by three chair-lifts and a *Gondelbahn* — a cable railway with four-passenger cabins. The latter takes 12 minutes to climb up to the Wallberghaus (refreshments) at 1,620m (5,313ft) from where the Wallberg summit (1,722m, 5,648ft) can be reached on foot in about 45 minutes. The motorist can use a toll road to reach Moosalm at 1,113m (3,650ft) for splendid views, but to reach the Wallberg must then go on foot for about an hour to get to the Wallberghaus.

Less than 10km (6 miles) east of Tegernsee is the little Schliersee with the resort of the same name (population 6,300) the only real centre on the lake and including the outlying villages of Fischhausen, Neuhaus and Spitzingsee. At the beginning of the present century **Schliersee** had only 700 inhabitants but the tourist influx following the construction of the railway soon changed this. Another factor in the village's rise to fame was the founding of the Schlierseer Bauern-theater (Peasant's Theatre) by the landlord and actor Xaver Terofal in 1892. The proud theatrical tradition is carried on today by the theatre group of the local *Trachtenverein* (Traditional Dress Club) and the idea has been adopted by many other villages in Upper Bavaria.

There are two *Gondelbahnen* and two chair-lifts, supplemented in winter by no less than fifteen ski-tows. The church, consecrated in 1715, retains the late Gothic tower of an earlier church but it only received the present pointed dome in 1873. The atmosphere of the bright, spacious interior is enhanced by the stucco and the chancel ceiling picture. The church contains a number of priceless relics as well as examples of the creative work of the several important artists.

A little above the church on the way to the lower station of the Schliesbergbahn — a small-cabin cableway — there is a hill sur-mounted by the chapel of St Georg. The hill is called the Weinberg but this has nothing to do with grapes, but is a term used in some parts of Upper Bavaria for a Kalvarienberg and means 'hill of weeping'. St Georg's chapel is from the fourteenth century and was renewed in the early part of the seventeenth. The central feature of the high altar is a mounted St George despatching an angry dragon.

It is possible to walk right round the lake in about 2 hours. From the parish church go southwards along the east shore, past boat moorings, the Kurpromenade and the Park-Strandbad. The walk is waymarked 'K1' but is pretty obvious. It continues along Seestrasse and later Neuhauserstrasse. After $\frac{1}{2}$ hour the road moves away from the shore and about 150m past a boat mooring place keep right along a little road past boathouses and the outlying dwellings of Fischhausen. Ten minutes later, join a wide road and follow it as it curves to the right round the south end of the lake and eventually join a surfaced road northwards along the west bank. In **Fischhausen** there is another pilgrimage church of St Leonhard (1670) situated at the roadside but with enough space round it for the traditional ride, celebrated here on the saint's day, 6 November.

Continuing northwards, the woods rise to the left on the slopes of the Brunstkogel. When the track climbs a little to the left, cross the railway and turn right to walk parallel with the line, noting the tiny island of **Wörth** on the lake , once the site of a gruesome prison with cells so small that the prisoner could either sit or stand but not both!

In **Krainsberg** cross back over the railway and immediately turn left to continue following the line northwards. Cross a road running down to the Freudenberg 'peninsula', go straight on for 100m then turn right into a woodland path to the Hotel Freudenberg. Keep left at the entrance, cross a little stream then keep right over a gangway to the Tegernseer Weg along the north shore back to the church. A good walk at all seasons; even in winter the paths are kept clear.

This chapter gives an overview of the lakes in the popular area between München and the Alps. East of München the large Chiemsee and some smaller lakes are explored in Chapter 5, while the new Franconian Lake District south-west of Nürnberg is described in Chapter 8.

Additional Information

Places to Visit

Benediktbeuern
Historische Fraunhofer Glashütte
Fraunhofer Strasse 2
83671 Benediktbeuern
☎ 08857-2512
Open: Monday to Saturday 10am-12noon, 2-5pm Sunday 1-5pm.

Grossweil
*Freilichtmuseum des Bezirks
   Oberbayern an der Glentleiten*
82439 Grossweil
☎ 08841-1095 or 1098
Open: April to November, Tuesday to Sunday 9am-6pm (5pm in November). Open Easter and Whit Mondays.

Wolfratshausen
Märchenwald im Isartal
Kräuterstrasse 39
82515 Wolfratshausen-Farchet
☎ 08171-18760
Wolfratshausen exit on A95 München-Garmisch then east of town
Open: 2 weeks before Easter to mid-October daily 9am-6pm.
Restaurant and kiosk.

Local Events and Festivals
Bad Tölz
Leonhardifahrt — 6 November.
Best known of the St Leonhard's Day rides. Similar in Rottenbuch and Waldkirchen.

Diessen
South German Töpfermarkt — Ascension Day. Pots and pans, vases etc.

Staffelsee
Fronleichnam — 2nd Thursday after Whitsun.
Corpus Christi procession on lake.

Long Distance Paths
König-Ludwig-Weg — 110km (69 miles)
Starnberg to Füssen

Starnberger See Rundweg — 48km (30 miles) Circuit of the lake.

Steam Railway
Tegernsee-Gmund-Schaftlach
Bayerischer Localbahn Verein e V
Postfach 1311
83684 Tegernsee
Steam passenger trains most Sundays end-July to September and St Nikolaus excursions early December. Refreshments on trains.

Tourist Information Centres
Fremdenverkehrsverband
Sonnenstrasse 10
80331 München
☎ 089-597347
General information about Upper Bavaria.

Fremdenverkehrsverband
Starnberger Fünfseenland
Postfach 1607
82306 Starnberg
☎ 08151-13008
General information about Starnberg and the five lakes.

For local details, accommodation lists, etc write to 'Tourist Information' giving postcode and name of town:

83646 Bad Tölz
83671 Benediktbeuern
86911 Diessen
82431 Kochel
82418 Murnau
83700 Rottach-Egern
83727 Schliersee
83684 Tegernsee
82432 Walchensee
82405 Wessobrunn
82515 Wolfratshausen

4
MÜNCHEN
(MUNICH)

Neither the revolution after World War I, the collapse of the monarchy, the deluge of bombs in World War II, nor the confusion following that war, have left traces which make the Bavarian metropolis unworthy of admiration. München (Munich) is sometimes called Germany's secret capital. After Berlin and Hamburg, München, with 1.2 million inhabitants, is the third biggest city in Germany. The population growth, especially since World War II, means that less than one-third of the population now consists of born *'Münchner'*. Some 200,000 are foreigners, and there are some100,000 students at the university and other centres of learning. The general opinion of Germans from other parts seems to be that the quality of life in München is better than in any of the other big cities.

To a large extent, the history of München is that of Bavaria itself. Perhaps today's citizens, and the annual throng of tourists, should give a retrospective vote of thanks to Duke Heinrich of Bavaria and Saxony who, in 1158, knocked down the Isar bridge, belonging to the bishop of Freising, at Föhring and had it rebuilt further upstream to capture the lucrative salt trade from the Reichenhall district. The move brought in a rich reward in tolls and taxes and the village called Bei den Mönchen quickly became known as it grew in importance.

By 1175 the citizens decided to build their first town wall so that their bridge should not suffer the same fate as the Föhring bridge. The size of the town increased five-fold under Emperor Ludwig dem Bayern; it had long since outgrown the original town wall and in 1319 he started the building of a new wall with four main gateways which, with the exception of some of the latter, was only removed around 1800.

The eighteenth century found München in an impoverished state and many of the citizens hungry. Then Benjamin Thompson, who had fled from the American War of Independence, arrived in München. He was the originator of *Erbsensuppe* — pea soup made from dried peas, ham and herbs. Thus he was able to provide some nourishment for more than a thousand hungry citizens each day. By this time Thompson had been given the title of Graf Rumford and the people found the *Rumford-Suppe* an improvement on their previous diet of potatoes. The *Münchner's* aversion to potatoes has endured to this day. Graf Rumford went on to join the Bavarian civil service in 1784 where he re-organised the army and founded workhouses!

In 1806 Maximilian became king of Bavaria as Maximilian I Josef, with München as the seat of government. He died in 1825 and was followed by his son who became King Ludwig I. Under his rule, München blossomed into a glittering centre of art and partly from his private purse, the king financed many fine buildings including the Pinakothek, the Glyptothek and the Feldherrnhalle. His aim was to build a city which would have such a reputation that nobody could claim to know Germany without knowing München. The scandal of his association with the dancer Lola Montez — Maria de los Dolores Porris y Montez — finally resulted in his abdication in 1848 when his son Maximilian II took over the throne. The new ruler fostered learning and amongst other things built the Maximilianeum, today the home of both houses of the Bavarian parliament.

Maximilian II was succeeded in 1864 by his son Ludwig II. Although Ludwig supposedly hated München, the city continued to flourish during his reign, especially as a result of his patronage of Richard Wagner. This period too, saw the building of the Neues Rathaus in neo-Gothic style. After the death of Ludwig II in 1886 his brother Otto should have succeeded to the throne but he was in poor mental health and in consequence Prince Luitpold governed as regent for 25 years. Luitpold's son became King Ludwig III but World War I broke out 2 years after his accession, and he died in exile in Hungary in 1921.

München City Centre

Visitors can obtain information for exploration of München from the City Information Office which can also assist in finding accommodation. The city makes special efforts to cater for young visitors and with a special youth information centre. A booklet *München – Leitfaden für Jugendgruppen* (Guide for Young People) contains a wealth of useful information. See 'Fact File' for more details.

Enjoying München means seeing the sights: reminders of the royal Bavarian past, the Residenz, Schloss Nymphenburg, the baroque

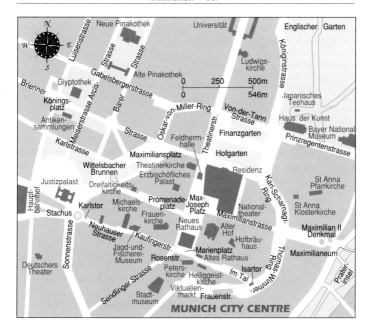

MUNICH CITY CENTRE

and rococo churches and the spacious parks. A shopping tour through the extensive pedestrian zone and across the big food and flower market together with a visit to the famous Hofbräuhaus and some museums or art galleries should be included. Inevitably, all this takes time but then, München is not a place to be rushed.

Most people have heard of the *Oktoberfest* and most have a vague idea of what the term means. For a festival known all over the world, the *Oktoberfest* has a remarkably short history. Surprisingly, it originated in horse-racing, long a popular sport in Bavaria. In 1810, a non-commissioned officer in the National Guard suggested that racing, which had been dropped as an economy measure, should be revived as a suitable way of celebrating the marriage of Crown Prince Ludwig (later King Ludwig I) to Princess Therese. King Maximilian gave his consent and the races were run on 17 October of that year, sixty horses from all over Bavaria taking part. So successful was the event that the fields where the races had taken place were named Theresienwiese in honour of the princess and they have kept the name ever since.

The king agreed to the races being held annually and until the beginning of this century they formed an essential element of the festivities. In 1811 they were accompanied by an agricultural show which still continues every 2 years. In 1818 booths and beer tents similar to those seen today made their appearance. The Silver Wedding of Ludwig and Therese in 1835 was marked by a procession which was the forerunner of today's splendid opening procession when decorated brewers' drays, carnival floats and tableaux, also Dirndl-clad waitresses and civic dignitaries parade from the Bavarian State Parliament building to the festival grounds. The *Oberbürgermeister* (Lord Mayor) taps the first barrel of beer and the festival is then officially open. It now lasts for 16 days, finishing on the first Sunday in October when there is another procession.

Some of today's beer tents can seat 5,000 people but in addition to the serious business of beer drinking there is ample opportunity for eating and drinking in the numerous restaurants or from the many stalls selling meat and fish delicacies, sweetmeats, candy floss, ice cream and so on. There is an enormous fun-fair with hair-raising rides including an alarming roller-coaster. Visitors need not feel intimidated by the noisy crowds in the beer tents. After finding an empty seat they will immediately be welcomed by their neighbours and, even if they cannot speak a word of German, they will quickly become involved in the general conviviality and be introduced to the art of *Das Schunkeln*, the linking of arms and swaying back and forth in time — more or less in time, anyway — with the raucous beat of the brass band. Outside, the crowds seem to spend much time just promenading up and down the broad avenues, looking at the sideshows, stopping for the odd drink or snack or trying out the latest heart-stopping device in the fun-fair. The festivities go on well into the night — indeed, it is a wonder that any work is done at all during the *Oktoberfest* weeks — but eventually everybody wanders or staggers off home or back to hotels for a good sleep in preparation for the next evening's session.

The other principal time of merry-making in München is the pre-Lenten carnival period, 7 January until Ash Wednesday. Here it is called *Fasching* and it is celebrated a little differently. Balls always played a prominent part in the München scene and in 1893 a society was formed to inject some order into the various *Fasching* balls and parades. The first *Fasching* prince was chosen in 1894 and this is now an annual appointment; he is accompanied by a princess of his own choice and they reign supreme throughout the season, supported by suitable male and female retinues. The balls are splendid and varied with constant endeavours to find new themes.

But if the *Münchner* make the most of the secular festivities, they are no less positive in their approach to the various religious festivals. *Fronleichnam* (Corpus Christi) is celebrated with a colourful festive procession and the beautiful squares of the inner city are gaily decorated to match. Advent sees the beginning of Christmas music concerts in many of the churches and also the Christmas market which is held in the Marienplatz in front of the new town hall. It was previously called the *Münchner Kripperlmarkt* because only crib figures were sold but nowadays all the usual Christmas oddments are to be found there and the name *Christkindlmarkt* seems to have been adopted as in Nürnberg and several other towns. Traditionally, Sunday church-going is followed by the *Frühschoppen*, the morning or early lunch-time drink, sometimes with sausages and bread, so that man's earthly needs are not forgotten after the spiritual ones have been taken care of. Even the priests sometimes take this opportunity to mingle informally with their parishioners.

The centre of München is dominated by the distinctive twin towers of the **Frauenkirche**, a late Gothic brick building which has become the city's symbol. The church in its present form was built in the fifteenth century and was consecrated in 1494 although the towers were not then complete and only received their onion-domes in 1524–5. First class restoration work after the damage done in World War II means that the building is now seen at its best and probably in better condition than at any time since its construction. It is a hall church with ten bays and unusually high side-chapels. The nave is separated from the side-aisles by twenty-two octagonal pillars. Much of the medieval content has been lost or destroyed but the fourteenth–sixteenth-century stained glass windows in the chancel have survived more or less intact. Most important is the Scharfzandt window (1473) in the centre. The numerous gravestones and memorials include the grave slab of the famous architect J. M. Fischer who was responsible for no less than thirty-two churches, twenty-three monasteries and numerous secular buildings.

Many churches in München contain works by the two Asam brothers (painters, stucco workers and master-builders) who belonged to the group of most significant artists of the seventeenth and eighteenth centuries. Some of their most important works of the brothers are to be found in the frescos of the Trinity Church, the parish church of St Anna im Lehel, the little palace of Maria Einsiedel in Thalkirchen, the St Johann Nepomuk church and in the decoration of Freising cathedral.

The church of St Johann Nepomuk, in Sendlinger Strasse, is commonly referred to as the **Asamkirche**. It was built 1733–46 and shows how passionately the brothers pursued their work. In this case they were more than just decorators to the order of some patron for Egid bought the land with his own money and between them the young men financed the construction of the building. Here they were able to pursue their ideas to the ultimate; shape, colour and light work harmoniously together. The walls are covered with red stucco marble. The massive high altar is framed by four twisted columns and the lower part contains a glass sarcophagus with the wax figure of St Nepomuk.

The Franciscan monastery church of **St Anna im Lehel** in St Anna-Strasse, not far from the Nationaltheater, was consecrated in 1737. It was badly damaged in World War II but afterwards was rebuilt in its original form. Most of the stucco and paintings were irretrievably lost but the ceiling paintings were restored in 1971–2. Altars by the Asam brothers and a pulpit survived in part and were also restored.

In Neuhauser Strasse the 1291–4-built core of the former Augustinian monastery church at No 53 has survived; it was extended in the fourteenth and fifteenth centuries and radically altered in 1618–21. Thereafter it was de-consecrated and served first as a toll hall, then as police headquarters and finally as the **Deutsches Jagd-museum** (Hunting Museum) which is its present function. In the same street, part of the pedestrian precinct, is the **Bürgersaal,** built for the Marianist congregation in 1709. Under glass above the baroque doorway is a Madonna on the Crescent Moon. It is a two-storey building and the walls of the lower have fifteen Stations of the Cross painted in bright colours on wood. Here too is the grave slab of the Jesuit Rupert Mayer (1876–1945), a well known priest and resistance worker. The baroque oratory in the upper storey has fourteen views of Bavarian places of pilgrimage painted around 1710.

Still in Neuhauser Strasse, the Jesuit church of **St Michael** was built in 1583–9 as a spiritual centre of the sixteenth-century Catholic renewal movement. It is, to say the least, a spectacular building. The façade was only restored in 1972 after war-time bomb damage; there is a figure of Christ on the gable, below that Emperor Otto is shown as victor in the field at Lech in 955 and then follows a series of the emperors and dukes who established Christianity in Bavaria. There is a bronze statue of St Michael (1592) in a niche between the two doorways and the saint is also portrayed with the Devil on the massive high altar (1589). The interior is dominated by the huge barrel vault with a span of more than 20m (65ft).

The Marienplatz in front of the **Neues Rathaus** is the city's main square. It is part of the pedestrian zone and provides a good and safe place for the crowds who gather at 11am each day (also at 5pm in

A rooftop view of München from the tower of Alte Peter, with the old town hall in the foreground

The Viktualienmarkt, München

✻ summer) to see the *Glockenspiel* on the 85m-high (278ft) tower of the town hall. The mechanical display shows a procession of brightly painted figures representing Duke Wilhelm V on the occasion of his marriage to Renate von Lothringen. Beneath this is the *Schäfflertanz* (Coopers' Dance) first mentioned in 1463 and previously performed every 7 years at carnival time by members of the guild.

⌂ Across the square is the church of **St Peter**, the oldest parish church in München. The unusual tower, completed in 1386, has become a München landmark. The balcony round the tower is open to the public and provides a good view of the city. It is, however, a little alarming if the enormous bells are struck while one is up aloft. The pillared basilica is over 90m long (295ft) and nearly all the famous artists working in München in the fifteenth–eighteenth centuries contributed to the interior decoration.

⌂ The **Theatinerkirche** on Theatinerstrasse, the Catholic parish church of St Kajetan, was built by Elector Ferdinand Maria and his wife Henriette Adelaide in thanks for the long-awaited birth of an heir to the throne. Despite the long period of construction and decoration (1663-1768) and the many different craftsmen involved, the end result is a remarkably unified whole and no visitor with even the slightest interest in architecture should fail to visit it.

⌂ The **Feldherrnhalle** just across the Odeonsplatz from the Theatinerkirche, is at the south end of Ludwigstrasse which King Ludwig I had built as a show street modelled on the Loggia dei Lanzi in Florence. The hall was built in 1840–4 and has statues representing the famous Bavarian generals Tilly (1559–1632) and Wrede (1767–1838) while the army memorial is in honour of the dead in the Franco-Prussian war. Facing the Theatinerkirche across Odeonsplatz is one corner of the **Residenz** (begun in 1836), not a single building but a complex linked by a series of fine courtyards. It replaced the Alter Hof which was being hemmed in by the growing city, but even after the Residenz had been completed the old building was not abandoned. It was badly damaged in World War II but excellently restored in 1946–66 and now houses the finance department with the mint appropriately adjacent.

The Residenz is entered from Max Joseph-Platz and the present buildings include the Königsbau (King's Building), the Alte Residenz, the Festsaal, Cuvilliés Theatre, the ruined court church, the Residenz Theatre and the National Theatre. The courtyards are charming, the most important being the Königsbauhof which contains G. Petel's statue of Neptune (1641). The Grottenhof is surrounded by arcades with the Perseus fountain (1590) in the centre.

⌂ Do not leave the central area without seeing the **Altes Rathaus** at the end of Marienplatz and the nearby **Viktualienmarkt** (open-air food and flower market) with its charming sculptures of the music hall figures Karl Valentin and Ida Schuhmacher. Then for interest or thirst, the **Hofbräuhaus** with its many rooms, cellars and terraces and its historical connection as an early meeting place of Hitler's followers in the 1920s, justifies a little time. At most of the museums there is a modest admission charge but it is worth noting that at the art galleries, **Alte Pinakothek** and **Neue Pinakothek**, there is no charge on Sundays. The world-famous **Deutsches Museum** occu- pies an island in the River Isar and provides many days of interest. Its numerous departments include mining, shipping, railways (with an extensive model layout), aircraft, musical instruments, chemistry, ceramics, printing, glass technology, photography and so on.

München is one of Europe's foremost cultural centres with music of all kinds featuring prominently. The summer season commences in June with a splendid concert series held in the gorgeous baroque palaces at Schleissheim and Nymphenburg. At the same time there are serenade concerts in the Residenz. All these lead up to the opera festival which usually runs from mid-July to the beginning of August. At other seasons, the Bavarian Radio Symphony Orchestra, the München Philharmonic, the Bavarian State Orchestra and the München Bach Chorus carry on the great musical tradition. Opera is not confined to the festival season either and the works of composers who had a special connection with München are often performed, including Mozart, Wagner, Richard Strauss and Carl Orff. The Bavarian State Opera performs at the Nationaltheater but the Kammerspiele Playhouse and the Light Opera House on Gärtner- platz should not be overlooked. Nor should the rococo Cuvilliés Theatre in the Residenz where a Mozart opera is a rare delight.

München caters for every taste and lovers of modern music are not forgotten either. 'Pop' concerts take place frequently and the München *Jazz-Szene* has its own special programme. The *Münchner Rocksommer* in the **Alabamahalle** (Schleissheimer Strasse) is now an annual event. **Das Theater der Jugend** (Youth Theatre) puts on shows in the Schauburg am Elisabethplatz in Schwabing, catering for different age groups. For children, the **Münchner Marionetten- theater** in Blumenstrasse has performances afternoons and evenings all year and there is also the **Münchner Märchenbühne** (Fairy-tale Stage) at Dachauer Strasse 46. Concert and theatre tickets can be quite expensive but there may be reductions for children, groups, students or pensioners. At the Nationaltheater and some others, standing places are offered at low cost, useful for hard-up young-sters.

München and the Surrounding Area

München has many parks and gardens, the largest (372ha, 807 acres) and most well known being the **Englischer Garten** running down to the banks of the Isar. It is a favourite spot with the *Münchner* in summer and sun-worshippers bare all for maximum effect. The spectacular Chinese pagoda here stands at the centre of the biggest beer-garden in München, which has room for 6,000. There are many other restaurants, beer gardens and the Japanese Tea House. One of Europe's foremost zoos, the **Tierpark Hellabrunn** is easily reached by 31, 52 or 57 bus or by S-bahn lines 7 or 27 to Mittersending station. The zoo is on the banks of the River Isar south of the city centre and covers an area of 360,000sq m to house some 5,000 animals. It is regarded as one of the most advanced zoos in the world and is in beautifully landscaped surroundings. Another popular goal during the summer is **Grünwald** a short way to the south, reached from the city by tram or S-bahn and tram, where the Isar provides an attractive bathing and sunning place.

Equally attractive but more formal surroundings can be found at the several *Schlösser* within easy reach of the centre. Nearest is **Schloss Nymphenburg**, north-west of the *Hauptbahnhof* and not too far to walk if one has time. Otherwise take U-bahn line 1 to the Rotkreuzplatz terminus and tram 12 from there, or S-bahn lines 1–6 to Laim and change to a 41 or 68 bus. With the 24-hour ticket you can change between the various modes of transport without formality.

The central pavilion of the extensive Nymphenburg complex was built from 1664–74 as a summer residence for Henriette Adelaide, mentioned earlier. Wings built in 1715–16 by J. Effner show French influence and the same architect built the Pagodenburg (1716–19), the Badenburg (1718–21) and the Magdalenenklause (1725–8). The Amalienburg in the extensive grounds was built in 1734–9 and the central section has remained the focal point of the *Schloss*. The *Festsaal* (banqueting hall) was refurbished in 1756–7 with frescos and stucco. The adjacent rooms are also lavishly decorated. The park was transformed into a picturesque garden in 1804–23 in the strictly geometrical French style.

The *Schloss* complex incorporates two museums; the Mar-stallmuseum is a history of the electors' horses and stables with a display of many ornate state carriages. The Zoologische Staatsamm-lung is a museum of zoology. Adjoining the Nymphenburg park on the north side are the Botanic Gardens with extensive hothouses and outdoor beds featuring plants from all over the world. **Wasser-schloss Blutenberg** (1435) lies a little to the west of Nymphenburg and can be reached via S-bahn line 2 to Obermenzing. This former hunting lodge now houses the international youth library and is not open to the general public. The exquisite late-Gothic chapel is, however, open every afternoon.

Schloss Schleissheim is 13km north of the city centre, the nearest S-bahn station being Oberschleissheim on line 1. There are really three separate palaces here. The Altes Schloss was built as a country retreat for Duke Wilhelm V in 1597 with completion in 1616. It is a simple gentleman's residence of the period. The Neues Schloss is the most important: the foundation stone was laid in 1701, but technical problems and political upheaval resulted in construction being suspended with only the shell complete. Work to complete it re-started in 1719; C. D. Asam and J. B. Zimmermann were responsible for the vault fresco above the staircase and the stucco decoration of the banqueting hall respectively. This is where the famous Schleissheim summer concerts take place.

All in all, the central part of the Neues Schloss is one of the finest examples of German baroque. Under King Ludwig I in 1847–8, the staircase was completed to the original design and the façade was reworked by Leo von Klenze in the early nineteenth century. World War II was responsible for a certain amount of damage but this has since been made good. The Gartenschloss Lustheim, built 1684–7, was modelled on Italian baroque palaces. Central in the building is the great hall, the distinctive feature of which is a mirror vault. The interior of the palace is uniformly outstanding. Today it houses a significant collection of porcelain including much famous and priceless Meissen ware.

Two stops further out, Lohhof is the nearest S-bahn station to **Schloss Haimhausen**, once owned by a count of the same name and a purely private creation. The original seventeenth-century building was elegantly modernised starting in 1747. There is an exterior staircase similar to that at Nymphenburg. Today the *Schloss* makes a fine setting for a display of antiques in thirty rooms and occasional special exhibitions.

Dachau, a town of some 40,000 inhabitants on line 2 of the S-bahn suffers the drawback that its name will forever be associated with some of the worst atrocities committed by the Nazi regime before and during World War II. At Alte Römerstrasse 75 there is a concentration camp memorial with exhibits relating to the history of the camp and of persecution under the Nazis. Nevertheless, the town is completely charming and has an air of stolidity with its old gabled houses, and one can understand why, from the middle of the nineteenth century, it attracted large numbers of artists — their association at one stage numbered some 300 members. The much-travelled Ludwig Thoma lived at Augsburger Strasse No 13 from 1893 until 1897. In his peasant stories he described the town as having a 'rough, old Bavarian zest'.

Dachau is proud of its cultural life which centres largely upon the *Schloss*. The original eleventh-century castle on the site was replaced by a new building in 1546–73. Rebuilding took place in 1715 but it fell into disrepair in the early nineteenth century and only the southwest section survived. The banqueting hall (*Festsaal*) is the most important element in the building today. It is approached by a noble staircase and has a splendid coffered wooden ceiling, also a grisaille (shades of grey) frieze painted in 1567. Unfortunately the *Festsaal* can only be seen during exhibitions or concerts.

Places of interest encircle München like satellites. **Freising** (population 35,000), a bare 32km (20 miles) out, is one such place. It is the northern terminus of S-bahn line 1 and has more than enough sights to keep the visitor occupied for a day. It lies at the foot of the Domberg above the River Isar and developed as one of the spiritual and ecclesiastical centres of south Germany. It was a cathedral town from the eighth century until the see was moved to München in 1821. Churches, chapels, clerical residences and the buildings of the bish-

op's palace can be seen today. Watching over the town from the
Domberg, the Romanesque cathedral of St Maria and St Korbinian
was rebuilt in 1160 although it was altered in the seventeenth century
by Renaissance rebuilding and additions. Then in 1723–4, the interior was decorated with extravagant rococo paintings and lavish
stucco. The choir stalls and vaulted ceiling date from the 1480s. The
high altar of 1625 now has only a copy of Rubens' painting *Woman of
the Apocalypse*, the original of which was removed to the Alte
Pinakothek in München after the 1803 secularisation. In the crypt is
the famous 'beasts column' on which dragon-like monsters battle
with men. Experts have puzzled for years over the precise meaning
of the carvings. The cathedral is a building of contrasts and contains
treasures which really should be examined item by item if time
permits.

As well as the early Gothic Johanniskirche (1320) nearby, the path
between the *Dom* and the bishop's *Residenz* has yet another rare
attraction. This is the Diocesan Museum which has a collection of
valuable works of art. The display of Christmas cribs is quite outstanding and if there are children in the party these will keep them
happy for a long time. The oldest brewery in the world (1040) is to be
found nearby in the former Benedictine abbey of Weihenstephan.
The Benedictine monks were making beer here before München had
even been founded and they continued to do so until 1803. Appropriately, the Technical University of München has taken over the
premises and has here its departments for brewing and food technology as well as for agriculture and garden design. There is even a state
school of flower art, not so surprising really in a land where flowers
and plants feature prominently in almost every household. Freising
is a pleasant and restful base for the exploration, not only of
München, but of a very pleasant rural area as well.

To the north-east of München at the terminus of S-bahn line 6, is
the little town of **Erding** 35km (22 miles) from the city. From the
visitor's point of view it is rather like Freising although less than half
the size. Cycles may be hired to explore the rather flat Erdinger Moos
(moor) south and east of the River Isar. The eye is immediately
attracted by the Landshuter Tor, also called the Schöner Turm
(Beautiful Tower) built in 1400 as part of the encircling wall. In 1648
the town was almost completely destroyed by fire so the dignified
houses with their balconies, gables and little towers nearly all stem
from the eighteenth century. Happily, the monumental Gothic parish church of St Johannes (1450) survived. A distance of 5m separates
the church from its bell-tower which was formerly the station of the
town watchman. Despite the age of the church most of the furnish-

ings are nineteenth century but the most valuable item is the so-called Leinberger Crucifix made by H. Leinberger in the 1520s, Gothic with the first hint of baroque.

Ebersberg (population 8,000) is the terminus of S-bahn line 4, almost due east and 32km (20 miles) from the city. The former *Kloster* church of St Sebastian has an imposing dome-capped white tower. The building has suffered so many alterations over the years that no one architectural style is dominant but the foundations of the original building (1312) can be identified. It is said that the skull of St Sebastian was brought to Ebersberg from Rome in 931 thus giving the *Kloster* its name. The market place is graced by baroque and Biedermeier houses; the town hall (1529) has net vaulting and a carved wooden ceiling.

Round now to the south side of the city, the station of Ebenhausen-Schäftlarn on S-bahn line 7 gives access to one of the most significant *Kloster* complexes in the München area. Standing in open country with a backdrop of wooded hills, the *Kloster* at **Schäftlarn** looks most impressive. The present buildings were erected at the beginning of the eighteenth century to plans by Viscardi. The tower (1712) was erected before the church (1735–51) following the collapse of an earlier tower. Consecration was in 1760 and both church and buildings escaped the ravages of secularisation in 1803 and were given back to the Benedictine order 50 years later. The church was excellently restored in 1954–9 and is regarded as a gem of Bavarian rococo architecture. A pleasant beer-garden nearby provides a place for a rest and a drink when the sight-seeing has been done.

To complete this outer circuit of München go west on S-bahn line 4 to **Fürstenfeldbruck**, two separate places with about 31,000 inhabitants. Bruck is the old settlement which grew up around a crossing place over the River Amper. Fürstenfeld is the place where a famous monastery was built in the thirteenth century. Do not neglect Bruck, a town of some charm with a Leonhardskirche containing the text 'God Bless the Horses'. The long market is enhanced by the old judges' house (1626) with ornamental balconies and the parish church of St Magdalena should not be missed.

The macabre origin of the *Kloster* in no way detracts from the beauty of the present church, one of the most important sacred buildings in Upper Bavaria. Duke Ludwig the Strong suspected that his wife, Maria von Brabant, was being unfaithful and had her beheaded. When it was revealed that his suspicions were entirely without foundation Ludwig was filled with remorse and as a penance founded the *Kloster* on the *Fürstenfeld* (Duke's Holding) in 1263. The early Gothic brick church on the site was replaced in the

The former monastery church at Fürstenfeldbruck

eighteenth century by the present building. Work started in 1701 but was interrupted by the War of Spanish Succession; the long delay meant that elements of German baroque crept in. Although the church was consecrated in 1741 it was not until 1766 that the interior was finally finished. By then, secularisation was not far off and when that time came it was threatened with destruction by cannon fire. Only by the spirited intervention of one Louis Philipp Weiss, a keeper of post-horses, was the deed prevented. The *Kloster* buildings continue today in secular use.

The façade of the church is quite striking with figures of St Benedikt and St Bernard on the balustrade and a statue of Christ the Redeemer in a central niche. Inside, there is a rather bewildering mixture of colours and different styles: Italian, French, Bavarian and the individual contributions of the distinguished masters responsible. The frescos in the choir and main aisle are by C. D. Asam and the side-altars of St Sebastian and St Peter and Paul are the work of his brother Egid Quirin. As in many other great churches, the problem here is to spare time to see all there is to see. Every corner holds something of interest; of particular value is the late Gothic gilded wooden statue of the enthroned Madonna with the child Jesus which was part of the high altar in the earlier building. The great organ is the only one in Bavaria still essentially the original two-manual instrument of the first half of the eighteenth century. It was built by Johann Georg Fux (1670–1738), 'Citizen and organ-maker of Donauwörth'.

Returning to München, one of the city bus tours starting from the *Hauptbahnhof* could be interesting. Throughout the year there are daily round tours lasting about an hour and taking in all the principal sights. A slightly extended version includes the ascent of the Olympic Tower — a wonderful viewpoint — and lasts about $2\frac{1}{2}$ hours. Another variation is a tour taking about the same time and including some inside visits, for example, to the Nymphenburg Palace or the Frauenkirche. More ambitious is 'München by Night', starting at 7.30pm on Friday and Saturday evenings and lasting until midnight. This is a tour through the illuminated streets and buildings, with visits to typical night-spots, including a restaurant. The price of the trip is fully inclusive — not cheap but certainly 'a night to remember'.

Additional Information

Places to Visit

Dachau

Schloss
Open: May to September, Saturday and Sunday 2-5pm. Café-restaurant

KZ (Concentration Camp) Memorial and Museum
Alte Römerstrasse 75
85221 Dachau
☎ 08131-17041
Open: Tuesday to Sunday 9am-5pm.
Film in English 11.30am & 3.30pm.

Freising

Diözesanmuseum
Domberg 21
85354 Freising
☎ 08161-92432
Open: Tuesday to Sunday 10am-5pm.

München

Alte Pinakothek (Art Gallery)
Barar Strasse 27
80333 München
☎ 089-23805215 or 6
Open: Tuesday to Sunday 9.15am-4.30pm, also Tuesday and Thursday 7-9pm. Open Whit Monday, otherwise closed as Deutsches Museum. Admission free on Sunday and holidays.

Neue Pinakothek (Art Gallery)
Barer Strasse 29 (entrance on Theresienstrasse)
80799 München
☎ 089-23805195
Open: Tuesday to Sunday 9.15am-4.30pm, also Tuesday 7-9pm. Open Easter and Whit Mondays but closed on Good Friday, 1 May, Whit Sunday, Corpus Christi, 24, 25, 31 December. Admission free on Sunday and holidays.

Deutsches Museum (Science and Technology)
Museuminsel (Ludwigsbrücke)
80538 München
☎ 089-21791
Open: daily 9am-5pm but closed 1 January, Good Friday, Easter Sunday, 1 May, Whit Monday, Corpus Christi, 17 June, 1 November, 24, 25, 31 December. Railway section includes large model layout. Restaurant and café.

Deutsches Jagd- und Fischereimuseum (Hunting and Fishing)
Neuhauser Strasse 53
80331 München
☎ 089-220522
Open: daily 9.30am-5pm (9pm Monday and Tuesday). Closed some holidays.

Residenz and Museum
Max-Joseph-Platz 3
80539 München
☎ 089-290761
Open: Tuesday to Sunday 10am-4.30pm (last admission 4pm). Accompanied children under 15 free.

Englischer Garten
Always open. Admission free. Restaurants, cafés and beer gardens.

Tierpark Hellabrunn (Zoo)
Siebenbrunner Strasse 6
81534 München
☎ 089-661021
5km S of city centre
Open: April to September daily 8am-6pm, October to March 9am-5pm. Children's amusements. Restaurant.

München-Nymphenburg
Schloss and Amalienburg
Open: April to September, Tuesday to Sunday 9am-12.30pm, 1.30-5pm, October to March 10am-12.30pm, 1.30-4pm. Closed 1 January, Shrove Tuesday, 1 November, 24, 25, 31 December.

Marstallmuseum (Carriages etc)
Open: April to September, Tuesday to Sunday 9am-12noon, 1-5pm, October to March 10am-12noon, 1-5pm, October to March 10am-12noon, 1-4pm. Closed as *Schloss* above.

Badenburg, Pagodenburg and Magdalenenklause
Open: April to September, Tuesday to Sunday 10am-12.30pm, 1.30-5pm. Café.

Botanic Garden
Menzinger Strasse 63
80638 München
☎ 089-17861310
Open: daily 9am-5pm (Greenhouses 9-11.45am, 1-4.30pm)

Chapel of Schloss Blutenberg (Late Gothic)
Near Nymphenburg
Open: daily 2-5pm. Admission free.

München-Schleissheim
Altes Schloss, Neues Schloss, Schloss Lustheim
Open: Tuesday to Sunday 10am-12.30pm, 1.30-5pm (4pm October to March). Closed 1 January, Shrove Tuesday, 1 November, 24, 25, 31 December. Restaurant.

In addition to those listed, there are many more museums and galleries in and around München — brochure from Tourist Information Office.

Local Festival
München
Oktoberfest — 16 days finishing 1st Sunday in October. Beer tents and enormous fun fair.

Tourist Information Centres
Fremdenverkehrsverband
Sonnenstrasse 10
80331 München
☎ 089-597347
General information about München and Upper Bavaria.

Fremdenverkehrsamt München
Sendlinger Strasse 1
80331 München
☎ 089-23911
Accommodation lists and detailed information about München.

Radius Touristik
Im Münchner Hauptbahnhof
Arnulfstrasse 3
80335 München
☎ 089-596113
General information service, guided city tours by bicycle or by foot and tram; ticket agency for public transport and sightseeing tours, etc.

See 'Fact File' for addresses of Youth Hostels, facilities for cycle hire, etc.

5
THE INN VALLEY
& THE CHIEMGAU

East of München, in the south-eastern corner of Bavaria, is an area of great charm. Numerous holiday and health resorts have grown up along the river banks and round the numerous lakes, and there are literally hundreds of villages in the rural countryside. The land is closely veined with small rivers and streams so that most villages have a water course of some sort. The area has many camping and caravan sites and is very favourable for caravan touring since there are few significant hills, a fact which makes it popular with cyclists too. The southern fringe of Chiemgau has already been touched upon in Chapter 2 so this chapter concentrates on the more low-lying part of the area which, nevertheless, lies generally at an altitude of 500m (1,640ft) or more.

In the north-east of the area, not far from Passau, join the River Inn at Neuburg. The river forms the frontier with Austria. **Neuburg am Inn** (to distinguish it from Neuburg an der Donau visited later) with a population of 3,300, is a holiday resort overlooked by the mighty Schloss Neuburg perched on a steep rock 100m (328ft) above the valley. It was built in the eleventh century and in the course of its long history has withstood attacks of all kinds. In 1908 Prinzregent Luitpold gave it to a Passau artists' association which, with similar organisations, has turned it into a hotel and recreation home for the artistic community. There are splendid views over the Inn valley and Austria from the *Schloss* which, with its fourteenth-century chapel, is well worth a visit. During the Passau *Europäischen Wochen* (European weeks), serenade concerts are given in the castle courtyard.

At **Neuhaus** (population 3,000) where the River Rott flows into the Inn, a bridge connects with the Austrian town of Schärding. From the Inn-Promenade Schloss Neuhaus can be seen on an island. Today it is a house of the Institute of Englischen Fräulein — a religious order based on the principles of the Jesuits and devoted primarily to the education, religious instruction and upbringing of young girls. Its headquarters is in Rome with around 3,000 sisters distributed over its several houses.

It is surprising to come across an organisation named after English girls in Bavaria but there is a good reason. In 1585 one Mary Ward was born into a Roman Catholic family near the Yorkshire city of Ripon in England. Although she is said to have been beautiful and to have had many admirers, her heart was set on a life in the church and in 1606 she went to St Omer in France to a severe order of St Clare. As a lay sister she was not subject to the harsh discipline she sought and she left in 1607 resolved to found a community of like-minded Englishwomen. After much opposition she had, by 1621, founded houses in Spitalfields, London and in Köln and Trier. But she was not satisfied with this limited achievement so she went to Rome to put her case to Pope Gregory XV. She was allowed to establish a house in Rome where an eye could be kept on her. For a time things went well but by November 1626 she had decided to return to England via Germany. In München, Elector Maximilian I permitted Mary and her companions to remain since he favoured the education of girls. In 1627 the emperor of Austria invited Mary to found a house in Vienna. Opposition continued and at one stage she was arrested in München and imprisoned in the convent at Anger. Constant harassment undermined her health and in 1637 she returned to England where she died near York in 1645 and was buried at Osbaldwick where her gravestone may be seen in the church.

Two kilometres upstream from Neuhaus is a major technical achievement, the Schärding-Neuhaus power station with its dam which has turned the River Inn here into a 16km (10 mile) long and up to 300m (984ft) wide artificial lake. Turn aside from the Inn to reach **Bad Füssing** (population 4,800), a spa with three thermal springs delivering water at 56°C (133°F) from a depth of 1,000m (3,280ft), the most powerful sulphur springs in Europe. These feed the spa's bathing facilities: the open-air pools have a water temperature of 36–38°C (97–100°F) and are available throughout the year but there is a thermal *Hallenbad* as well.

Aigen, close to the river, with a pilgrimage church dedicated to St Leonhard is the scene of an annual *Leonhardiritt*. It was founded in the thirteenth century to celebrate the finding of a wonder-working *Marienbild* (picture or statue of Mary) washed up from the Inn.

One of the more pleasant things about this area is the bird sanctuary on the banks of the Inn with marked nature trails. A little further upstream between Ering and Simbach, beside another Inn *Stausee* (reservoir), there is a more extensive bird protection area (*Vogel-schutzgebiet*), well worth a visit.

Bad Füssing is at one corner of the so-called Rottal spa triangle, the other resorts being Birnbach and Griesbach both of which lie to the north-west. **Birnbach** is 25km (16 miles) from Bad Füssing. Although its inhabitants number less than 1,300 there is a wide range of leisure activities for every age group. The thermal springs which feed the open-air swimming pools maintain water temperatures of 24–38°C (75–100°F). **Griesbach**, 10km east and about 20km from Bad Füssing, has three thermal springs producing water up to 60°C (140°F) to supply the pools in the pleasant spa which has grown up around the old village. The *Kur* is claimed to be specially beneficial for sufferers of rheumatic and arthritic conditions. In addition to the usual activities and entertainments there is an 18-hole golf course.

Another border town with a major crossing over the Inn to Austria is **Simbach** (population 5,400). This pleasant country town makes an ideal base for visiting the *Vogelschutzgebiet* and for rambling in the very attractive countryside to the north between the valleys of the Rivers Inn and Rott. Fifty-three kilometres of marked *Wanderwege* are centred on Simbach and excursions into the Austrian Salzkammergut are only a matter of crossing over the river bridge. The Gothic church in **Erlach** is worth visiting and the *Heimatmuseum* has a number of items of interest. **Kirchdorf am Inn** a few kilometres up river is close to another *Stausee* which provides a natural bathing place and a broad boating lake.

Germany's great rivers are frequently dammed to provide a head of water for the many hydro-electric power stations. The Inn between here and Passau is a case in point, but these developments have not necessarily harmed the landscape. On the contrary, the new 'lakes' provide opportunities for sailing, wind-surfing and other water activities which would hardly have been possible with a river in its natural state. Six kilometres beyond Kirchdorf the Inn swings sharply northwards with both banks in Bavaria. The B12 running west from Simbach should be followed until it crosses to the south bank of the Inn then fork left into the B20 to reach Burghausen in 10km. Although it is on the Salzach, **Burghausen** is the outstanding example of the distinctive 'Inn valley' style of architecture and a few hours should be spent here. Do not be put off by the fairly uninteresting outskirts of the modern town but seek out the *Burg* and the old town on the banks of the river. There is good parking space near the *Burg* which occupies a long, level terrace high above the town. There are fine views down to the river and the colourful houses beneath, and several paths or flights of steps lead down.

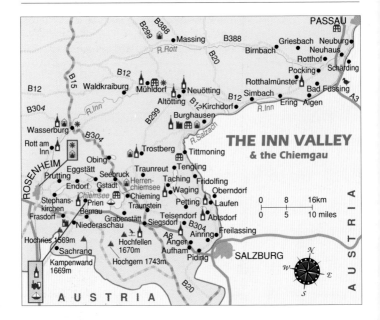

Much that is important in Burghausen is at the upper level. The six sections of the ancient *Burg* extend for some 1100m along the terrace and form the largest castle complex in Germany. The present building dates from the thirteenth to fifteenth centuries and is protected on the flat north side by numerous ditches, gates and courtyards. The south buildings towering over the town include the three-storey Dürnitzstock which has a storage hall with two aisles, over which is the heated dining room, also with two aisles. The upper storey was formerly the ballroom and there is fine fifteenth-century groin vaulting in both apartments. The choir of the *Burg* chapel dedicated to St Elisabeth, was built in the Romanesque style but gave way to Gothic around 1255. The nave has net vaulting from about 1475. The Fürstenbau (Princes' Building) now houses a department of the Bavarian State Art Collection. At the entrance to the *Burg* is the municipal photographic museum and the *Heimatmuseum* is in the inner courtyard.

Down in the town, the fourteenth-century *Rathaus* and the six-teenth-century Regierungsgebäude (Government Building) colour-fully dominate the many fine houses which line the broad main street. This is a photographer's delight. The parish church of St Jakob

Kraiburg

(1360 with later modifications) and the Spitalkirche Heilig Geist (fourteenth century with eighteenth-century baroque) are both worth a visit. There are often concerts and exhibitions, particularly, it seems, during the spring months. There is an underground car park (*Tiefgarage*) in the main street and the new pedestrian zone to the south is most attractive. The feeling of the south is very marked here in Burghausen and can be experienced in many other towns in this area.

Return to the Inn valley at Neuötting about 10km (6 miles) along a picturesque road to the north-west of Burghausen but first turn aside to see **Altötting** (population 12,000) lying a little back from the river. Pilgrims daily make their way to the Gnadenkapelle here, as they have been doing for hundreds of years. The principal object of the pilgrimage is the so-called 'Black Madonna', a 64cm-high (2ft) blackened figure of Mary, probably made in Lorraine about 1300 and which was brought here in 1360. Altötting is sometimes called Herz Bayerns (Heart of Bavaria); in fact this has some validity for in wall compartments opposite the miraculous image are the hearts of six kings, two queens, two electors and Field Marshall Tilly. The continuous stream of pilgrims has resulted in a rather brash commercialism growing up around the chapel with the usual tawdry souvenirs. Those needing a little peace should seek out the modern Stations of the Cross near the Stiftskirche with its two soaring spires, an up-to-date representation in red marble of the beliefs of Christians for nearly 2,000 years. Altötting has its *Hofdult* around the end of May/beginning of June and a *Christkindlmarkt* takes place early in December when there are also concerts of Advent music.

Neuötting has none of the frantic scramble associated with its neighbour. It is a typical Inn-Salzach town and was fortunately spared by World War II so that the market area, with its colourful façades and arcades, is 'original'. It also has a distinguished church, a fine example of Upper Bavarian brick Gothic started in 1410 and not finished for some 200 years. The original plans were adhered to, however, despite the fact that tastes had changed in the meantime. An excursion 25km to the north from here ends at the excellent open-air museum at **Massing** in the River Rott valley. The museum is a collection of Lower Bavarian farmhouses and gives a good insight into the rural way of life in years gone by.

In contrast to Neuötting, **Mühldorf**, 12km west along the Inn, saw action at the end of the war including the blowing up of the Inn bridge. The figure of a town guard from 1659 was thrown into the river by the explosion but the fragments were recovered. The rebuilt figure now stands watch again with shield and halberd outside the

Münchener Tor, one of the town's historic gateways. With around 15,000 inhabitants, Mühldorf is another typical Inn valley town with colourfully painted house fronts — some from the fifteenth and sixteenth centuries, four fountains from the seventeenth and eighteenth centuries and arcades around the long-stretched Stadtplatz or market street. The late Gothic *Rathaus* was rebuilt from three houses after a serious fire in 1640 and was complemented by the Frauenkirche in 1643.

Waldkraiburg is a larger town with the Inn snaking past it on the south side. A pleasant enough place, but not one which tourists need go out of their way to inspect. On summer Sundays there are concerts in the *Stadtpark* and there are regular concerts, drama, opera and operetta in the town theatre. **Kraiburg** on the south side of the river is quite another matter. A little gem of a place which should not be missed, its square surrounded by colourful houses and dominated by the immense St Bonifatius church. **Wasserburg** (not to be confused with the Bodensee Wasserburg) is an important centre and is the point at which the Ferienstrasse (Holiday Road) (see Chapter 7) crosses the Inn to continue its route to the Alps. By now, the Inn has turned south to head for Austria again and a great curve of the river encircles the old town. The most striking view is obtained by entering from the south-east on the B304. The bridge over the Inn is crossed and through the Brucktor gateway is the town centre Marienplatz with the *Rathaus*, the Marienkirche and the Kernhaus with a rococo façade.

The Marienkirche is a fourteenth-century building but the baroque interior was not completed until the second half of the eighteenth century. The older furnishings include a fifteenth-century Madonna, late fifteenth-century figures of St Blasius and St Apollonaria and a font from 1520. The parish church of St Jakob has a fine baroque pulpit from 1638–9 while the *Burg* of 1531, no longer intact, has most attractive stepped gables. The *Heimatmuseum* has a fine collection of Bavarian farmhouse furniture. Civil engineers may well be interested in the Wegmachermuseum (Road-making Museum) which has some 1,500 exhibits including road surfaces, bridges and every conceivable item of equipment to do with road-making, maintenance, snow-clearing and so on.

Although Wasserburg (population 13,400) may not be the place for a prolonged stay, it is certainly worth spending a night or two here in order to see the town in the evening or early morning, free from the daily throng of tourists. In February, Wasserburg is the venue of the biggest pigeon market in the world; Whitsun is the time for a big spring fair with a pleasure park; in July the wine festival includes a Venetian night when the old town is illuminated, while on the first Saturday in August there is a great flea market.

Little **Rott am Inn**, 10km south of Wasserburg, is mainly renowned for its former Benedictine abbey church of St Marinus and Anianus. Rott was the seat of Benedictine monks from the twelfth century on. The enormous fresco in the dome depicts the glorification of the saints of the Benedictine order. The church, standing on the threshold of classicism, represents the mature final stages of baroque and in contrast to the plain exterior, the inside is truly magnificent.

Some of the lesser-known places in the area are also rewarding. One of these is **Tuntenhausen**, 11km south-west of Rott, a village overlooked by most guide books but with a very old (1441) pilgrimage church. The exterior is lined with large pictures of numerous miracles which form a unique documentation of folklore, complemented by the many memorial tablets inside the church. The most original picture is known as the *Tuntenhausener Tod*, a seventeenth-century painting on wood of Death with a poised arrow, illustrating the saying *'Fleuch wo du wilt, des Todes Bildt, stäts auf dich zilt'* ('Hide where you will, Death is always aiming at you'). Wherever you stand in the church the arrow seems to be aimed in your direction.

Returning to the river, enter the busy town of **Rosenheim** (population 53,000) 27km (17 miles) from Wasserburg and by far the biggest town in the area. Rosenheim celebrates several festivals each year, the most important being the autumn fair during the first fortnight of September. The town stands where the old Roman road from Augsburg to Salzburg crossed the Inn and also on the old trade route from the Brenner Pass to Regensburg. Rosenheim clearly belongs to the group of Inn valley towns and the old centre around the Max-Joseph-Platz displays a similar architectural style to Wasserburg and Mühldorf, although only a few of the arcades remain following serious fires in the sixteenth and seventeenth centuries. The parish church of St Nikolaus, Heilig-Geist-Kirche (Church of the Holy Ghost) and Heilig-Blut-Kirche all justify a visit. The *Heimatmuseum* housed in a fourteenth-century town gateway is worth a visit and the town art gallery largely features the works of nineteenth- and twentieth-century painters from München and the Chiemgau. Do not miss seeing the stucco and courtyard of No 20 and the former *Rathaus* (1444) at No 22 Max-Joseph-Platz.

Bad Aibling (population 12,500) just west of Rosenheim, is a pleasant spa with all the appropriate facilities. Art-lovers may be interested in the *Heimatmuseum* which includes the studio of Wilhelm Leibl (1844–1900) who lived and painted in this area for a

Wasserburg town hall

VNDE SVPRBIT HOMO
NASCI POENA LABOR
POST HOMINEM VERMIS POST
SIC IN NON HOMINEM

CVIVS CONCEPTIO CVLP
VITA NECESSE MORI
VERMEM FOETOR ET HORR
VERTITVR OMNIS HOMO

The seventeenth-century painting in Tuntenhausen church of Death aiming his arrow

number of years. One of his well known paintings *Drei Frauen in der Kirche* (Three Women in Church) of 1881 now hangs in the Hamburg Kunsthalle; it was painted in the church at **Berbling** just to the south and the artist is said to have spent no less than four summers working on it. The church is worth seeing anyway for it is much more than the usual village place of worship. It was restored in 1983 and shows rococo at its best; indeed, it is often called the Wieskirche of the Mangfall valley, a bit of justifiable exaggeration perhaps.

East of Rosenheim several resorts south of the motorway deserve attention, for they occupy an exceptionally picturesque corner of Chiemgau. **Frasdorf** (population 1,400) like many other villages, celebrates spring by erecting a maypole on 1 May. Throughout the year there are fortnightly folk-music or dance presentations but it is also an ideal centre for rambling in the Alpine foothills. The neighbouring villages of **Törwang** and **Grainbach** both have churches — originally Gothic — as their focal points. From Grainbach, the Hochriesbahn climbs to the summit of the Hochries (1,570m, 5,150ft). The *Bahn* is in two sections, first a chair-lift for 250m (820ft) and then a cable car for the remaining 670m (2,200ft). It is cheaper to pay for both sections together and for families the *Familienkarte* offers substantial savings on a return journey. Refreshments are available at the upper station (not far from the Austrian border) from where there is a choice of routes to take one back to the valley on foot if desired. The summit offers marvellous views towards the Wilder Kaiser mountains in Austria to the south. Another village in this group, **Rossholzen**, is worth visiting because its church has a late Gothic winged altar and a number of naive but realistic memorial tablets portraying the one-time water traffic on the nearby Inn.

Aschau, in the valley of the little River Prien, is divided into two parts, **Niederaschau** to the north and **Hohenaschau** to the south. It is a *Luftkurort* of 4,300 inhabitants and is the terminus of a branch railway from Prien on the main München-Salzburg line. The village is attractive with its variety of flower-bedecked houses and the twin towers of its baroque parish church. This spacious late Gothic building was given baroque treatment in 1702 and the main aisle was extended in 1752–3. However, the symbol of Aschau is not the church, pretty though it is, but the imposing castle, Burg Hohenaschau, which dominates the skyline. It is the mightiest of the many fortresses in the Chiemgau and in 1561 was converted from an uncomfortable *Burg* into a spacious Renaissance *Schloss* which was later rebuilt in the baroque style. The building is well worth a visit for its monumental 'Gallery of Ancestors' (larger-than-life stucco statues) in the state ballroom and the chapel, and with an early baroque

Italian high altar from Verona. Aschau has a lively programme of events from May to September for its summer visitors: in winter, attention focuses mainly on winter sports activities. In this corner of Chiemgau there are several splendid opportunities for mountain walks which, while not specially difficult, do reach fine vantage points.

From beside the main road in Hohenaschau, the *Gondelbahn* climbs up to the Kampenwand for the start of a walk of 7.5-8km. As the car glides over the tree tops, look down into the clearings for glimpses of chamois and other wildlife. The actual summit at 1,669m (5,474ft) is reached along a path about 1km in a north-easterly direction from the upper station (1,464m, 4,800ft) (refreshments) and a little beyond that there is an *Almhütte* selling refreshments.There are wonderful views north over Bernau and the Chiemsee.Continue first north-east then north for nearly 1km. The Sulten (1,473m, 4,831ft) is on the left and the Gederer Wand (1,399m, 4,590ft) on the right. A path going sharply back to the left (west) before passing the Sulten is the shortest way back down to Hohenaschau but it is very steep. Less demanding is the path past the Sulten which gradually curves to the left (west) descending steadily and often quite steeply. After about 2.5km keep left when the path forks, continuing westwards past the Maisalm (refreshments) to join and follow a stream running down to the valley. The main road is reached in Niederaschau, turn left and follow it back to the starting point. Look out for posters advertising an *Almkonzert* or *Almtanz*, usually on a Sunday afternoon. There will be refreshments and the enjoyment of folk-music and dancing there on the mountain can make the workaday world seem very far away.

Beyond Aschau, **Sachrang** is the last village before the Austrian border. Its idyllic setting amongst the mountains close to the source of the Prien makes this a fine centre for mountain walking. Sachrang is an unsophisticated resort; but the summer visitor is entertained with occasional film evenings and a fortnightly (on Fridays) *Almtanz* or *Heimatabend* (folk-evening) or guided mountain walks. The little village church was built at the end of the seventeenth century, when Italian artists were brought in to work on the stucco and paintings.

From the church (at 738m, 2,420ft) walk due north up the hillside to start a rather strenuous 10km ramble; climb steeply for nearly 2km until the path makes a T-junction with another and turn left into this. Continue climbing, now walk due west for about 1km to reach a mountain hut, the Spitzsteinhaus at 1,237m (4,057ft) right on the Austrian border. Refreshments should be available here (*Ruhetag* Tuesday). To ascend to the summit of the Spitzstein (1,596m, 5,235ft) go north from here on a well used steep path on the Austrian side of the border and reach the summit in about 1km. Note that this involves a climb of about 360m (1,180ft) from the Spitzsteinhaus. From the summit there is a choice of return route.

1. Continue northwards along the ridge to the Brandelberg (1,517m, 4,976ft) and (by now back in Bavaria) on to the Feichtenalm about 2km from the summit where a path turns down to the right, east at first and then curves to the right to drop steeply down into Innerwald and Huben (refreshments) then follows the main road back into Sachrang in under 2km.

2. Return the same way to the Spitzsteinhaus, continue south on the Austrian side for 1km or so — do not take any paths going west off the ridge — and look out for signs to Café Kaiserblick. From the café there is a fine view to the Kaiser mountains and down to Sachrang below. Continue downhill, sometimes fairly steeply, on one of several obvious paths to reach the village.

Whether one chooses route 1 or 2 there is little difference in the distance covered or the time required. These are most rewarding walks and the summer visitor will be astonished at the variety and abundance of wild flowers to be found. Remember to carry your passport, for the border is not obvious in these mountains.

From some of the heights around Frasdorf or Aschau one can look north to the 5km-long Simssee near Rosenheim, a delightful lake in pretty surroundings. The principal resort on the Simssee is **Stephanskirchen** near the south end, only 6km from Rosenheim. There are numerous bathing places including a particularly fine beach at **Krottenmühl** near the north end where there are also good eating places. **Prutting** is a village about 2.5km west of the Simssee and 2 or 3km beyond it are two more lakes, the Hofstättersee and the Rinssee, each about 1.5km long. The many paths and small farm roads make for pleasant and level walking around the lakes. Prutting is equally well placed for access to the small lakes or to the larger Simssee, connected to the village by a direct footpath.

A little beyond the end of that lake, **Endorf** (population 5,100) is principally a health resort with important mineral springs. No single large village this, but the core of a group of no less than fourteen little communities. A lively programme of entertainment is organised, especially in the summer months when *Kur* guests are joined by many holidaymakers. Concerts, theatrical productions (including a religious one June/July), film evenings and so on ensure there is always something for the visitor to look forward to. Between here and the village of Eggstätt, 6km to the east, there is another cluster of idyllic little lakes. **Eggstätt** (population 1,700) is also a health resort on a modest scale. Despite the proximity of the busy Chiemsee this

The little steam train which runs from Prien to the harbour at Stock on the Chiemsee

The lake steamers which connect Prien-Stock with Herrenchiemsee and Frauenchiemsse

area is relatively unspoiled and many happy days may be spent just wandering from one little lake to another, enjoying the (protected) natural surroundings. Look out in July and August for announcements of *Almtänze* (folk dances) and *Dorffeste* (village fairs).

The Chiemsee with an area of 80sq km is Bavaria's largest lake and at the same time the largest entirely in Germany. **Prien** (population 9,000) at the west end is not only the biggest town near the lake but the only one served by main line trains. In fact, the town centre and station are 1.5km from the lake shore. A magnificent museum piece of a steam railway, the nineteenth-century Prien-Stock-Bahn connects the DB station with the pier at Stock where the lake steamers depart. The strange tramway-type locomotive is known affectionately as 'Feurige (fiery) Elias'

Prien is a *Kneippkurort* and a town worth visiting if only for the *Heimatmuseum* in a house of 1681 which gives a comprehensive picture of the one-time peasant life around the Chiemsee. There is a busy programme of events in Prien and the surrounding villages and various excursions on foot, by bicycle or by steamer are arranged from May to September. There is a bathing beach on the Chiemsee at **Stock**. Less than 3km to the south in the village of **Urschalling**, the little twelfth-century chapel is the site of remarkable Romanesque and Gothic wall paintings which were hidden for centuries under countless coats of distemper and only came to light during restoration work in 1941–2.

Travel into the mountains, to Rosenheim or even to München is easy from Prien but it is the steamer trips on the lake which bring many people here and in particular the opportunity to go ashore on the main islands, **Herrenchiemsee** and **Frauenchiemsee** (Herreninsel or Fraueninsel). Herrenchiemsee is the bigger of the two and most visitors coming off the steamer hasten past the Altes Schloss towards Ludwig II's dream palace (1869–86) which, conceived during his 'French' period, is modelled on the French baroque palace of Versailles. However, the Altes Schloss (built 1700) is also of interest; it was part of the monastery which once stood here (hence the *Herren* [men or monks] in the name) and is where Ludwig stayed during his frequent visits to the island, which he bought in the first place to protect it from speculators. .

The new palace is a truly spectacular building and the great hall, the mirror gallery and the state bedroom are amongst the finest of Ludwig's creations. It is a wonderful experience to take the steamer to the island from Prien or one of the other lake resorts, enjoy a leisurely meal in the Schlosshotel and then walk through the trees to the palace for a concert of chamber music in the great hall (no seats).

Then back to the mainland, if one is lucky, in the moonlight.

Frauenchiemsee is the site of a *Kloster* founded by one Irmingard in 772 for nuns of the Benedictine order. Her grave was only rediscovered in the course of excavations started in 1961. To enjoy fully the delights of this little island, it should be visited outside the peak holiday season when every calling steamer disgorges a crowd of visitors. The meringue swans are a delightful speciality of the Klostercafé where liqueurs and gorgeous marzipan are also on sale.

Take time to walk right round the island for the wonderful views in every direction but especially southwards towards the mountains. Frauenchiemsee is a favourite haunt of artists and an exhibition of their work is held during the summer months.

A circuit of the Chiemsee is a must, even if traffic is a problem at times. Going north from Prien, pass through a succession of resort villages: **Rimsting** (population 2,680) is only 3km along this road and then comes **Breitbrunn** (population 1,300) with its picturesque baroque church and extensive views over the lake to Frauenchiemsee and the mountains beyond. **Gstadt** is right on the shore, with steamers, boats for hire and a bathing beach. **Seebruck**, at the northernmost tip of the lake, is where the lake waters enter the River Alz on the way to the Inn. One of the lake's sailing centres, Seebruck also caters for bathing and other water activities with a large bathing beach, a *Freibad* and an enormous area for just sunning and lazing. This was once the site of the Roman settlement of Bedaium where a fortress was erected to protect the important Salzburg-Rosenheim road. Many Roman remains are exhibited in the Heimathaus.

Now, for a short while, the lakeside road becomes the Ferienstrasse which has come across country from Wasserburg. **Chieming** (population 3,500) marks the easternmost limit of the lake and is devoted largely to sun and water worshippers. The lake steamers call here from May to September. The Ferienstrasse now turns off east to **Traunstein** but the lake circuit continues south along the shore towards **Grabenstätt** (population 3,100), a flower-bedecked health resort lying about 2km from the shore, because the road has to make a detour round the marshy delta of the River Tiroler Ache, a wildlife sanctuary. The nearby Tüttensee is one of Bavaria's warmest natural bathing places.

Shortly after leaving Grabenstätt join the motorway for the westward journey along the south lake shore. The next junction — **Feldwies** — gives access to a 3km-long sandy strand which is a favourite weekend goal for the *Münchner*. At the Bernau exit from the motorway turn north to complete the circuit of the lake past Urschalling and back into Prien. For those relying on public trans-

King Ludwig II's palace at Herrenchiemsee, built to rival the Palace of Versailles in France

The Great Hall of Mirrors at Herrenchiemsee

port, the stations at Übersee and Bernau near the south shore of the Chiemsee are served by local trains.

If one follows the Ferienstrasse north from Seebruck **Pavolding** is reached in about 5km. Here the remarkable Heinrich Kirchner lived and worked. He was teacher of sculpture in the Münchner Art Academy from 1952 until 1970 and died in 1984. In and around the village are the enormous and astonishing bronze figures which he created — a sight not to be missed. In another 2-3km is **Seeon** with its idyllic little lake, the Klostersee, and the former Benedictine monastery church of St Lambertus on its shore. Originally Romanesque, the building was rebuilt in Gothic style around 1430 and converted to baroque in the seventeenth century. The cemetery with its separate chapel (1349) is a surprise, for many of the headstones and memorials bear the unfamiliar double cross of the Russian orthodox church and Russian inscriptions. This was the burial place of the Leuchtenberg-Romanovs and a recent headstone marks the grave of Anastasia, the pretender to the Russian throne, who was buried here after her death in America in 1984.

A little further north on the B304, **Obing**, with its little lake and bathing beach, is worth a visit. Here in a peaceful land of little lakes, streams and woods is an environment ideal for those seeking escape from the workaday world. In the fifteenth-century parish church of St Laurentius there are three examples of the work of a notable local wood-carver, his *Mother-of-God*, *St Laurentius* and *St Jakobus* in the late Gothic style. The name of the artist is unknown and he is merely recorded as Meister von Rabenden. **Rabenden** is, in fact, the next village 5km eastwards and in the little church there, the high altar and two side-altars make an impressive unit and the principal figures, *Jakobus*, *Simon* and *Judas Thaddäus* are most lifelike.

Four kilometres more, and in **Altenmarkt**, the River Traun adds its Alpine waters to the northward flowing Alz. It is a friendly little town of about 3,000 inhabitants and the picturesque river with its waterfalls invites the traveller to linger. Immediately south of the town, the Klosterkirche Baumburg occupies an elevated site with good views of the countryside and can be seen for miles around with its unusual pointed domes. It is the former church of the Augustinian canons. The first building here was consecrated in 1023 and the present one was built on the Romanesque foundations in 1754–7. Externally quite plain, the church is lavishly decorated inside with rococo stucco work by the Wessobrunn school, excellent carving on the altars, pulpit and choir stalls and *Putti* (symbolic children's figures) everywhere. Concerts of sacred music are given here during the summer months.

Just north of Altenmarkt, **Trostberg** (population 6,200) is known as the northern gateway to the Chiemgau. It is a pleasant town with a long history and one in which markets play an important role. In March, May, October and November there are market days on the third Saturday and Sunday in the month; from May to October there is a flea market on the first Saturday in each month. Although this romantic old town does not really make many concessions to the tourist trade, the Gothic parish church is worth seeing; the *Heimatmuseum* housed in the Heimathaus, built in 1943, is notable for its series of furnished rooms depicting the life-styles of the baroque, rococo and Biedermeier periods. Returning to Altenmarkt, follow the River Traun and the B304 south to **Traunreut** in about 8km, where the main interest for the holidaymaker may well be the *Freibadzentrum* with its heated swimming pools, huge water-chute and extensive sun-bathing area.

Continuing south on the B304, bypass Traunwalchen, and in 10km reach **Traunstein** (population 17,400), the principal town in this corner of the Chiemgau, a *Luft-* and *Kneippkurort* with all the amenities. Originally settled by the Romans, Traunstein blossomed in the fourteenth century when it became a river crossing place for one of the old salt routes. There is less of a historic town centre than one would expect due to a series of disastrous fires. The baroque church was restored after the last fire in 1851 and graces the 250m-long (820ft) and 85m-wide (280ft) Stadtplatz.

Traunstein is one of several places where the Easter Ride is still practised. Here it is known as the *Georgiritt* and the brightly decorated procession, including St George on a white horse, makes its way to the little church at nearby **Ettendorf** where the horses are blessed on behalf of all the animals on the farms, and on returning home, horses and riders are treated to a special Easter meal. In addition the town hosts a spring festival in May, a folk-festival in August and a *Christkindlmarkt* in December.

The visitor with time available should follow the Traun a further 5km south, crossing the motorway to the little town of **Siegsdorf**, focal point of a holiday region of about 7,000 inhabitants. Since the region includes mountainous country reaching heights of over 1,200m (3,936ft) there are winter facilities with ten ski-tows. The region embraces the village of **Bergen**, 4km west of Siegsdorf, where there is a cable railway in two sections to the summit of the Hochfelln (1,670m, 5,477ft). Again there are group and family tickets offering substantial reductions. Siegsdorf is ideally situated for mountain walking, modest rambling round the Chiemsee or for excursions a little further afield to the Inn valley or the Berchtesgaden area for example. There is a heated *Freibad* with an adjoining unheated pool.

From Traunstein the B304 heads directly for Salzburg and if this picturesque road is followed for about 16km, arrives at **Teisendorf**, a useful little resort with — between mid-June and end of August — folk-evenings, slide or film shows, guided rambles and mountain walks.

About 4km south of the village is Kloster Höglwörth, an ancient seat of the Order of Augustinian Canons which was refounded in 1125. After falling into disrepair the church was rebuilt in the seventeenth century and contains striking stucco work. This rural *Kloster* looks more like a fortress and there is no doubt that the monks built with an eye to their security in an isolated location.

Two kilometres below the *Kloster*, the parish church of St Peter and St Paul (1450) in **Anger** has a number of interesting sculptures from the sixteenth and seventeenth centuries. King Ludwig I was of the opinion that Anger was the most beautiful village in Bavaria and it is a very fine spot with its surrounding farmhouses, mostly from the eighteenth century, making a homely, attractive picture. Today, an important factor is the freedom of the village from traffic thanks to the proximity of the motorway.

A pleasant walk of 16-18km (10-12 miles) by well defined footpaths southwards from Teisendorf brings one to the former *Kloster* and its church, then down to the little wood-fringed lake which belonged to the *Kloster*. From here the route runs south-east into Anger and then due east for about 3km to the summit of the Höglberg (827m, 2,712ft). One could return by the same route or shorten the distance slightly by taking one of several paths or tracks which run more or less directly north-west back to Teisendorf.

Anger, with its close neighbour **Aufham**, south of the motorway, has a fairly ambitious programme of events from June to September.

The River Saalach flows north-east marking the Austrian border, followed closely by the B20; **Ainring** (population 8,500) is reached in about 8km (5 miles), a little town whose entertainments include candlelit evenings with light music and dancing, Bavarian evenings with *Schuhplattler* (clog dancing) and brass band concerts. Note here the castle-like parsonage (1532) and the late Gothic church with interior baroque decoration. At the border town of **Freilassing** the Saalach joins the Salzach which now marks the frontier northwards.

Continue on the B20 from Freilassing for 14km (9 miles) to **Laufen** (population 5,000), a town rich in tradition. It was a salt trading post in a favourable position on a bend of the Salzach. Now, with its arcades and a few lovingly restored houses, it is a charming haven, an unexpected bonus. The parish church Maria Himmelfahrt is the oldest surviving hall church in Germany. It was built from 1332 on the site of a Romanesque basilica, the tower of which it inherited. The painter J. M. Rottmayr, born in Laufen, was responsible for the fine painting (1690) on the south side altar. A low arcade with beautiful net vaulting and frescos runs round part of the church and leads to the fourteenth-century Michaelskapelle which has been partly re-built recently.

The present *Schloss* is the result of building and rebuilding in 1424 and 1606 on the site where there has been a castle since at least 790. The sixteenth-century *Rathaus* received its present façade in 1865. Three towers remain from the old town walls which have otherwise disappeared.

Just over the border in the Austrian village of **Oberndorf** that best-known of Christmas carols *Stille Nacht, Heilige Nacht* (Silent night, Holy night) was composed in 1818 by Franz Gruber. There are various legends about how the song came to be written; one describes how, after mice had eaten through the organ pipes in St Nikolaus' church, the priest Joseph Mohr asked his friend Franz Gruber, local teacher and organist to compose a tune which could be accompanied by guitar. Father Mohr wrote the words and the first performance was given on Christmas Eve. It was an immediate success and quickly spread to surrounding areas; Tirolean singers from the Zillertal sang it when on tour in New York in 1839 and thereafter it was quickly adopted all round the world. The church for which the song was written was later destroyed by floods and the story is now beautifully recalled in the stained glass windows of the *Stille Nacht Kapelle*. A recently opened museum fills in the detail.

A few kilometres south-west of Laufen, the idyllic Abtsdorfer See near the village of **Abtsdorf** is a quiet oasis among the old farms. The village church surprisingly contains a glittering world of frescos and pictures of the saints including St Urban, the patron saint of wine-growers, an indication perhaps that in some long-forgotten past there were vineyards here.

Waging, Petting, Taching and **Tengling** are the unlikely names of a group of village resorts in a miniature lake district 10–20km west of Laufen. The principal lakes are the Waginger See and the Tachinger See and the shores are liberally sprinkled with spacious camp sites. The lakes are amongst the warmest in Upper Bavaria so it is small wonder that the majority of holidaymakers here are those for whom water activities are the main attraction. Bathing, sailing, surfing and angling are the order of the day in this essentially summer holiday area. The organised entertainments too are angled towards the outdoor life, with forest and lakeside rambles, conducted cycle tours and gymnastic sessions. The lake shores are little built-up although Waging itself is a market town with well over a thousand years of history. The seventeenth-century church has stucco in the style of the Wessobrunn school.

The nearby towns of **Fridolfing** and **Tittmoning**, both on the B20, are really part of the same group. The former is a friendly rural town while Tittmoning is a romantic little place with a historic town square, fountains and statues. It is typical of the towns along this Austrian border — like Laufen it belonged to Salzburg until 1816 — and is comparatively little known so that it has many modest treasures to reveal to the visitor prepared to spend a little time here.

The mighty *Rathaus* of 1580 was renovated in 1751; the gilded busts of twelve Roman emperors over the first and second floor windows are a reminder that this too was once in Roman possession. The castle was erected in the thirteenth century as a bulwark against the Bavarians (!) whose troops besieged it and caused a lot of destruction in 1611. Today, twenty-five rooms constitute the *Heimathaus*, a museum with many valuable exhibits, inspection of which is limited to conducted tours during afternoons.

A glance at the map reveals that the area covered in this chapter is really but a small corner of Bavaria yet it is probably the most attractive part for those who enjoy the outdoor life. There is much of historical and cultural interest but it is not surprising that sun and water dominate the activities in an area where the climate during the summer months is usually reliably warm and dry.

Additional Information

Places to Visit

Burghausen
Burg and Gemäldegalerie
Burg 48
84489 Burghausen
☎ 08677-4659
Open: April to September daily 9am-12noon, 1-5pm, October to March, Tuesday to Sunday 10am-12noon, 1-4pm. Closed 1 January, Shrove Tuesday, 1 November, 24, 25, 31 December.

Herrenchiemsee
Neues Schloss & König Ludwig II Museum
Verwaltung
Altes Schloss
83209 Prien/Chiemsee
☎ 08051-3069
Open: daily April to September 9am-5pm, October to March 10am-4pm. Closed 1 January, Shrove Tuesday, 1 November, 24, 25, 31 December. Fountains play mid-May to September. Schlosshotel restaurant.

Massing
Bauernhofmuseum
Schusteröd
84323 Massing
☎ 08724-577
Open: Tuesday to Friday 10am-
12noon, 2-6pm, Saturday, Sunday
and holidays 2-6pm.

Oberndorf
'Silent Night' Museum
Oberndorf (Austria)
☎ 06272-7221
Open: Tuesday to Sunday 9am-
12noon, 1-5pm (on 24 December
9am-6pm).

Wasserburg
Wegmacher-Museum
In der Strassenmeisterei
Herderstrasse 5
83512 Wasserburg/Inn
☎ 08071-7437
Open: Monday to Thursday 8-
11am, 1-3pm. Admission free.

Steam Railway
Prien
Chiemseebahn
Information: Chiemsee-Schiffahrt
Ludwig Fessler
Postfach 1162
83209 Prien
☎ 08051-6090
Steam trains daily mid-May to
September between Prien DB
station and Stock pier.

Tourist Information Centres
Fremdenverkehrsgemeinschaft-
  Inn-Salzach
Kapellplatz 2a
84503 Altötting
☎ 08671-506219
For general information about the
Inn and Salzach river areas.

Verkehrsverband Chiemsee eV
Rathausstrasse 11
83209 Prien
☎ 08051-2280 or 3031
For general information about the
Chiemsee and Rosenheim areas.

Verkehrsverband Chiemgau eV
Ludwig-Thoma-Strasse 2
83278 Traunstein
☎ 0861-58223
For general information about the
Chiemgau.

For local detail, accommodation
lists etc address inquiries to
'Tourist Information' giving the
postcode and name of the town:

83352 Altenmarkt
84503 Altötting
83229 Aschau
83043 Bad Aibling
94072 Bad Füssing
84364 Birnbach
84489 Burghausen
83093 Endorf
83395 Freilassing
94086 Griesbach
83410 Laufen
84453 Mühldorf
83209 Prien
83358 Seebruck
83313 Siegsdorf
84529 Tittmoning
83278 Traunstein
83308 Trostberg
83329 Waging
83512 Wasserburg/Inn

6
THE EASTERN MARCHES

There is a great difference between the Chiemgau of Chapter 5 and the eastern marches of Bavaria. Much of this eastern strip is densely wooded, the Bayerischer Wald (Bavarian Forest) and the adjoining Böhmerwald (Bohemian Forest) on the Czech side of the border constituting the largest forested area in Europe. There are many communities in the forest though and it is a popular holiday area. This is a land of glorious scenery, well appointed resorts and a climate which favours summer and winter visitors alike. The northern part of the area has the Oberpfälzer Wald (Upper Palatinate Forest) and there are many smaller wooded parts in addition to the two major forests. Like a rather crooked spine, one of Bavaria's tourist roads, the Ostmarkstrasse, runs northwards from Passau and serves as a loose link between the various places to be visited.

A pleasant introduction to the southern end of the Bayerischer Wald is a walk along the well-marked Ilztalwanderweg (Ilz Valley Way), a charming riverside trail. The total distance is 70km (44 miles), but it can be walked in short stages. The Ilz is a small river which feeds into the Donau at Passau. It has its source near the Czech border between the Rachel and the Lusen mountains. The walk will be of particular interest to nature lovers who will find rare and often protected varieties of flora and fauna. In the river, mussels, which earlier supported a modest pearl-fishing industry, are now rare but crabs, trout and pike are among the commoner inhabitants. Many colourful birds flit among the branches and on the ground, lizards, including the fire-salamander, are to be found. Along the way there are information boards drawing attention to points of interest in the locality. There are plenty of seats and picnic areas, many natural bathing places and, of course, never far away, a hostelry of some sort for refreshments or an overnight stop.

The *Wanderweg* starts at Veste Oberhaus (youth hostel — see also Chapter 7) high above the city of Passau on the north bank of the Donau and runs in a generally northerly direction. After a few kilometres is the first of several bridges which enable the walk to continue on either the left or right bank and, of course, to vary the route for the return. The final crossing point is at a water-mill, the Schneidermühle where there is a *Wanderparkplatz* and information board, about 35km from Passau. One can wander a little further upstream on the east bank to view the ruins of Diessenstein Castle. **Fürsteneck**, east of the river is probably the best place in this vicinity to seek refreshment or accommodation.

Tucked away in this furthest corner of Bavaria, 30km (19 miles) east of Passau along the B388, the little health resort of **Wegscheid** offers the visitor a peaceful haven in an area which must be regarded as well off the beaten track and all the more attractive for that. There are several earlier churches of interest including St Anna Kapelle (1716) with a late baroque central part, little onion-capped towers and an octagonal cupola; the Wasserkapelle (1770) has an over life-sized Christ with water flowing into a granite basin from the wounds. The 1822 *Rathaus* incorporates some earlier parts.

Activities include roller-skating and there are many walks; favourite excursions are to the Friedrichsberg (930m, 3,050ft) about $1\frac{3}{4}$ hours' walk to the north for splendid views or to the rocky summit of the Eidenberger Luessen (733m, 2,404ft) an hour to the south. At the foot of the latter mountain is a woodland nature trail, a circular walk of about 4km through the romantic Bärenlochklamm (Bear's Cave Ravine).

Hauzenberg (population 3,500) is about 16km north-west of Wegscheid along a picturesque road and it too is a health resort, although at first it may seem that the principal sights in the area are the enormous quarries from which the famous blue granite is obtained. This material is in great demand all over the world and has long contributed to the Hauzenberg economy. Rowing boats may be hired on the nearby idyllic Freudensee which is a favourite spot for anglers and here there are the ruins of a former hunting lodge (fifteenth century) of the prince-bishops. Behind the ruin is the quarry where King Ludwig I had eighteen octagonal monoliths, each 6.70m (22ft) long, cut for his Befreiungshalle in Kelheim (see Chapter 7). They should have gone by water up the Danube but because of the weight — some 40 tons each — could not be transported to the river side and were abandoned until 1908 when two of them were taken for the university building in Amalienstrasse, München.

Walks include the Frauenwaldberg (948m, 3,110ft) the Steinberg

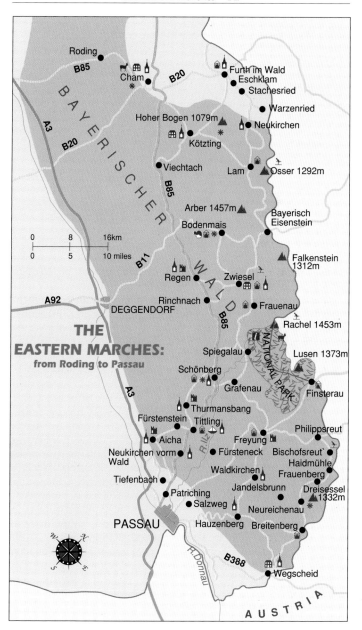

(830m, 2,722ft) and the Staffelberg (793m, 2,600ft). Along this eastern fringe there are many walking possibilities and although the rambles mentioned in no way constitute mountaineering, many of them do, nevertheless, involve quite strenuous climbs.

Back near the Austrian frontier, **Breitenberg** (population 2,000) is a peaceful summer resort with the opportunity of forest rambling northward to the Dreisessel (1,332m, 4,369ft) and to many lesser summits. Of interest here is the Webereimuseum. The growing of flax and spinning and weaving of linen are amongst the oldest occupations in this area and this little museum traces the history of the craft from the earliest times. There are demonstrations on old machines, and furniture, implements and utensils of the rural life of the past are displayed. A few kilometres north of Breitenberg is one of the many *Dreiländerecken* (literally 'three countries corners') in and around Germany; here all the constituents still exist and the frontier stone at 1,320m (4,330ft) with the inscriptions CS, Ö and B marks the point agreed in 1765, by Bohemia (now the Czech Republic), Austria and Bavaria.

Since it is so near, this is a good opportunity to go up through the trees to the Dreisessel for wonderful views over the forests of all three countries. The summit area is often quite busy for a motor road now terminates only a short distance below. As one climbs, the row of blue and white posts marking the border of Bavaria is seen in the trees on the right. At the top one has to walk round a tip of the Czech Republic to reach the summit shop and *Gasthof*.

The Dreisessel, despite its prominence, is not actually the highest of the summits in the small group. Its neighbours Höchstein and Bayerischer Plöckenstein overtop it by 20m (65ft) and 50m (164ft) respectively and Böhmischer Plöckenstein over the border by 66m (216ft). Towns and villages around the Dreisessel have combined to make a holiday and health resort area under the name Ferienland um den Dreisessel: **Haidmühle**, neighbouring **Frauenberg** a scattered place at the start of the 9km road to the summit, and **Bischofsreut** lie at an altitude of 830–1,000m (2,722–3,280ft). There is a good network of footpaths including a *Waldlehrpfad* (forest nature trail) and a *Trimmpfad* (keep-fit course).

The *Hallenbad* has a sauna and a solarium and for children there are several play areas and a fairy-tale wood. Winter guests are not forgotten either and 65km of trails for cross-country skiing are serviced by several ski-lifts and the longest double ski-tow in Germany.

Neureichenau which, with its outlying villages, has a population of around 4,500 is also a health resort and again caters for winter visitors as well as summer ones. It has a fine *Hallenwellenbad* while nearby **Jandelsbrunn** is well fitted to cater, as it claims to do, for those who seek peace and relaxation in natural surroundings during their holidays.

The biggest town in the group is the *Luftkurort* of **Waldkirchen** with some 9,000 inhabitants, a busy little centre with good shopping facilities. Waldkirchen has always been an important place, lying as it does on one of the old salt routes from Passau to Bohemia. Indeed, the prosperity of the whole region was bound up for centuries with the lucrative salt trade. Because of a history of devastating fires, there is little of real historic value. The parish church of St Peter and St Paul built in 1861 was destroyed the following year and after being rebuilt, endured until 1945 when it fell victim to the destruction which marked the end of World War II. Once again it was rebuilt and with its impressive steeple is now a dignified church which enjoys the title 'Cathedral of the Bavarian Forest'. The fine organ is well worth hearing.

On the nearby Schulerberg (657m, 2,155ft) a citizen, one Bernhard Linus, had a chapel built (1663–5) which was dedicated to his patron saint Borromäus. Rebuilt in 1756 the little church has ceiling frescos depicting the Holy Trinity, Borromäus and a view of Waldkirchen before the fire of 1782. Every Easter Sunday the men of the town are up early for the *Emmausgang* (traditional procession) and go to worship at the chapel. Later in the year the chapel is the goal of the riders taking part in the *Leonharditag* procession on 6 November. They ride three times round the chapel and the horses are then blessed by the priest. Waldkirchen's many amenities include a heated *Freibad* and a *Hallenbad* with sauna, solarium and the unique Mediterraneum — a room with Mediterranean flora and a suitably warm temperature. Waldkirchen caters for winter ramblers by keeping 25km of surrounding footpaths clear of deep snow.

These Dreisessel resorts are more or less enclosed by the B12 on its way from Passau to the Czech border near Philippsreut and thence on towards Prague. From Waldkirchen and many other resorts in the Bayerischer Wald, 2-day coach excursions are run to the Czech capital. Those intending to participate should book locally in advance and provide two passport photographs.

Ten kilometres north on the B12, **Freyung** (population 6,000), a *Luftkurort*, is one of several resorts claiming to be the gateway to the Bavarian Forest National Park. It is a good centre for visiting, not only the National Park, but all the other sights in the southern part of the forest. The town takes its name (Frey=*Frei*=free) from the fact that early settlement in this corner of the prince-bishopric of Passau was encouraged by the freeing of the residents from most of the taxes and duties that would normally have been imposed upon them. The parish church Maria Himmelfahrt burned down in 1872 and was rebuilt in neo-Gothic style but it contains some treasures from the earlier building. There are a few interesting houses in the town which is dominated by Schloss Wolfstein perched on a rocky eminence 37m (120ft) above the little River Saussbach. The present building dates from 1590 and today houses some government offices and the art gallery for the *Landkreis* (administrative district) of Freyung-Grafenau. The *Heimatmuseum* is to be found in the Schramlhaus (about 1700) and specialises in exhibits showing the history of the area. A popular walk is through the Buchberger Leite, a rocky ravine through which the Saussbach tumbles.

The Ostmarkstrasse leaves Passau as the B85 and 10km 6 miles) from the city the pleasant village resort of **Tiefenbach** lies just to the west of the road. Here, as at almost every other place in this southern part of the forest, there are holiday 'packages', often with a rambling theme, which are exceptional value. Details are available from the local information office. About 17km (11 miles) from the city, **Neukirchen vorm Wald** (to distinguish it from the dozens of places called Neukirchen, three in the forest), with a population of around 2,000, is a peaceful resort where outdoor activities predominate; the countryside around is especially charming in spring and autumn. The Gothic parish church was given the baroque treatment in 1724 and contains some interesting relics. Half an hour's walk to the north of the village, the little baroque Kolomannkirche is also worth a visit.

At **Aicha** (also **vorm Wald**), 7km to the west, the *Schloss* (about 1600) is of interest for its unusual and charming three-storeyed arcades or galleries around a courtyard. It is barely 6km now to **Fürstenstein**, again a little to the west of the B85, and whose mighty *Burg* can be seen from afar on its granite ridge above the village. Rebuilt after a fire in 1860 more as a *Schloss* than a *Burg*, the impressive building now houses a boarding school of the Passau branch of the Englischen Fräulein and the interior is not normally open to the public. The nearby Englburg belongs to the same order which has a small *Pension* there. These old fortresses are two of the three castles of the so-called Dreiburgenland.

Back on the B85, the little market town of **Tittling** (population 4,000) is the principal place in this Dreiburgenland and is a useful centre with a lot of activity around the little Dreiburgensee with swimming and other water pursuits. A main attraction is the Museumsdorf Bayerischer Wald, an open-air museum containing a large number of old houses, mills and other buildings representing

On the summit of the Rachel

Bavarian band at Grafenau

forest life between the fifteenth and nineteenth centuries. The museum lies on the road to **Thurmansbang** (population 2,000) with its baroque parish church of St Markus (1763). Between Tittling and Thurmansbang is the little Maria-Bründl Kapelle (1712) on the right of the road. In front of the chapel there is an unusual little tower with onion-dome which protects a spring. Back towards the B85 is the third of the three castles of the Dreiburgenland, the Saldenburg, which is now a youth hostel.

After 6km the main road bypasses **Schönberg** (population 2,200) so turn off to visit this charming town with a fine market place surrounded by houses reminiscent of the Inn valley style and a statue of St Nepomuk dating from 1737. Schönberg enjoys a particularly mild climate and is an ideal centre for walkers, with many marked footpaths at hand, some of which are kept clear in winter. Many of the leisure facilities are shared with **Grafenau** (population 4,000) about 6km to the east. Grafenau was on one of the principal salt trade routes and this is remembered each year on the first Saturday in August when the town centre is closed to traffic for the *Salzsäumerfest*, a rural fair with demonstrations of the old crafts of spinning, pottery, woodwork, glass-blowing, etc. Several bands provide music and there are colourful processions, including the arrival of the salt-carriers who have wandered the salt route with their pack-horses for several days prior to the *Fest*. The centre of all this activity is the spacious Marktplatz around which the houses are again reminiscent of the Inn valley.

The fire-damaged church was rebuilt in baroque style but retains the Gothic choir and tower of the previous building and has a number of interesting relics. The Spitalkirche of the Holy Trinity (1759) not only has an interesting rococo altar but also thirteen Stations of the Cross made of sheet-zinc, colourful representations from the middle of the eighteenth century which were only discovered in the attic of the building in 1951. The Bauernmöbel Museum (Farmhouse FurnitureMuseum) can be found in two historic houses (eighteenth to nineteenth centuries) on the way to the *Kurpark*. A minor curiosity is the little Snuff Museum, said to be the only one in the world, in Spitalstrasse opposite the post office. On the slopes above the park is Grafenau's huge *Freibad* complex. A full-sized sport pool and a diving pool are at the upper level, below is the leisure pool which caters for paddlers and the not-so-good swimmers and at one end of this is the *Wellenbad* where the wave-making apparatus operates for 10 minutes every half-hour. Toddlers have their own little paddling pool away from the main pools which are surrounded by 25,000sq m of grass for sunbathing. There are lockers (free) for several thousand bathers and a restaurant, snack bar and ice-cream kiosk are at hand. Even by Germany's high swimming pool standards, this is an outstanding centre. Not far away is the *Sommerrodelbahn*, an exciting dry bob-sleigh run, a popular venue with the youngsters and even with the not so young. The rambling possibilities here include designated walks of 11–30km which follow the old salt routes towards the eastern frontier.

The Nationalpark Bayerischer Wald is a short distance north-east of Grafenau. It was founded in 1970, is the property of the state and consists of an area of some 13,000 hectares of unspoiled forest and mountain landscape. National parks exist to protect the environment and its flora and fauna. The first-time visitor should go to the Nationalpark-Haus to learn about the area. Animals — brown bears, wolves, lynx, red deer, bison and many others — are kept in large enclosures quite close to the *Haus* and parking area. The park includes some 200km of *Wanderwege* and the principal routes are marked so that one may visit the areas of interest, eg forest history, geology, landscape, etc. Two prominent summits, the Lusen (1,373m, 4,503ft) and the Rachel (1,454m, 4,770ft) are good for distant views but there are many other summits in the 800–1,100m (2,600–3,600ft) range.

The waymark *Auerhahn* (Capercailzie) leads to a strenuous but rewarding walk of 9.5 miles which includes the summit of the Rachel. Start at the *Wanderparkplatz* called G'fäll at 950m (3,116ft) reached by a good road north from **Spiegelau** in about 6km. The path goes north from the car park climbing steadily, at first through mixed woods and then through spruce. In the spruce wood note two wayside monuments but keep to the designated path; at certain seasons deviations are forbidden in order to leave the wildlife undisturbed.

About 2km from the start is another wayside shrine and then a stiff climb for about 600m to the Waldschmidthaus, a mountain inn at 1,360m (4,460ft), open May-October and the mountain rescue centre for the Rachel. Suitably refreshed, the final climb to the summit at 1,454m (4,770ft) ends after 500m or so. Even if one is not breathless from the climb, the views from the top are certainly breathtaking. On a clear day, the chain of Alps far to the south can be seen, to the south-east above the lesser hills, a glimpse of the Donau between Passau and Linz. South-eastwards along the frontier the Lusen and Dreisessel are in view, and north-westwards the Grosser Falkenstein (1,312m, 4,300ft) and the Grosser Arber (1,457m, 4,780ft) can be identified. The Lusen shows up especially clearly because the whole of its summit is made up of enormous granite blocks. On the Rachel the vegetation reaches almost to the top and the impression is quite different. In the valleys on the west side of the frontier the cheerful red roofs of the various villages can be picked out but to the east there is little sign of habitation.

Leaving the summit the waymark is joined for a while by the green arrowhead of the Nördlicher Hauptwanderweg, a long-distance path which links the main summits along this border. There is a steep descent for about 1,200m and a fine view at the Rachelkapelle, a tiny wooden chapel perched at the edge of a steep drop down to the little Rachelsee far below. The story is that a rider lost in a snowstorm reached this near-precipice which was hidden from his view. His horse would not go a step further despite liberal use of spurs and whip, thus saving the life of its impatient master. In gratitude, the man had the chapel erected here.

The path continues to fall steeply until it passes along the east side of the Rachelsee, another essential stop to admire the view. Note the information board here about the *Urwaldlehrpfad* (Primeval Forest Nature Trail) and another a little later about the *Eiszeitlehrpfad* (Ice Age Nature Trail). The route continues to fall, less steeply now, for another 2.5km to a fork in the track near a shelter. Go right, follow the waymarks for about a kilometre then join a minor road for a few more minutes back to the starting point.

An essential piece of equipment for exploring the National Park is the 1:40,000 map *Wandern und erleben Nationalpark Bayerischer Wald* published by Morsak Verlag, Grafenau. This map shows the degree of difficulty of the various paths; for example, the walk described above demands the stoutest footwear, preferably boots.

A little over 20km (13km) north-east of Grafenau, **Finsterau** is a pleasant little holiday resort on the fringe of the National Park at the foot of the Lusen. The road ends at the frontier 4km beyond the village so there is little traffic to disturb the peace. There is another rural museum here, the Freilichtmuseum Finsterau with a good range of rebuilt farmhouses, a smithy, an inn (still serving refreshments) and other items of interest. Summer visitors will come mainly to ramble in the National Park; there is a ski-school for those here in winter.

Spiegelau, already mentioned, an *Erholungsort* of 2,800 inhabitants a little further west on the National Park boundary, has Erasmus Moosburger to thank for its existence, for he founded a glass factory here in 1530. The business has changed hands many times and now specialises in crystal glass, the production of which may be seen by visitors for a short time each working day. An excellent centre this with plenty for the visitor to do.

Glass-making is also an important feature in nearby **Frauenau** where the official Glasmuseum is to be found. Three thousand years of glass technology are exhibited here and there are displays of ancient and modern products. The nearby glass factory of Valentin Eisch may also be visited; it is one of only a handful of such factories left from more than sixty once working in this area. Frauenau (population 3,500) is another *Erholungsort*. It was founded in 1324 by Hermann, a lay-brother from Kloster Niederalteich who sought a hermit's existence here. It became a place of pilgrimage and in 1759–67 a church was built, called Zu Unserer Lieben Frauen Au from which the village derived its name, although the church is now called Maria Himmelfahrt. There is a fine ceiling painting of the Ascension by a student of the Asam school and excellent rococo stucco from 1767. A late Gothic *pietà* (1480) graces the high altar. Skiing instruction, skating and horse-sleigh rides are available in winter.

Still east of the Ostmarkstrasse **Zwiesel** (population 9,300) is an important rail and road traffic centre. The railway divides here into branches for Bodenmais, Bayerische Eisenstein and Grafenau, the latter reached through Frauenau and Spiegelau. Once again glass-making has played a significant part in the development of the town where, behind the *Rathaus*, is the excellent museum Wald-Heimat-Glas with imaginative displays on several themes. On the ground floor is an outstanding diorama of the primeval forest, with models of animals and birds which have long since disappeared. The glass section includes a display of old snuff bottles while in another room there are examples of religious folk art. The three-storeyed *Rathaus* of 1838 has a classical façade and provides a backdrop for a statue of Nepomuk (1767) who is flanked by St Georg and St Florian. The neo-Gothic parish church (1891–6) has an 86m-high (282ft) steeple — unique in this area — and inside, has a more than life-sized statue of the weeping Saviour. Folk music and folk singing are the subjects of competitions held in Zwiesel in late spring and September. There is always plenty going on here and winter sporting activities mean that it is always 'season' in Zwiesel. In January and February snow is even more certain here than in some better-known Alpine centres.

Rejoin the Ostmarkstrasse at **Rinchnach** (population 3,000), a peaceful summer resort. The present parish church was built in 1729 and lovers of baroque architecture have called this the most beautiful church in the Bavarian Forest. C. D. Asam contributed two altar pictures sometime between 1730 and 1735 and these remained comparatively unknown until they were 're-discovered' for the artist's 300th birthday celebrations in 1986.

Regen (population 11,000) is an *Erholungsort* right on the Ostmarkstrasse, a lively and attractive town with all the facilities one would expect in a place of this size. An unusual folk festival here is the five-day annual *Pichelsteinerfest* which takes place around the last Saturday in July. In 1874, some youths returning from a festival stole potatoes from the field of a man named Pichler, but when accosted explained that they had only been collecting stones. The lads took their booty to the woman who was cooking up the remains from the festival and she threw the potatoes into the cauldron and concocted a nourishing stew. Making such a dish became an annual event and a regular folk festival gradually emerged. Today's hot-pot has a rigid recipe and must contain at least three kinds of meat — beef, veal and pork — potatoes and diced carrots all simmered slowly with parsley, onions and herbs without being stirred. The cook has a place of honour in the festival procession. Celebrations in the evenings include rides in lantern-lit 'gondolas' on the River Regen.

Extraordinarily, the village of **Bichlstein** not too far away claims to have invented the same dish in 1847 and celebrates the *Pichlsteiner Bergfest* there on the first Sunday in August to prove it!

Easter Monday is another colourful day in Regen. The event is the *Osterritt* (Easter ride) and the day starts with an open-air service. The riders assemble and process to the Wieshof and then to the town square where the gaily decorated horses are blessed. The day ends with an Easter dance in the evening. The spacious square contains a number of rather fine old houses and the attractive Marienbrunnen (fountain). The parish church of St Michael (1655–7) replaced a Romanesque-Gothic building burned down in 1648. The squat tower has an open lantern topped by the familiar onion-dome but there is also a north tower (dating from about 1270) from the earlier church.

An hour's walk south of the town, Burg Weissenstein towers over the valley, an impressive ruin. Not quite all ruin though, for the old granary now houses a small but interesting museum. This part of the castle was, from 1918 until his death in 1974, the home and workplace of the poet and writer Siegfried von Vegesack and, until 1935, of his poetess wife Clara Nordström. The ground floor has memorabilia of the couple; the first floor is mainly of geological exhibits, the second floor is given over to special exhibitions changing each year while the third floor contains literary archives with particular reference to the Bavarian and Bohemian forest areas. Finally, in the attic — Vegesack called it his paradise and used to retire there when working on a particularly demanding poem — there is a display of old equipment connected with flax growing and linen production.

Regen is a good centre for the exploration of the surrounding attractive countryside. A curiosity sometimes found in this part of

Bavaria is a row of *Totenbretter*. The term cannot easily be translated into English. A *Totenbrett* is a wide board and in days gone by was used to convey the corpse to the place of burial. Unlike a coffin, the *Totenbrett* was not buried but was used as a permanent memorial to the departed. The boards were often elaborately carved or colourfully painted and often had verses or a passage relating to the life of the deceased inscribed upon them. Today the boards are no longer used for the original purpose but the old custom is not entirely abandoned and rows of *Totenbretter*, almost like an ornate fence, may be seen outside villages or around churches and chapels. Another similar practice is the production of *Votivtafeln* — memorial tablets — which take many forms and often incorporate a picture of the person being honoured or remembered. They are frequently to be found in churches and chapels which have become places of pilgrimage and a complete wall may well be covered by them.

Twelve kilometres north from Regen along a picturesque road, the *Luftkurort* of **Bodenmais** (population 3,400) enjoys a favourable climate and is a recommended resort for those suffering from nervous complaints or convalescing. A map and guide to many walks stands in the Marktplatz and this is a favourite starting point for an excursion to the Grosser Arber, whose summit (1,457m, 4,778ft) is 6km north of the village. Glass-making is important in Bodenmais and visitors are welcomed at the Joska Glass Factory. There is a small charge for admission to the main factory but two exhibitions of the products — which may be purchased — are free. Bodenmais has a long history of mining silver and many other minerals. A visit to the historic silver mine of Barbara-Stollen is now possible. The parking place for the mine is at the lower station of a two-seater chair-lift and one may travel effortlessly to the mine entrance at the middle station. Alternatively walk up to the entrance along several signposted footpaths. Museum Bodenmais in Bahnhofstrasse traces the mining history of the area and has a comprehensive display of minerals.

West of Bodenmais, back on the Ostmarkstrasse is **Viechtach**. The oldest building in the town, the Bürgerspital (1432) houses the Kristallmuseum, a remarkable collection of some 1,200 varieties of crystal found naturally in the district. The rococo parish church of St Augustinus (1766) is well worth a visit for its stucco decoration by travelling craftsmen of the Wessobrunn school and fine wood-carvings on the choir stalls and the confessional boxes. The baroque-treated Gothic St Anna-Kapelle is close at hand as is the seventeenth-century *Rathaus*. Viechtach (population 6,500) is a *Luftkurort* on the River Schwarzer Regen and has a superior camp site — Komfort-Campingplatz — with nearby *Hallenbad* and sauna and a large modern open-air leisure complex in a very attractive location. For railway enthusiasts the museum trains to Gotteszell will be of interest.

Leaving the B85 travel north to **Kötzting** (population 6,100), famous for its *Pfingstritt* or Whitsun ride, a custom dating back to 1412. The ride takes place on Whit Monday when the residents are

The fishers' pulpit in Weissenregen pilgrimage church is a remarkable example of Bavarian craftsmanship of the late baroque period

given a musical 'early call' at 5am. At eight o'clock hundreds of horsemen ride, accompanied by solemn music, to the village of **Steinbühl** 6km away. The procession is headed by the Cross and lantern carriers, the priests and attendants are followed by men in traditional costume and mounted on splendidly groomed and decorated horses. After a service at Steinbühl, the procession returns to Kötzting, where it is greeted by fanfares and bell-ringing. The festival officially opens the previous Saturday afternoon; on the Sunday there are entertainments including the performance of two Whitsun plays, with other events during the week.

Kötzting has its share of old buildings. The group in the southwest corner of the town includes the parish church (1769), the St Anna-Kapelle (seventeenth century) and the remains of the fifteenth-century *Schloss*. As a recognised *Erholungsort* with *Kneipp-Kur* facilities, this town has a good reputation for hospitality and there are a number of attractive eating places. The many well-marked paths offer a choice ranging from a modest afternoon stroll to a two-day mountain tour of 30km. Especially recommended is the short ramble (waymark blue fish) from the car park (also the bus station) near the railway to the pilgrimage church of **Weissenregen** clearly visible on its hill to the south-west. The carved *Gnadenbild* (Miraculous Image) of the fourteenth century is outshone by the remarkable pulpit known as the Fischerkanzel in the form of a boat with three apostles endeavouring to draw in the great draught of fishes which Christ has bestowed upon them. Among other figures in this elaborately carved, coloured and partly gilded masterpiece are Jonah and the whale. Return directly along the surfaced path to Kötzting or continue to follow the blue fish signs past the church to extend the walk to about 8km.

Leaving Kötzting eastwards it is 16km (10 miles) to the resort of **Lam** (population ,2500) close to the Czech border at the foot of the Osser (1,292m, 4,238ft) in the valley of the Weisser Regen. This is a delightful small *Luftkurort* with facilities for open-air recreation, not only in summer but in winter when many of the footpaths are kept clear for walkers and one can go ski-rambling. The summit of the Osser can be reached on foot from Lam in $2\frac{1}{4}$ hours with quite a lot of fairly steep climbing. Many *Totenbretter* are to be found in this area.

Returning again to the Ostmarkstrasse continue northwards on the B85 towards Cham. **Cham** (population 16,000) is a busy *Kreisstadt* with some industry but it is an old town founded in the eighth century with many reminders of the past. From the car park near the river there is a good view of an old tower topped by a stork's nest. The parish church of St Jakob has parts from the fourteenth to eighteenth centuries and it was enlarged as recently as 1894. The Gothic choir and fine rococo stucco make inspection worthwhile. There are several more churches which justify a brief visit. Nearby, the fifteenth-century *Rathaus*, rebuilt in 1937, has attractive stepped gables and houses the *Heimatmuseum*. Further along there is the late Gothic Gasthaus zur Krone, an old lodging place of the nobility.

In Schwanenstrasse the Gasthof Luckner is a reminder of a prominent son of the town, Graf (Count) Nikolaus von Luckner, born in 1722 and guillotined in France in 1794.

There is a lot to see and do around Cham. Water activities are plentiful with swimming, sailing, surfing and angling in many little lakes. On the Lamberg near Chammünster there is a red deer enclosure. South of the town on the B20 is the Churpfalz-Park at **Loifling**, a modern pleasure park with the usual attractions — Ferris wheel, old-timer train, roundabouts, boating lake and so on. What is rather unusual about this complex of 10,000sq m is that it is laid out in a garden setting with some 3km of footpaths among 7,000 roses, herbacious borders, into baroque and 'paradise' gardens, through a dahlia display and so on. There is a good restaurant too.

Two modest festivals appear in the Cham calendar. The *Frühlingsfest* (Spring Festival) takes place from the Wednesday before Ascension Day until the Monday after. There are the usual folk activities of *Frühschoppen* (morning drinks) and clay-pigeon shooting followed by food and drink in a festival tent. The *Chamer Volksfest* lasts for eleven days starting on the Friday of the last week in July.

About 40km (25 miles) westwards, is the narrow neck of the forest north of Regensburg. The tourist will find much of interest in the area. **Roding** is about 13km from Cham along the B35, a very old town with many historic buildings. There are fine houses around the Marktplatz: the *Rathaus* (1660), parish church (1753) and many more. Turn off the main road shortly after Roding to **Walderbach** with its buildings around the former Augustinian and Cistercian *Kloster* or the *Heimatmuseum* for demonstrations of rural crafts; then on to **Reichenbach** for the absolute riot of glorious baroque in the former Benedictine Klosterkirche and to **Nittenau** where Napoleon made an overnight stop as he retreated westwards after his defeat before Moscow in 1812.

North-east of Cham along the B20 the road passes through the lower ground which marks the geographical division between the Bayerischer Wald and the Oberpfälzer Wald. **Furth im Wald** (population 10,000) is an *Erholungsort* close to the border and the proximity of Bohemia is reflected in the statue of St Johann Nepomuk (1767) which stands in the town square shaded by four huge chestnut trees nearly 150 years old. The old buildings include the baroque parish church of 1727 and the eighteenth-century Leonhardikapelle, the scene each Easter Monday of a *Leonhardiritt*. There are three museums of interest: the Hammerschmiede Voithenberghütte (black-smith's workshop), the Stadtmuseum housed in the Stadtturm (tower) of 1866 with a varied range of themes including geology, mineralogy, botany, zoology, local history and the Furth dragon (more about this later) and finally, the Waldmuseum covering aspects of forest flora and fauna.

Furth has a good programme for its summer and winter visitors — it is in a popular skiing area — and being close to a frontier crossing point is a good starting place for coach excursions into the Czech Republic. However, most visitors will find plenty to do near at hand. Horse-drawn coach rides — sleigh rides in winter — folk evenings, visits to the various deer enclosures, these are the things which contribute to a fine family holiday atmosphere far removed from the throng of tourists found in better-known resorts.

On the second Sunday in August, the ceremony of *Drachenstich* (Spearing the Dragon) provides the theme for a colourful annual spectacle. A play tells the ancient story. It goes back to 1431 when the Imperial army was defeated at the Battle of Tans and the Bohemian hordes invaded and ravaged Bavaria. The local dragon chose this moment to emerge from the wood and the terrified inhabitants thus had a double reason to seek the safety offered to them by the noblewoman of Furth Castle. She was even prepared to sacrifice herself to the dragon to save the people but in the nick of time Sir Udo, lord of the castle, returned from the war and slew the monster. This is the climax of the play and a wedding follows to celebrate the heroic deed.

The present dragon is 18m (59ft) long, 3m (10ft) high and weighing over a ton. This fearsome creature is propelled by an internal combustion engine but it is nevertheless finally killed by the modern Sir Udo to the accompaniment of church bells, trumpets and applause. The grand procession which follows has about 1,100 participants in costume and about 200 horses.

Furth is the biggest of a cluster of resorts in the *Feriengebiet* (holiday area) called Hohen-Bogen-Winkel, to the north of the Schwarzriegel or Hoher Bogen (1,079m, 3,540ft). **Neukirchen bei Heilig Blut** (population 3,450) got its name from a 'miracle' around 1450 when a follower of John Huss, the Bohemian religious reformer, split open with his sabre the head of a wooden Mary figure and blood flowed from the 'wound'. The inevitable pilgrimages started shortly after. The parish church Maria Geburt (fifteenth century and later) and the

Interior of the Benedictine monastery church at Reichenbach

Franciscan *Klosterkirche* share the same site and are divided by a double-sided altar containing a carved wooden image of Mary and child and a sabre-swinging Hussite.

The other resorts of this group are **Eschklam**, **Warzenried** and **Stachesried** and all share the various facilities of the area including the Hoher Bogen leisure centre with activities the year round. A two-stage chair-lift (total length 1,358m) takes the hard work out of the ascent and one alights at the middle station for the exciting run downhill by the *Sommerrodelbahn*, at 750m the longest dry bob-run in the Bayerischer Wald or in winter for the conventional bob-sleigh run on snow. Skiers can also alight at the middle station or can go right to the top where the Berghaus provides refreshments. The chair-lift is supplemented by two ski-tows.

Waldmünchen, 12km (7 miles) north-west of Furth, is a *Luftkurort* of 6,000 inhabitants in the Oberpfalz (Upper Palatinate). Here again there is a statue of Nepomuk (1769) in the Marktplatz together with fountains from 1776 and 1790. On the parish office (former Gasthaus Alte Post) there is a memorial tablet to the French writer and politician Châteaubriand who had an enforced stay here on his way to Prague in 1833 having mislaid his passport. He was, however, suitably impressed by the town's hospitality.

In 1742 during the war of Austrian succession, Bavaria was invaded in the name of Empress Maria Theresa by the Baron of Trenck with an army raised at his own expense. These violent soldiers were called Pandours — a word implying brutality — and they played havoc in the nearby town of Cham but it appears that Waldmünchen bought itself comparative peace by paying Trenck 'fifty gold coins'. Needless to say, this historic event is celebrated in the twentieth century by a pageant, *Trenck der Pandour vor Waldmünchen*, which is staged at 8.15pm usually on Saturdays during July and August. There are spectacular wild riding scenes and an accompanying colourful folk-festival.

The same event provides the theme for a long-distance walk *ohne Gepäck* called 'Der Pandurensteig' which runs from Waldmünchen to Passau, the last section joining with the llztalwanderweg mentioned earlier. The route touches many of the places of interest already mentioned. More details in 'Additional Information'.

After Cham, the B22 becomes the Ostmarkstrasse and at **Rötz** a short deviation 4km west leads to the Oberpfälzer Handwerks-museum where there is a collection of tools and machinery from as far back as the fifteenth century with enormous circular saws, grinding stones and mechanical hammers, as well as many smaller items. Well worth a little time and the modest admission charge.

Eighteen kilometres (12 miles) further along the B22, the skyline above the town of **Oberviechtach** is dominated by the grey profile of Burg Murach which even the Hussites were unable to overthrow. It is a pleasant little place, although a history of fires means that there are fewer medieval buildings remaining than might be expected. After one such fire, the Catholic parish church of John the Baptist was rebuilt using the choir and tower of the previous Gothic building. It contains excellent rococo decoration from 1775–6 and the choir-stalls should be specially noted. The parish church of St Andreas was also rebuilt (1826) after a fire and has two rococo altars from 1750. The pilgrimage church of St Johann and Nepomuk on the nearby Johannisberg has some noteworthy carving.

Honoured by the town is the Catholic priest Maximilian von Müller who, in 1705, organised the resistance of the Oberpfälzer farmers against the Austrian occupation. A better-known son of the town is Dr Johann Andreas Eisenbarth, a physician and surgeon who was well ahead of his time. His methods were sometimes ridiculed — as in a popular student song from 1803— but he nevertheless achieved considerable fame and served the both the Prussian and British royal houses. A memorial fountain is dedicated to him and the *Heimatmuseum* is largely given over to a permanent exhibition 'Dr Eisenbarth and his Time' where some of his bizarre surgical instruments — for example, a brace and bit — are displayed.

Tännesberg lies just to the east of the Ostmarkstrasse after about 12km (7 miles) and here in the idyllic Pfreimdtal there is a hut belonging to the Oberpfälzer Waldverein (Forest Association) for the use of youth and family rambling groups. The accommodation is provided on a self-catering basis and there is a river bathing place nearby, also a camp site. See 'Fact File'. A turning to the east leads into a pretty road to **Vohenstrauss** (20km, 13 miles, north of Oberviechtach), a resort of nearly 7,000 inhabitants and a place for a peaceful, relaxing holiday. The emblem of this little town is the unusual Renaissance Schloss Friedrichsburg (1586–93), with six round towers, one at each corner and one in the centre of each of the longer sides. The pretty Marktplatz with its shady trees invites the visitor to rest awhile. The interesting little *Heimatmuseum* (admission free) is to be found on the third floor of the *Rathaus* and there is a glass factory which may be visited.

About 16km (10 miles) north-west of Vohenstrauss, **Weiden**, on the Ostmarkstrasse, is the biggest town in the area with 43,000 inhabitants. It lies in the valley of the River Waldnaab and is one of the principal cultural venues of eastern Bavaria. It has been an important centre of communications since early times for the trade routes between Nürnberg and Prague and between Regensburg and Leipzig crossed here. The organist and composer Max Reger (1873–1916) came here as an infant and received his musical education from the organist Adalbért Lindner. In the Kulturzentrum is the Stadtmuseum and the Max Reger Collection; the composer is also remembered by the Weiden Music Festival which takes place in spring every fourth year — 1966, 2000, etc.

Other regular festivals here are *Frühlingsfest* around May Day, *Bürgerfest* (Citizens' Festival) the last Sunday in June, *Volks- und Schutzenfest* (Folk and Shooting Festival) around mid-September and *Christkindlmarkt* about 3 weeks up to 23 December. There are regular markets on Wednesdays and Saturdays and occasional Sunday fairs in the pedestrianised old town. There are concerts of all types of music, also exhibitions and art shows in several galleries. From mid-June to end-August there are Summer Serenade concerts in Max-Reger-Park on Wednesdays at 7pm and Sundays at 4pm. The Eisenbahn museum of the Model Railway Club should not be missed by those interested in the subject. Twenty-four trains operate on the large model railway layout.

The buildings and monuments of earlier centuries are lovingly cared for here and there are many which the visitor will find worth seeing. Amongst them the *Rathaus* (1539–45) with its modern *Glockenspiel* (chimes), the Altes Schulhaus (1529) now the culture centre, the fifteenth-century Michaelskirche and, of course, the Max-Reger-Haus. The interior of the neo-Romanesque St-Josefs-Kirche (1900) is considered to be one of the most successful applications of *Jugendstil* (*art nouveau*) in south German church architecture. Many well marked footpaths and cycling routes lead to other places of interest in the vicinity. The town is remarkably well endowed with restaurants, cafés, bars and discos and free car parking is available in the town centre. The Weidener Thermenwelt is a modern leisure complex with hot whirlpools, grotto solarium and a huge water-chute as well as the more conventional swimming facilities, and a bistro.

Only a few kilometres separate Weiden from its northern neighbours **Altenstadt** (population 4100) and **Neustadt** (population 5300), both '**an der Waldnaab**', attractive little towns in a sparsely populated area of considerable charm sandwiched between two *Naturparke*. Altenstadt is near the Süssenloher Weiher (lake), good for bathing and sailing. Neustadt is known for its lead-crystal industry and visits may be made to some of the factories. There are a number of well preserved old buildings; in the town centre are both the Altes Schloss (about 1558) with its external staircase, arcades, balconies and high, pointed gable and the Neues Schloss (1698–1720) in Italian

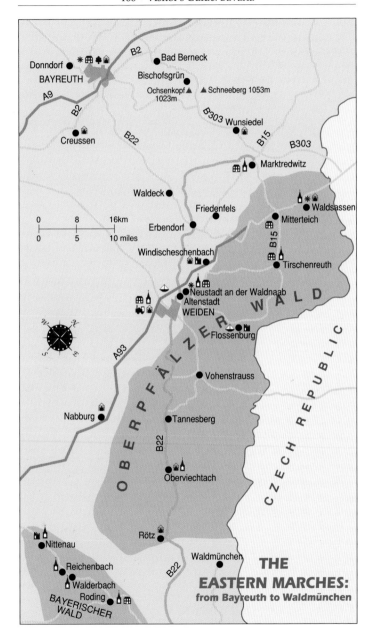

THE
EASTERN MARCHES:
from Bayreuth to Waldmünchen

baroque at the east end of the Marktplatz. Some rooms on the third floor have stucco and ceiling paintings from 1710–20. On a little hill outside the town is the rather unusual pilgrimage church of St Felix originally built in 1735 but enlarged 1763–5 and at the same time fully renovated. There is a rectangular church with rounded corners for the laity while the monks have a clover leaf-shaped choir. The ceiling is painted with numerous scenes from the life of St Felix.

There is a very fine camp site — claimed to be one of the best in Europe — on the little Gaisweiher (lake) at the foot of the Flossenburg, a castle ruin 15km east of Neustadt. A little aside from the Ostmarkstrasse **Windischeschenbach** (population 5,900) some 8km north of Neustadt, is another place famed for its lead-crystal industry. There is a lead-crystal museum, factory visits are possible and crystal, porcelain, ceramics and pewter may be purchased at favourable prices. A speciality of the town is *Zoiglbier*, a traditional brew rich in hops and free from carbonic acid which is best sampled in a *Zoiglbier-Stub'n* (bar) with a tasty home-made snack. At nearby Burg Neuhaus is the Waldnaabmuseum and the unusual 'Buttertub' tower.

A short distance north on the B22, the *Erholungsort* **Erbendorf** is on the fringe of the Steinwald *Naturpark*, at the centre of which the Platte rises to 946m (3,100ft), a good viewpoint. Friedrich Schiller's maternal ancestors came from Erbendorf and Max Reger stayed here and wrote his choral fantasy *Ein' feste Burg* which was to bring him acclaim as a composer of organ music. It was set to words by Martin Luther and became the hymn 'A safe stronghold our God is still'.

The Ostmarkstrasse now leaves the B22 to head for Marktredwitz which lies due north. The route now is through the Steinwald *Naturpark* to the *Erholungsort* of **Friedenfels**. The landscape is charming and there are many well marked paths. These can be followed to the ruins of Burg Weissenstein at 863m (2,830ft). The watch-tower can be climbed for an even better view. There is also a seven-day, 140km (87 mile) *Wanderung ohne Gepäck* called Burgenweg which, as its name implies, covers many of the old castles in the area.

The countryside between Friedenfels and Tirschenreuth (population 9,500) 18km (12 miles) to the east is speckled with thousands of little lakes — some hardly more than fish ponds — in what is known as the *Teichpfanne* (Pond Pan), a quite amazing landscape where holidays are geared towards water-orientated activities. Angling and sailing are popular and there are many other facilities. **Tirschenreuth** has much to offer the gastronome and it is not surprising to find that fish, especially carp, features prominently on the menus here. Buildings of interest include the *Rathaus*, a Renaissance building of

1582–3 and the parish church Maria Himmelfahrt dating from the end of the thirteenth century but completely renewed in 1669. There is a wooden relief *Heimsuchung Mariens* from the early sixteenth century which is much valued because examples of local late Gothic carving are rare in the Oberpfalz.

Waldsassen 16km (10 miles) north of Tirschenreuth and of similar size, has much for the visitor, not least the baroque basilica built 1681–1704. The interior decoration is striking with rich stucco work. In the adjoining *Kloster* the splendid library, built at about the same time, lost most of its valuable books during secularisation in 1803. Now the shelves are well filled again thanks in part to purchase and in part to the 'loan' of some of the stolen books from the state archives.

Four kilometres north-west of Waldsassen at **Kappel** is the unusual pilgrimage church of the Heilige Dreifaltigkeit (Holy Trinity) built in the seventeenth century on the site of earlier chapels. The design consists of three semi-circular niches with half-domes or conches in the angles of the basic trefoil, above each of which is a round tower capped with an elongated onion-dome. The interior is richly endowed with sacred treasures. The valuable organ has been beautifully restored but since the church now sees more tourists than pilgrims, Mass is only celebrated once a month and on the Sunday after the Feast of the Holy Trinity (3 June).

The route now leaves the Oberpfalz in a westerly direction and enters Oberfranken (Upper Franconia). **Marktredwitz**, the final place on the Ostmarkstrasse (population 20,000) is essentially an industrial town but the Protestant parish church of St Bartholomäus has a Renaissance pulpit with inlaid work from 1613 and a late Gothic tabernacle from around 1490. The old *Rathaus* (fourteenth century) is enhanced by a pretty balcony while the new *Rathaus* is a late eighteenth-century building in the classical style.

The B303 west to Bad Berneck is the Fichtelgebirgsstrasse and passes through the attractive scenery of the Fichtelgebirge Nature Park. **Wunsiedel** (population 10,000), a little to the north of the road, is the regional capital and economic centre of its area and although it is quite industrialised has some attractions for visitors. Some 100,000 people come each year to see the festival play which has been performed since 1890 in the rocky labyrinths of the Luisenberg on the north slopes of the Kösseine (939m, 3,080ft), a unique natural stage encircled by the forest.

On the Saturday before Johannistag (24 June) there is the *Brunnenfest*. The twenty or so fountains in the town are decorated with garlands and ornaments; in the evening they are illuminated with lanterns and candles and at each there is music and folk singing. The festival goes back to the ancient ceremony of *Brunnenputzen*, the essential annual cleaning in days when the fountains were the source of the town's water supply. The ceremony can be likened to that of 'Well Dressing' in parts of England. Wunsiedel was the birthplace of the poet Jean Paul (1763–1825) and he is remembered, along with Max Reger in the Fichtelgebirgsmuseum.

Continuing on the B303, the summit of the Schneeberg (1,053m, 3,454ft) can be seen on the right. If time permits, the 20-minute ascent of nearby Ochsenkopf (1,023m, 3,357ft) by chair-lift is a rewarding excursion. At the top there is a café and a stone tower with extensive views over the countryside. The Fichtelgebirge is rich in semi-precious stones and one could quite easily form a small mineral collection here. Nearby **Bischofsgrün** (population 2,500), a *Luftkurort* and winter sports centre, is a good base for a relaxed and peaceful interlude. The modern hotel Berghof has a pleasant restaurant.

The long journey from Passau ends at **Bad Berneck**, 41km (26 miles) from Marktredwitz. This is an attractive little spa with around 4,500 inhabitants and it is encircled by seven hills. The town is a *Kneippheilbad* and *Luftkurort* and its praises have been sung by many famous people including Jean Paul the poet and the composer Carl Maria von Weber, who concluded that it was 'just made for artists'. The town's rise to fame is fairly recent. From 1857 a health establishment offered a cure based on skimmed goat's milk and vegetable juices. Then about 1900 a factory owner from Waldsassen fell in love with the place and gave his fortune to the town for its development. A *Kurhaus*, chapel and the *Kneipp* centre were built and a town garden was laid out. Nowadays there are facilities from minigolf to a modern *Hallenbad* in the sports centre near the River Main.

The B2 leaves Bad Berneck in a southerly direction and enters the Richard Wagner festival town of **Bayreuth.**

In 1848 Wagner started to think about a setting for his projected music drama (he preferred the term to opera) *Siegfried*. He first thought of Zürich and then started to consider some of the smaller German cities, especially Weimar. However, he had earlier gained a favourable impression of Bayreuth and confirmed this during a visit in spring 1871. Writing to his friend Dr Karl Landgraf in May of that year '… it is now decided that my great Stage Festival Play shall take place in the summer of 1873 in Bayreuth, at which time I also intend to take up my permanent residence in your city … His Majesty the King of Bavaria has granted his permission … and will give considerable financial support ….'

Villa Wahnfried, Wagner's home at Bayreuth, with a bust of his patron King Ludwig II

The sun temple at the Eremitage, Bayreuth

The 1873 target was not achieved; building work on the new festival Theatre was only completed in 1875 and even a first perform-ance in 1876 appeared to be in doubt. However, all was ready in time and the opening celebrations included the complete 'Ring' cycle. Famous visitors to Bayreuth for the occasion included Kaiser Wilhelm I and King Ludwig II. Many musicians also came to pay honour including Bruckner, Grieg and Tschaikovsky. A full house at every performance was still insufficient to generate enough income to cover the costs and even the costumes had to be sold afterwards to help the funds. It all looked like a gigantic flop but Wagner, although disheartened, did not give up and in 1882 the festival resumed with a performance of *Parsifal*. Richard Wagner died in Venice on 13 February 1883. His wife Cosima — daughter of Franz Liszt — carried on the work and the survival of the festival owes much to her. Later his son Siegfried took over the reigns of manage-ment from 1906 until 1930 and was in his turn succeeded by his English wife Winifred whom he had married in 1915. She kept the festivals going in splendid style but was discredited by her friend-ship with Hitler — a great admirer of Wagner's works — and her public career ended at the close of World War II. She lived on until 1980 and did a lot of work behind the scenes.

Those wishing to attend performances of Wagner's works in the Festival Theatre must book a very long time in advance.

This town of 70,000 inhabitants is good for a visit at any time; there is always plenty to see and do. The Festival Theatre can be visited as can the Margrave's baroque opera house (1745–8), a little gem of a theatre. It was built at the suggestion of the Margravine Wilhelmina (1709–58) who was no mean musician herself and did much to foster the cultural life of the town.

Wagner was not the only famous resident. Johann Paul Friedrich Richter (1763–1825), known as Jean Paul, spent much of his life here and with Franz Liszt (1811–66) is buried in the town cemetery. The Wagners' graves are behind his house Villa Wahnfried, now the Wagner museum, in the Hofgarten. A little outside the town is the Eremitage with its spectacular fountains, cascades and extensive park. It was created between 1715 and 1750 to enable court society to spend time pretending to be hermits or shepherds, an eighteenth-century social game.

The Eremitage has its own Altes Schloss and Neues Schloss with the sun temple, a magnificent example of late rococo work with its fine rotunda surmounted by a gilded chariot drawn by four horses. Back in the town, the Altes Schloss has an octagonal tower (1565–6) with a spiral ramp for horses; the three wings are from the seventeenth century. The Schlosskirche was added in 1753–6 with rococo stucco and contains the graves of the Margravine Wilhelmina and her husband Friedrich. The Neues Schloss (1753–4) has room decorations which reveal Wilhelmina's inclination towards natural motifs, trees, birds, insects and dragons! — things Chinese were in vogue at the time. The building now houses the Stadtmuseum and a branch of the Bavarian State Collection of paintings of the sixteenth to eighteenth centuries. The Schreibmaschinen-museum (typewriter museum) and the Freimaurer (Freemasons') Museum, a library and exhibition on the history of freemasonry in Germany are also worth seeing.

Six kilometres west of Bayreuth in the village of **Donndorf** on the B22 is the Schloss Fantaisie with a fine park. The interior of the *Schloss* is not open to the public. Fourteen kilometres to the south on the B2, **Creussen** is the home of the Krügemuseum, a historical display of Creussen stoneware in colourful array.

Additional Information

Places to Visit

Bayreuth

Neues Schloss
☎ 0921-65313
Open: Tuesday to Sunday, April to September 10am-12noon, 1.20-5pm; October to March 10am-12noon, 1.30-3.30pm. Closed 1 January, Shrove Tuesday, 1 November, 24, 25, 31 December.

Markgräfliches Opernhaus
☎ 0921-65313
Opens 9am in summer, otherwise as next above.

Eremitage — Altes Schloss
☎ 0921-92561
Open: Tuesday to Sunday, April to September 9-11.30am, 1-4.30pm; October to March 10-11.30am, 1-2.30pm. Closed as Neues Schloss. Fountains play May to mid-October 10am-5pm on the hour.

Richard-Wagner Museum
Haus Wahnfried
Im Hofgarten
95444 Bayreuth
Open: daily 9am-5pm. Music at 10am, 12noon, 2pm.

Deutsches Freimaurer-Museum
Im Hofgarten
95444 Bayreuth
Open: Tuesday to Friday 10am-12noon, 2-4pm, Saturday 10am-12noon.

Deutsches Schreibmaschinen-Museum
Bernecker Strasse 11
95448 Bayreuth
☎ 0921-23445
Open: Monday to Friday 2-5pm. Advance confirmation requested. Admission free.

Bodenmais

Museum Bodenmais
Bahnhofstrasse 1a
94249 Bodenmais
☎ 09924-656
Open: weekdays 9-11am, 2-6pm,
Sunday 10am-12noon. Closed
Sunday in winter.

*Historisches Erzbergwerk im
   Silberberg*
BHS Bergwerk
94249 Bodenmais
☎ 09924-304
Open: April to September 9am-
5pm, October, Easter and Christmas 10am-4pm. Reduced admission charge for school parties.

Creussen

Krügemuseum
95473 Stadt Creussen
(14km S of Bayreuth)
☎ 09270-607
Open: Tuesday to Sunday 9.30am-
12noon, 2-5.30pm.

Finsterau

Freilichtmuseum Bayerischer Wald
94151 Mauth-Finsterau
☎ 08557-221
Open: mid-December to April 1-
4pm, May to September 9am-6pm,
October 9am-4pm.

Frauenau

Glasmuseum
Am Museumspark 1
94258 Frauenau
☎ 09926-718
Open: 20 December to mid-May
10am-4pm, mid-May to end
October 9am-5pm.

Furth im Wald

Waldmuseum
Steinbruchweg 9
93437 Furth im Wald
☎ 09973-609
Open: daily 9am-12noon, 1-4pm.

Grafenau

Bauernmöbel-Museum
Kurpark
94481 Grafenau
☎ 08552-2085 (Verkehrsamt)
Open: July and August daily 2-
5pm, other months Tuesday,
Thursday and Sunday only.

Schnupftabakmuseum
Spitalstrasse 4 (In Stadtmuseum)
94481 Grafenau
☎ 08552-2081
Open: mid-December to end-
October daily 2-5pm.

Nationalpark Bayerischer Wald
Information centre 8km NE of
Grafenau
Extensive animal and bird
enclosures. Admission free.

Rötz-Hillstett

Oberpfälzer Handwerksmuseum
92444 Rötz-Hillstett
☎ 09976-423
Open: mid-April to mid-October,
Tuesday to Sunday 10am-5pm.

Tittling

Museumsdorf Bayerischer Wald
94105 Tittling
☎ 08504-8482
Open: daily 9am-5pm.

Viechtach

Kristallmuseum
Spitalgasse 5
94234 Viechtach
☎ 09942-8107
Open: summer daily 9am-12noon,
2-6pm. Closed in November. Other
winter months, Tuesday to
Saturday only at same times.

Weiden

Stadtmuseum & Max-Reger-Sammlung
Kulturzentrum Haus Bauer
Pfarrplatz 4
92637 Weiden

☎ 0961-81412-4 (Kultur u Fremdenverkehrsamt)
Open: Monday to Friday 10-11am,
2-3pm. Admission free.

Eisenbahnmuseum
Modelleisenbahnclub eV
(Adjoining DB station)
92637 Weiden
☎ 0961-805631
Extensive model layout with 24
trains in operation certain days,
usually Sunday and holidays.

Wunsiedel
Fichtelgebirgsmuseum
Spitalhof 1-2
95632 Wunsiedel
☎ 09232-2032
Open: Tuesday to Saturday 9am-
5pm (9pm Thursday March to
October), Sunday and holidays
10am-5pm.

Zwiesel
Wald-Heimat-Glas
Stadtplatz 29
94227 Zwiesel
☎ 09922-2041 (Stadtverwaltung)
Open: mid-May to mid-October,
Monday to Friday 9am-5pm,
Saturday and Sunday 10am-
12noon, 2-4pm; in other months
Monday to Friday 10am-12noon, 2-
5pm, Saturday and Sunday 10am-
12noon.

Leisure Centres
Cham
Churpfalz-Park
93413 Loifling bei Cham
☎ 09971-30300
8km S of Cham on B20
Open: daily April to October 9am-
6pm. Restaurant.

Neukirchen
Freizeitzentrum Hoher Bogen
93453 Neukirchen bei Hl Blut
☎ 09947-464 or 1078
Open: all year. Cafes and bars.

Weiden
Thermenwelt
Raiffeisenstrasse 7
92637 Weiden
☎ 0961-3893319
Open: all year. Bistro.

Local Events and Festivals
Furth im Wald
Drachenstich — Second Sunday in
August
Historic pageant and festival

Grafenau
Salzsäumerfest — First Sunday in
August

Kötzting
Pfingstritt — Whit Monday.
Colourful procession with religious
theme. Similar in Furth im Wald

Regen
Pichelsteinerfest — 5 days around
last Saturday in July

Long Distance Paths
Der Goldene Steig — four walks in
Bavarian Forest, often over historic
salt caravan routes:

1. *Prachatitzer Weg* (28km):
Röhmbach, Waldkirchen, Bischofsreut.

2. *Winterberger Steig* (23km):
Hinterschmieding, Herzogsreut,
Philippsreut.

3. *Bergreichensteiner Weg* (30km):
Freyung, Kreuzberg, Finsterau.

4. *Gulden Strass* (12km): Grafenau,
St Oswald, Lusen.
Combine sections for a longer tour.

Der Nördlicher Hauptwanderung (182km): From Waldmünchen through the highest mountains and the nature reserve near the Czech border to the Dreisessel.

Ilztalwanderweg (70km): Nature trail traversing both banks of River Ilz. South end at Passau.

The following can be taken as *Wandern ohne Gepäck* (hiking without luggage) — details from Fremdenverkehrsverband, Regensburg:

Burgenweg (140km): From Friedenfels in the Steinwald to Rötz visiting many ruined and preserved castles.

Pandurensteig (174km): From Waldmünchen through the Bavarian Forest to Passau.

Tourist Railway
Viechtach-Gotteszell
Information: ISN eV
Postfach 1329
82194 Gröbenzell
☎ 089-8114652 (Herr Bauer)
Three trains in each direction with historic motive power on alternate Sundays from end May to August and in October. Family tickets.

Tourist Information Centres
Fremdenverkehrsverband
Landshuter Strasse 13
93047 Regensburg
☎ 0941-5074410
General information about Lower Bavaria and Upper Palatinate.

Kultur- und Fremdenverkehrsamt
Altes Rathaus
92610 Weiden
☎ 0961-81412-4
Information about Weiden and general information about eastern Bavaria.

For local detail, accommodation lists etc write to 'Tourist Information' giving postcode and name of town:

95460 Bad Berneck
95444 Bayreuth
94249 Bodenmais
93413 Cham
94078 Freyung
95688 Friedenfels
93437 Furth im Wald
94481 Grafenau
93444 Kötzting
95615 Marktredwitz
93453 Neukirchen bei Hl Blut
94154 Neukirchen Vorm Wald
94089 Neureichenau
92660 Neustadt a d Waldnaab
92526 Oberviechtach
94209 Regen
95643 Tirschenreuth
94105 Tittling
92648 Vohenstrauss
94065 Waldkirchen
93449 Waldmünchen
95652 Waldsassen
94110 Wegscheid
92670 Windischeschenbach
95632 Wunsiedel
94227 Zwiesel

7
THE DONAU &
THE GERMAN HOLIDAY ROAD

This chapter explores the long corridor lying right across the centre of Bavaria. The 1785km-long Holiday Road (Deutsche Ferienstrasse Alpen-Ostsee) is the longest of Germany's named roads; its northern terminal is at Puttgarden on the Baltic coast and its southern at Berchtesgaden near the Austrian border. One of the routes outlined in this chapter embraces part of the Holiday Road which is joined at Dinkelsbühl. About 70km (43 miles) south of Dinkelsbühl in the west of Bavaria, the River Donau, which has its source in the Black Forest, enters Bavaria and the course of this river is traced eastwards into Austria.

From their starting points on the western border of Bavaria the Holiday Road and River Donau draw steadily closer until they finally meet and cross at Kelheim, west of Regensburg, after which the Holiday Road leaves the river to go south to Landshut.

Dinkelsbühl to Kelheim

The first route begins by leaving **Dinkelsbühl** and heading eastwards along the Ferienstrasse; this is a route to be enjoyed in a leisurely fashion. The small towns follow closely upon each other and most are worth a brief sightseeing stop.

The hill named Hesselberg (689m, 2260ft) is soon seen on the left, a site of significant historical discoveries including the remains of a bronze casting workplace dating from about 1800BC. The main road to the Hesselberg starts in the village of **Gerolfingen** about 14km (9 miles) from Dinkelsbühl and climbs steadily to the parking area near the summit. Walkers can start from the preceding village of **Wittels-hofen** and follow the geological trail to the summit, 5-6km. Near the car park there is an information centre with detailed drawings and descriptions (only in German) of the many features of interest.

As one explores the area it is obvious why this has been a fortified place since the earliest times for the steep slopes alone would have been sufficient to deter all but the most determined attacker. Even if one is not interested in the historical aspect, the detour to the Hesselberg is worthwhile just to reach a pleasant picnic spot with spectacular views all round.

About 20km (12 miles) from Dinkelsbühl is **Wassertrüdingen** (population 6,000) lying between quiet forests and soft hills. A short pause here to visit the town church is worthwhile. It is a remarkable building with seating on three levels. The high altar is in the form of a triptych depicting biblical scenes in graphic detail. The little River Wörnitz is good for fishing. A folk festival takes place in the 8 days following Whitsun. This is a good walking area and there are conducted rambles, often with a geological theme. Information from the *Rathaus*. The Holiday Road follows the Wörnitz a mere 10km (6 miles) to **Öttingen**, a small Swabian health resort with a good range of facilities for young and old and well preserved timbered and baroque houses. In July there is a water festival on the Wörnitz.

Ten kilometres or so in a south-easterly direction is the resort of **Wemding** (population 5,200), reached after passing the pilgrimage church Maria Brünnlein built in 1748–52, one of the most beautiful rococo churches in Bavaria. The beautiful town centre is a photographer's paradise and should not be missed. The annual festival here starts on the Wednesday before Ascension Day and lasts for five days.

Another splendid medieval town is **Weissenburg in Bayern** which lies to the north of the Holiday Road 30km (19 miles) from Wemding. The old defensive wall is largely intact with gateways and towers, the Ellinger Tor being particularly fine. The oldest parts of St Andreaskirche date from 1327 and it holds many valuable treasures. It is overshadowed by the *Fünfeckturm* (five-side tower), originally part of the town wall. Just across the street is the information office and the Römermuseum, an outstanding collection of Roman relics from the many sites in the area. Cross the railway near the station to visit the nearest of these, a carefully restored bath house. Only 5km to the north is the charming little baroque town of **Ellingen** dominated by the Residenz (1708), a mighty rococo palace.

Twelve kilometres (8 miles) south of Weissenburg and back on the Holiday Road, **Treuchtlingen** (population 12,000) is a modest town with a thermal open-air pool, *Hallenwellenbad*, and sauna. There is a fine central play area for children who can sometimes enjoy a free ride on the nearby miniature railway. In the nearby village of **Graben** is one of the few remaining sections of the canal built by Karl der Grosse (Charlemagne) in 793AD. Treuchtlingen has many modestly

Öttingen on the German Holiday Road

The market square,
Wemding

The palace at Ellingen

priced *Ferienwohnungen*, thus catering well for family groups.

The River Altmühl here is one of Bavaria's lesser known but nevertheless very beautiful waterways and it is followed through its finest scenery until it joins the Donau at Kelheim. River, road and railway keep close company through the first 20km or so of the Altmühltal. The river has carved a broad cleft deep into the Franconian Jura; on the fringes are rocky cliffs and the river winds through meadows, fields, woods and colourful settlements.

Pappenheim, 5km from Treuchtlingen, is a small resort (population 2,400) where several hostelries offer specialities of the region. The ninth-century church of St Gallus is worth a visit, as is the fourteenth-century *Kloster* church, now the Protestant church. There is a splendid view from the tower of the ruined castle above the town. The annual folk festival is during the third week in July, and on the first Sunday in August there is an open-air church service up at the castle. There is a spacious swimming pool complex.

The Naturpark Altmühltal, with 290,800 hectares (710,000 acres) is one of the biggest nature reserves in Germany. The autumn colours in the valley are very spectacular and the natural attractions and the cultural and historical sights are pressed closely upon one another with a richness seldom found elsewhere. Five kilometres beyond Pappenheim is **Solnhofen** where fossils of the feathered *Archaeopteryx* — the ancestor of today's birds — have been found. An interesting museum on the subject is near the station, while a model railway layout may be seen in the school building.

Dollnstein is a typical village of the area, often busy on summer Sundays when railway enthusiasts greet the steam trains on the *Urdonautalbahn*.

Eichstätt (population 13,000), the last town on this part of the route directly accessible by train, is a former bishop's seat and the home of numerous ecclesiastical and government institutions. The baroque town centre, the cathedral, the Residenz, the parish church and numerous other buildings make an attractive picture with the imposing castle Willibaldsburg dominating the skyline. The Willibaldsburg houses both the remarkable Jura-museum devoted largely to the fossil finds of the area and also the Historisches Museum, the main attraction being the skeleton of a 60,000-year-old mammoth.

Turn north off the main road for a brief visit to the Gungolding landscape preservation area with its juniper bush-clad slopes. At Arnsberg catch a glimpse of the lovely Schambachtal to the south and before the health resort of **Kipfenberg** cross the remains of the Limes, a first-second century Roman fortification. Kipfenberg has a romantic castle perched on steep rocky slopes. The medieval and earlier fortifications including the Limes provide the theme for a festival in August. A pleasant hour could be spent in the Fastnacht-museum devoted to the pre-Lenten customs of the area.

Turn north for a few kilometres, pass beneath the Nürnberg-Ingolstadt motorway near the Altmühltal junction and almost immediately reach the picturesque village of **Kinding** which is a good centre for excursions — two side valleys feed into the Altmühltal here — and amongst other sights the fourteenth-century Kirchen-burg Castle and the haunted ruin Rumburg may be visited. The Erholungszentrum Kratzmühle is an extensive recreation area with a lake for bathing and many facilities for the holidaymaker.

From Kinding there are two possible routes to Beilngries, 5 or 6km to the north-west. The Holiday Road closely follows the river but the scenic road via Haunstetten goes past the stately baroque palace of Hirschberg which may be visited although access to the interior is somewhat restricted due to its use as offices, although the chapel can always be visited. **Beilngries** is a health resort of 3,500 inhabitants; the medieval centre is very attractive with a well preserved town wall. There is a wide range of facilities for the holidaymaker with many marked paths and routes for cyclists.

The Ferienstrasse now enters the lower Altmühltal. There are usually many anglers along the river bank for this is a fine fishing river. Pike, carp, tench, barbel and other fish may be caught here.

The road now crosses the southern tip of the Oberpfalz and, still following the River Altmühl, **Dietfurt** is reached in about 10km. This town of seven valleys is another little health resort, a meeting place of roads and rivers and the place where the original canal of King Ludwig I joins the Altmühl. It is a place which will become of increasing interest with the development of international traffic on the waterway. Five of the original six Gothic town towers still exist, overshadowed by the 65m-high (213ft) spire of the parish church of St Ägidius (Giles) the interior of which is decorated in the baroque style. There are relics from the fifteenth and sixteenth centuries. Do not miss the famous Chinese fountain in the Marktplatz. Dietfurt is an excellent centre for walking — routes from the information office — and the rivers are a paradise for anglers.

Following the now canalised Altmühl arrive, in about 14km (9 miles), at **Riedenburg,** known either as 'the pearl of the valley' or the 'town of three castles'. Either way, the Rosenburg (built 1112) is the jewel in the crown of this pleasant town in an area noted for its scenic beauty and its hospitality. The Falconry Museum in the Rosenburg has spectacular daily flying displays by eagles, vultures and falcons.

The Kristallmuseum near the quay has the largest crystal mass in the world weighing some 7.8 tons. If desired the remainder of the journey to the Donau at Kelheim could be made by steamer.

In another 3km, Schloss Prunn towers above the valley; this is where the *Nibelungenlied* (Lay of the Nibelungs) was discovered in 1575. In the next 4km to **Markt Essing** (population 1,100) pass a series of natural monuments, rocks and caverns. Essing itself huddles beneath towering cliffs and is a useful centre for exploring the various caves in the vicinity including the Schulerloch with its rare rock drawings. The old village centre is bypassed but one can park and walk into the market place over an ancient wooden bridge for a worthwhile visit.

A few minutes later reach **Kelheim**, the end of this first stage of the journey along the Holiday Road and the end, too, of the Altmühl which now loses its identity as it merges with the Donau. Kelheim (population 15,000) is on the site of an early Stone Age settlement.

The old town has typical remains of fortifications, town gates and decorative house fronts. Worthy of note is a late Gothic Madonna over the south side portal of the parish church. In and around Kelheim, the Befreiungshalle (Liberation Hall) comes repeatedly into view, which is, exactly what its founder intended. The 45m-high

The fourteenth-century church and the old palace at Pappenheim

Kipfenberg, dominated by its castle

(147ft) building tops the Michelsberg, which itself rises 100m (328ft) above the town.

King Ludwig I believed in all things German and in German unity; he wanted to erect a monument in memory of the Wars of Liberation. When in Greece in 1836 he decided to build a 'Byzantine' hall in this commanding position at the confluence of Altmühl and Donau. Work progressed slowly and in 1847, Leo von Klenze (builder of the Glyptothek and Pinakothek in München) took command and changed the style to Roman. Work was completed in 1863, just in time for the fiftieth anniversary of the Battle of Leipzig. The colossal round temple includes memorials to the victories and victors of the wars against Napoleon (1813–15). The climb up to the Befreiungs-halle is worthwhile just for the splendid view even if its historical symbolism is not appreciated.

The remarkable caverns in the Altmühltal are best visited on foot then one can move easily from one to another. Start from the car park beside the quays in Kelheim. Enter the town through the medieval Donautor (Donau Gate). Go left via the Altmühltor and over the river bridge through Riedenburger Strasse and Brandner Steig. The foot-path proper starts after passing the last houses and climbs up to the Maria-Fels, a rocky viewpoint. The path is then followed until it drops down into the Heidental. Take the path (waymark red N) which leads directly into the wood until the main Schulerloch is reached 5km from Kelheim. 40,000 years ago this giant stalactite cave was used as a dwelling place and it was inhabited again in the Bronze Age. From Easter until 1 November there are guided tours into the cave. In the nearby small Schulerloch the only Ice Age drawings in Central Europe are scratched on the walls.

Continue up the valley to Markt Essing (8km from Kelheim); the ruined castle Randeck nearby has a fine view over the valley and far beyond, even to the Alps in clear weather. Return from here by the same route or by going down to pick up the track (waymark red bar) along the river. Continue forward to the Felsenhäusl hut and bear right and upward to the Höhenweg (Hill Way) marked by a blue dot. Turn left and follow it to Schloss Prunn (12km from Kelheim) where there is a welcome terrace café. Down then to **Einthal** and over a pretty bridge to the Klammhöhle (more caves) and a prehistoric earthwork. Return along the river (red bar) which forms part of the great international waterway. It is possible to return to Kelheim by bus from Einthal but the walker can visit two more caves on the way, the Kastlhängehöhle and the Klausenhöhle.

Neu-Ulm to Kelheim

A hundred kilometres (62 miles) westwards at **Neu-Ulm** the Donau is joined, soon after its entry into Bavaria. This is Swabia and there is a noticeable difference in architectural style compared with Franconian Dinkelsbühl 70km to the north.

Ulm in Baden-Württemberg and Neu-Ulm in Bavaria are separated by the Donau but administered jointly. Train travellers are likely to have arrived at Ulm's busy *Hauptbahnhof*.

Neu-Ulm is comparatively new. In 1815 its population was no more than 260; by the time towns merged in 1971 it was able to add its 48,000 to the 99,000 of Ulm across the river. The holidaymaker need not linger long although the Catholic parish church of St John the Baptist, rebuilt in 1922-6, is worth a visit. The museum in the Edwin-Scharff cultural centre is noted for its display of locks and fastenings.

Take the B10 eastwards to **Günzburg** (population 19,000) where, in the old upper town, there is a pleasant historic atmosphere with buildings from the Middle Ages surrounding a fine market place. The palace of an Austrian margrave with its court church of 1579 and a rococo chapel justify a visit and the Liebfrauenkirche, built in 1735-41, is one of the most impressive rococo churches in Swabia. In the *Heimatmuseum* there is a large collection of archaeological finds. This is a popular cycling and rambling area and there is angling in the Donau for carp, tench, pike and trout. Fishing permits are available from Josef Sixti, Schlachthausstrasse 60.

A little aside from the Donau is **Burgau** (population 7,900) just 11km (7 miles) further along the B10. The town church (1791) shows the transition from rococo to classical style and has a fine ceiling painting (1829). The *Heimatmuseum* is located in yet another palace (1787) and there is a fine fountain, the Marienbrunnen (1728). The Auto-Motorrad-Museum has a collection of over seventy vintage cars and motor-cycles including such classics as the 1902 Peugeot and the Mercedes 'Stuttgart' of 1928. From November until March an ice rink provides ice hockey, skating and curling. There is a good network of well kept and well marked footpaths.

An agreeable 16km (10 mile) drive brings one back to the Donau which is crossed to reach medieval **Lauingen** (population 10,000), a former duke's seat with picturesque corners and some impressive sights. The late Gothic minster, with its princes' burial vault and cloister paintings, should be visited as should the classical *Rathaus* (1782–91), facing what is said to be the finest market place in Swabia. The Schimmelturm, a 55m-high (180ft) tower gives a splendid bird's

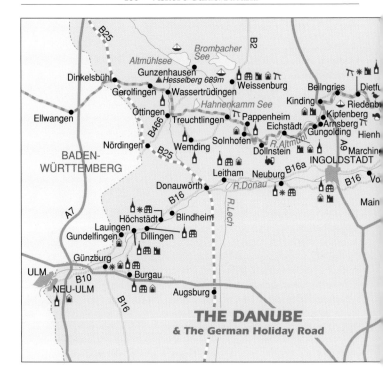

THE DANUBE
& The German Holiday Road

eye view of the town. The concerts in the great hall of the *Rathaus* have a good reputation and there are various other entertainments in this lively little town. The *Heimatmuseum* has a notable exhibition of minerals. There is an annual *Faschings* procession and a summer folk festival. Sports enthusiasts have tennis, riding, sailing, a bowling alley and swimming and there is fishing in the Donau and in several small lakes — Leo Mack, Donaustrasse 14 provides permits. At **Gundelfingen**, a few kilometres to the west, there is another motor museum with a collection of vintage vehicles.

Only 5km eastwards along the B16 is another town with very similar characteristics and equally well endowed with interesting sights. **Dillingen** (population 12,000), formerly the residence of the prince-bishops of Augsburg was, from 1549 until 1804, a university town, a fact which had considerable influence on the buildings. More than a short stop is required to see and appreciate the *Schloss*, the Studienkirche (former Jesuit church) (1610–17), the rococo

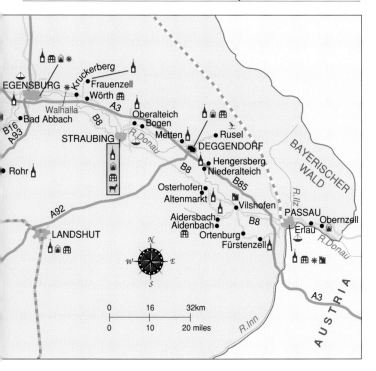

 Franciscan church (1736–8) and the golden hall of the former university — just a few of the architectural treasures. The town's many
attractions include concerts and theatre and again there is fishing in
the Donau — permits from Gästehaus Noll, Georg-Schmid-Ring 47
close by the camp site at No 45.

Six kilometres more and **Höchstädt**, at first glance rather less
attractive than the two previous stops, is nevertheless, well worth
closer inspection. Of particular interest to English visitors is the
memorial to the fallen of the great battle of the Spanish Succession on
13 August 1704 when the 'allied' forces of Austria and Holland, with
the English under the Duke of Marlborough, defeated the combined
armies of Bavaria and France here and at nearby **Blindheim** which
— as Blenheim — became the name of the family seat of the Dukes
of Marlborough in England. The Gothic parish church has a baroque
high altar and a richly decorated pulpit and once again the
Marktplatz, surrounded by old patrician houses, makes a fine centre.

The Renaissance palace houses a branch of the Bavarian National Museum with exhibits of Swabian sculpture, textiles and rooms furnished in eighteenth century style.

Towns, rather than scenery, have provided the theme since leaving Neu-Ulm but from **Donauwörth** (visited in Chapter 1) the motorist has to choose between the fairly fast B16 south of, but not near, the river and the quieter road on the north side running in part along the fringe of the Altmühltal *Naturpark*. The latter is more pleasant and allows a stop to visit the fine seventeenth-century *Schloss* at **Leitheim**.

Its rococo banqueting hall has fine ceiling and wall paintings. The *Schlosskirche* has rich stucco from 1696 while the *Schlossmuseum* exhibits important works of art from the eighteenth century. Concerts are given in the *Schloss* every Saturday May-October, usually chamber music or solo artists. Advance booking is essential.

Both roads converge at **Neuburg an der Donau** in Upper Bavaria (population 20,000) a pleasant town with the usual range of leisure activities. The *Neuburger Barockkonzerte* each September are well thought of. The Renaissance *Schloss* was built in 1530-45 with frescos from 1543 in the *Schlosskapelle*. Neuburg has many places of worship and the Hofkirche (1607), St Peter (1641–6), Church of the Holy Ghost (1723–6) and the Studienkirche (1700–1) are all worth seeing if time permits. Secular buildings of note include the *Rathaus*, the Münz (mint) and above all the Provinzialbibliothek (library) which has the fittings of the former Kaisheim abbey library.

It is 21km (13 miles) to **Ingolstadt**, a city of 100,000 inhabitants. Like most other German cities, Ingolstadt has a rich and varied cultural life to which the autumn concerts (*Musik-Herbst*) make an important contribution. The devastating bombing of the town at the end of World War II inflicted heavy damage on many fine buildings. The most important have since been painstakingly restored; the *Schloss* (1418–1500) is now even better than it was, for in the course of restoration, the towers have been built to the height originally planned. The *Schloss* today houses the Bavarian Army Museum. The minster (begun in 1425) is among the finest examples of late Gothic church architecture in Bavaria. The former oratory Maria de Victoria (1732–5), the fourteenth-century Moritzkirche, the Franciscan church (begun 1275) and the Spitalkirche (begun in the fourteenth century) are worthy of inspection.

Die Anatomie (1723–36) is the home of the German medical history museum but is of general interest. The Kreuztor (1385) and other parts of the fourteenth-century fortifications still exist. The Stadttheater (1966) is a good example of modern theatre architecture.

The rail traveller must now follow a more southerly route to Kelheim, perhaps interrupting the journey in **Abensberg**, a little town which could make a pleasant stop for a night with a visit to the little Aventinusmuseum housed in the former Carmelite *Kloster* where relics of the historian Johannes Thurmair, known as Aventinus, are on display. Nearby is the Lower Bavarian Bird Park.

The motorist should leave Ingolstadt along the road called Schlosslände on the north bank of the Donau and follow signs for Regensburg, shortly joining the B16a and after about 10km turn left into Vohburg continuing through Pförring, Marching and Irnsing to **Hienheim**.

There is an opportunity here for two short walks, each about 8km (5 miles). Leaving the village in an easterly direction, follow the small road towards Essing for about 2km to Hadriansäule, a monument in memory of the Roman emperor Hadrian who was responsible for building the Limes, the fortified wall marking the one-time boundary of the Roman Empire. Hadrian is also known for the great wall he constructed across Britain in 122–7. Turn left at the monument into a field track and follow the visible remains of the wall for a further 2km before turning left into a track out of the wood and into the village of **Weiler Ried** in about 1.5km. Visit the baroque chapel before returning to Hienheim along a minor road in about 3km.

The other walk includes a ferry crossing of the Donau. It is only a short walk from the village to the landing stage from where a small boat plies across to the village of **Eining**. Now go south-west along a minor road in the direction of Bad Gögging and very soon the remains of a Roman fort called *Abusina* are reached. It is about 2.5km to **Bad Gögging** where the Norman-style church of St Andreas, with its richly decorated portal, is built on the foundations of a former Roman bath. In 1976 new 650m-deep (2,132ft) borings tapped important reserves of therapeutic mineral waters which have resulted in the development of the town as a modern health resort.

Return to Hienheim by the same route or, on the south side of the river, use the alternative field paths.

Leave Hienheim by the Essing road and follow signs to reach **Kelheim** in about 16km. The route has bypassed the *Donaudurchbruch* (gorge) but, during the main holiday season passenger boats leave Kelheim every half-hour for an excursion as far as Kloster Weltenburg through an outstanding example of European scenery. Each year on the first Saturday of July, the spectacle called *Flammende Donau* takes place and the gorge is illuminated by thousands of Bengal lights. Early reservation on the cruise boats is essential.

To fully appreciate this delightful area, one should also explore it

Cycles are carried free
on the Urdonau Valley
Line

The Hofkirche, built in
1607, at Neuburg

on foot. Begin at the quay in Kelheim. Walk a little way west and leave the river bank near the end of the old Ludwigskanal to join a path up through the parkland of the Michelsberg and past the Befreiungshalle. The way is clearly marked. On the west side of the Michelsberg there are remains of the Keltenwall, another ancient fortification and shortly after this the path divides. The right fork (waymark 6) goes ahead through the wood on a pleasant little road and is slightly shorter than the left fork (7) which goes closer to the gorge with several fine view points. The hostelry 'Klösterle' provides for a rest and refreshment on the way. Just after passing another portion of the Keltenwall, both routes meet at a road. Join this and turn left down to **Stausacker** on the river bank where — from April to October — a boat goes across to **Weltenburg**.

The *Kloster* here was the first in Bavaria and is considered to be where the Christianisation of the country began. In the seventh century, monks founded a mission station on the tip of the tongue formed by a huge curve in the river and in 760 it became a Benedictine abbey. The present *Klosterkirche* was built by the Asam brothers (begun 1716). It is a masterpiece of their work and the visitor should not fail to see it. Refreshments are available here; the *Kloster* has it own brewery and a glass of its *Weltenburger Klosterbier* is very welcome under the trees on a warm summer day.

Performers at the Prince's Wedding pageant at Landshut take a break between scenes

Return to Kelheim by the same route — with the choice of paths 6 and 7 — or along the hill path (9) on the south side of the river. Or from April to October, save about 4km walking of the total 10km by travelling one way between Kelheim and Weltenburg by boat.

Kelheim to Landshut

The journey along the Holiday Road can now be resumed. From Kelheim, the first 10km or so lead back, parallel with the river, to Weltenburg and Eining but then the road turns south out of the Altmühltal *Naturpark* to reach **Abensberg**. Join the B301 and pass through extensive fields of hops, for this is the Hallertau or Holledau, the largest hop-growing area in Europe. This area is rich in art and cultural monuments — brick churches with onion-domed towers, well preserved *Klöster* and *Schlösser* and solid houses in the towns.

An outstanding example of church architecture is to be found in **Rohr** some 11km south-east of Abensberg. Little remains now of the Romanesque building of 1133 for in 1717 the site was cleared for the construction of a new church, consecrated in 1722. The fantastic high altar depicts the Assumption of the Virgin, borne up by angels towards an opening where the choir of angels and the figures of the Trinity await her. The apostles gather below in amazement and awe around the empty marble sarcophagus. During a service or organ recital, the atmosphere is tremendous and the whole creation is seen as originally conceived. In 1945 the buildings were taken over as a Benedictine abbey and the monks now care for this lovely church.

Mainburg, some 20km (12 miles) from Abensberg, is the centre of the hop industry; the Ferienstrasse now leaves the B301 to turn east for the final 40km (25 miles) to **Landshut**. This is the perfect picture of a medieval Bavarian town. The colourful façades of the buildings face each other across the broad Altstadt and the skyline is dominated by the 130m (426ft) high tower of St Martin's Minster. Through the simple entrance beneath the tower is the brick-built three-naved church, 92m (302ft) long and about 29m (95ft) wide and high, begun in the fifteenth century. The pulpit and high altar are original and are examples of the best of Gothic stonemasonry.

From the earliest days, Landshut (population 58,000) has been a place of royal residence. Parts of Burg Trausnitz, which once served as a fortress as shown by the drawbridge, date from the thirteenth century but many of its royal occupants introduced their own ideas of decoration and furnishing. From 1868, King Ludwig II had magnificent rooms on the second floor but these were destroyed in a serious fire in 1961. The damage has long since made good.

The famous historical pageant, the *Fürstenhochzeit* (Prince's Wedding) takes place every four years in June (1997, 2001, etc). This is probably the greatest folk festival in Europe and is in memory of Ludwig, Duke of Bavaria (1450–79) who successfully claimed the hand of Hedwig, the 17-year old daughter of the King of Poland, for his son Georg. Hedwig came to Landshut in the autumn of 1475 with a 'court' of no less than 642 persons. The wedding celebrations included church-going, jousting and feasting and this is recalled today when the wedding 'guests' in authentic costume walk from the new to the old town to the sounds of music and bell-ringing with 'Ludwig' in a sedan chair and 'Hedwig' in the golden bridal coach drawn by eight white horses with knights, jesters and gypsies all joining the merry throng.

Because there is so much to see and do in Landshut it is a very good base for the holidaymaker. There are many places of interest within easy touring distance and as the junction of several railway lines, it is equally good for those without their own transport. By train München can be reached in less than an hour, Regensburg in three-quarters of an hour and Passau in about an hour and twenty minutes.

Kelheim to Passau

Resuming the journey down the Donau for the 20km or so to Regensburg the motorist must choose between the pretty rural road on the north bank or the B16 on the south. The former is more pleasant but the latter provides the opportunity to visit the attractive spa of **Bad Abbach** which lies in between. This is no recently developed spa, for as long ago as the sixteenth century the Emperor Karl V came here for the *Kur*. A stop should be made in **Prüfening** on the western outskirts of Regensburg to visit the Benedictine abbey founded in 1109. The former *Klosterkirche* is now the parish church of St Georg, famed for its ceiling and wall paintings (1130–60) discovered in 1897.

Regensburg is the biggest centre of population in this chapter. With some 135,000 inhabitants it is a busy and lively city, as well as a bishop's seat and the seat of the government of the Oberpfalz. For a large part of its history it has been a place of royal residence and a centre of trade. The building of the huge cathedral was begun in the middle of the thirteenth century but the main work was not finished until 1525. At the time of its building, the cathedral would have accommodated every citizen of Regensburg three times over.

The former Benedictine *Kloster* of St Emmeram was one of the spiritual centres of Regensburg from the eighth century and was equipped and decorated by the Asam brothers in 1731-33. This is sufficient guarantee of a stimulating visit. The so-called Schottenkirche (Scottish Church) of St Jakob (1160–80) is the best-preserved Romanesque church in Regensburg. The wandering Irish monks of the eleventh century who settled here were followed by countrymen who were wrongly called Scottish. However, at the beginning of the sixteenth century, Scottish Benedictine monks did arrive and they occupied the *Kloster* until 1862. The church is well worth inspection.

The Museum der Stadt has been housed since 1931 in the former Minoritenkirche (1250–70). It must be one of the most comprehensive 'local' museums in Europe with more than 100 rooms of exhibits on three floors in the old church and in two modern annexes. It is, however, only one of half a dozen museums to be found in the city. Philatelists may learn something of the famous Thurn and Taxis postal service by visiting the museum in the *Schloss*.

Under Franz von Taxis (died 1517), a postal service between west and middle European states had been organised with Brussels–Vienna as its main artery. The headquarters of the postal service had been in Brussels but in 1731 it was moved to Frankfurt to be more central and finally, in 1748, to Regensburg. The various states gradually took over the postal functions for themselves, Bavaria in 1812, Württemberg in 1851 and Prussia finally bought out the rest of the family holdings in 1867, which was the last year that the now rare Thurn and Taxis stamps appeared. The museum tells the full story of this early example of international private enterprise.

The famous boys' choir, the Domspatzen (Cathedral Sparrows) sings regularly; in June there are serenade concerts in the cloisters of the museum; June to August is the time for organ recitals in the *Dom* following the April to June concerts in the splendid *Reichssaal* of the town hall.

There is a wide range of eating places in Regensburg and visitors should sample the delights of a speciality fish inn on the riverside and the Historische Wurstküche (Sausage Kitchen) near the 310m-long (1,016ft) Steinerne Brücke, the old stone bridge built in 1135–46. Legend has it that the sausage kitchen was first built to provide meals for workmen building the bridge and the nearby cathedral. A Regensburg speciality is *Schweinebratwürste über Buchenholzkohle gebraten*, little pork sausages grilled over a beechwood charcoal fire. The Prinzess-Conditorei-Café is said to be the oldest confectioners' shop in Germany. Their famous hand-made chocolates such as *Regensbürgerinnen* (Ladies of Regensburg), *Donaumuscheln* (Donau Shell Fish) or *Barbaraküsse* (Barbara's Kisses) make a lovely gift.

The turbulence of the Donau water around the piers of the stone bridge is known as the 'Regensburger Strudel' (commemorated in a well known student song) and it follows that the river steamer trip called 'Strudelrundfahrt' (round trip) has nothing to do with the well known apple pie! There are many river excursions from here, even a voyage as far as Weltenburg beyond Kelheim is possible.

On his way to Italy in 1786 Goethe wrote in his journal, 'Regensburg's situation is enchanting.' Four years later, Mozart was also favourably impressed, recording that he '… had a delicious lunch and drank an excellent wine to the accompaniment of divine music.'

A few kilometres downstream from Regensburg at **Donaustauf** is the gigantic national monument Walhalla. From Easter until the end of October it can be reached from Regensburg by steamer — 358 marble steps to climb from the pier! Walhalla is a copy of the Parthenon in Athens, with fifty-two columns 9m (30ft) high and 1.7m (5ft) wide at the base and the temple walls are of marble. The building is 20m (66ft) high and covers an area of 2,100sq m. Double doors 6.7m (22ft) high close the entrance, each leaf weighing 2.1 tons.

Why is a Greek temple on the banks of the Donau called Walhalla, the name of the place where according to Norse legend, Odin received the fallen heroes? Inevitably it was another brainchild of Ludwig I who wanted to create a shrine where German 'heroes'

Walhalla, Ludwig I's shrine to German heroes, is a copy of the Parthenon

could be honoured. Busts of the famous were installed and by the time of the opening in 1842 no less than 162 suitable persons had been identified. The 'German' qualification is interpreted freely and the busts include those of Dutch, Swiss and other national notables. The king laid an obligation upon his successors to continually review the ranks of the famous and since 1945 nine more marble busts have been added. This impressive monument occupies a fine vantage point above the river. A car park near the top saves the steep climb.

It is possible to make the rest of the journey to Passau by steamer but this is rather time-consuming. The motorist has the advantage of flexibility, but the train traveller can still reach many worthwhile places. After leaving Walhalla motorists should continue eastwards and after about 8km turn left to arrive after about another 6km at the Benedictine Kloster Frauenzell. Of the fourteenth-century church only a tower remains. The rest was pulled down in 1747 to make way for a new church and a somewhat motley collection of artists — although all of good repute — was assembled. It is well worth making the short detour away from the Donau to see this fine church.

Back on the main road, arrive at the little town of **Wörth** (population 2,000). The present *Schloss* dates from the sixteenth and seventeenth centuries, and since 1812 it has been owned by the princes of Thurn and Taxis. Wörth is a pleasant place for a peaceful holiday and well sited for excursions into the Bavarian Forest.

Leaving Wörth, pass under the motorway (A3) to reach **Straubing** (population 45,000) in about 20km (13km), the home of an ancient festival which, in scale, comes a close second to the famous Münchener *Oktoberfest*, yet is virtually unheard of outside Germany. The *Gäubodenvolksfest* takes place every year for two weeks in mid-August. In 1812 the king directed that there should be a regular agricultural show to display the achievements of the fertile Gäuboden area; the agricultural aspect is still important with some 400 exhibitors showing their wares and numerous specialist exhibits and displays. Over the years, the show has gradually come to be supported by a folk festival featuring an enormous fairground. Seven beer halls cater for nearly a million visitors to the show each year.

Then every four years (1996, 2000, etc) the production of the folk play, *Agnes Bernauer*, tells of the tragic death in 1435 of a beautiful girl of humble parentage who had fallen in love with Duke Albrecht III — and he with her — but there is no happy ending to this tale.

Straubing was once the Roman fort *Sorviodurum*, where a detachment of the Third Italian Legion from Regensburg was stationed. The Romans fled before Alemannic invaders in 233, but before doing so buried a hoard of beaten gold masks, leg protectors, etc and it was only in 1950 that these valuable relics were unearthed; they are now in the Gäuboden Museum.

The oldest church in Straubing is St Peter's, originally founded in 1029 and rebuilt in the late twelfth century as a three-naved Romanesque basilica. The cemetery of St Peter is worth inspection; there are three chapels there and the Agnes Bernauer chapel is of special interest for its memorial to that unhappy girl. Several other churches are well worth seeing but the visitor should at least see the remarkable Klosterkirche St Ursula. The jubilation of the colours, frescos and altars has been compared with the 'Hallelujah Chorus' from Handel's *Messiah* which received its first performance in 1742, the year in which this beautiful church was consecrated.

From September to May there are regular performances in the town theatre and from time to time concerts are given in the historic town hall. There are also trotting races which take place regularly. Straubing is a stopping place for the passenger ships between Regensburg and Passau. The town has the only zoo in east Bavaria.

Leave the town over the Donau bridge and follow signs for Bogen until, in about 8km, **Oberalteich** is reached. Here, the former Benedictine abbey (731) is the site of the present *Klosterkirche* of St Peter (1622–9) with rich baroque and rococo decoration. This imposing double-towered church is one of the notable memorials to Bavarian baroque. **Bogen** is a town of 7,000 inhabitants on the edge of the Bayerischer Wald overlooked by the Bogenberg (432m, 1,417ft) with splendid views all round. The Bogenberg has prehistoric ramparts and unusual plants are to be found here but most visitors make the climb to visit the late Gothic pilgrimage church of 1463.

Several picturesque roads go from Bogen into the heart of the forest but those without transport will find ample scope for walking on well-marked paths within 10 or 15km.

Continue in a south-easterly direction (signs 'Deggendorf') for about 20km (12 miles) to visit the Benedictine *Kloster* of **Metten.** The *Kloster* church is yet another example of Bavarian baroque at its best. In the east wing of the *Kloster* buildings the library, a little jewel of baroque ornamentation, should not be missed.

Deggendorf (population 22,500) is one of several towns claiming the title 'Gateway to the Bavarian Forest' and in this case with very good reason. It is a busy market town and shopping centre, the market place — Luitpoldplatz — being dominated by the free-standing late Gothic *Rathaus* with its distinctive stepped gable. The building dates from 1535 and embraces the town tower, begun in the fourteenth century and reaching its present form in 1790. Opposite is the *Heimatmuseum* with a comprehensive display of rural implements and folklore. The Church of the Holy Sepulchre is a Gothic basilica (1337-60) with a slender bell-tower added in 1727, one of the most beautiful baroque towers in Bavaria. The parish church Maria Himmelfahrt in the lower town near the 416m-long (1,364ft) Donau bridge has a canopied high altar (1749) originally intended for the cathedral in Eichstätt. The late Gothic pilgrimage church of Maria Schmerzen (1486–7) in the nature reserve on the Geiersberg (379m, 1,243ft) has a collection of votive tablets and a wonderful view.

Leisure activities are well provided for and there are 70km of *Langlauf* (cross-country) skiing trails. In **Rusel**, 10km north-east of the town, there is a *Langlauf* centre — details from the *Verkehrsamt* in Deggendorf. This is outstanding rambling or cycling country with ample rural accommodation. Tour suggestions from the *Verkehrsamt*. The annual folk festival takes place at the end of July/beginning of August, events — including horse racing — taking place over about 10 days. For those wishing to spend a holiday in a place with a good range of facilities and interests yet not in one of the larger cities, it would be hard to better Deggendorf.

About 8km beyond Deggendorf is the *Erholungsort* **Hengersberg** (population 5,500) with modern facilities and looked down upon by two hill-top churches, Michaelskirche on the Rohrberg and Maria Himmelfahrt on the Frauenberg. Both of are of interest.

Nearby is the Benedictine abbey Niederalteich which was secularised in 1803 when many of the interior appointments were stolen and the buildings partially destroyed; in 1918 the abbey was re-occupied and is now a centre for education and Christian unity. The church is a charming baroque building with frescos honouring those who previously led the order here, among them St Gotthard, abbot and later bishop of Hildesheim. The St Gotthard Pass in Switzerland is named after this first Bavarian-born saint.

Before reaching Passau there are several more places of interest on the south side of the Donau. There is a ferry near Niederalteich or the next bridge is a few kilometres downstream. A route taking in some of the following is recommended: **Osterhofen/Altenmarkt** (Damenstiftskirche — works by the Asam brothers), **Aldersbach** (another fine 'Asam' church), **Aidenbach** (attractive *Marktplatz*), **Vilshofen** (old town centre and churches), **Ortenburg** (*Schloss* and deer park), **Fürstenzell** (Cistercian *Kloster* church and buildings).

And so to **Passau** (population 52,000), the most easterly Bavarian city. It stands at the confluence of the Donau, Inn and Ilz rivers; the Romans, with an eye for strategic locations, built a fort here in AD 80. Today, this lively city stands with one foot in Austria, for that part known as the Innstadt is the only part of Germany south of the rivers, the Austrian border having been bent inland to accommodate it. Upstream, the Inn itself forms the border and downstream, the Donau does so. The rivers have played an important role in Passau's history and continue to have considerable influence on its life and culture.

From the busy waterfront quay opposite the *Rathaus*, cruises leave eastward for Linz and Wien (Vienna) and north-westwards for Straubing, Regensburg and beyond. Local sightseeing is provided by the Three Rivers Excursion — Donau, Ilz and Inn — a 45-minute trip with boats leaving every 30 minutes in the high season.

Few European cities can boast a finer situation and not only the river and hill scenery around but the architectural treasures of the city itself are a constant delight to the eye. As one might suspect, there is something not quite 'Bavarian' about it. The Inn has brought a taste of the building styles of its valley downstream but, at the same time, some of the streetscapes are reminiscent of towns south of the Alps or perhaps Passau has been influenced by the mysterious east.

Passau is sufficiently small and compact to be explored on foot —

Passau cathedral

indeed, this is the only way and there is no better place to start than at the *Dom* of St Stephan. There is a convenient multi-storey car park just north of the cathedral. Parts of the choir and transept, later overlaid with baroque decoration, of a late Gothic building (1407–1530) were incorporated in the later cathedral. A serious fire in 1662 almost totally destroyed the main aisle; financial considerations did not allow construction of a completely new building so parts of the old were used. The 'join' is undetectable and in the course of 20 years' work, the biggest high baroque church in Bavaria with a length of 101m (330ft), width 33m (108ft), dome 69m (226ft) high and two west towers 68m (223ft) high was created.

The exterior has been 'improved' on several occasions and the west towers were only given their present domes (based on Salzburg Cathedral) in 1897. A thorough renovation of the building was completed in 1980. Sheer size apart, this church may not have as much impact on the visitor as do some of the smaller, more intimate and more colourful baroque churches of Bavaria but it does have one outstanding asset. It is the home of the biggest church organ in the world, a modern instrument built in 1978–81. In fact it consists of no less than five independent organs, all of which can be played from the main five-manual keyboard. The potential of this vast instrument with its 17,388 pipes and 231 registers is demonstrated each weekday May-October 12 noon to 12.30pm with a longer concert on Thursdays from 7.30pm. There is a modest admission charge at these times and to be sure of obtaining entry it is advisable to be there about half an hour before the recital starts.

The cathedral west doors face the rectangular Domplatz, originally intended to provide a clear view of the imposing façade but now often full of parked cars. The finest baroque façade of the surrounding buildings belongs to the Palais Lamberg (1724) which today houses the Diocesan Museum. Round the south side of the *Dom* (Zengergasse) are historic buildings with ecclesiastical origins. Enter the Residenzplatz which takes its name from the 'new' bishops' Residenz of the seventeenth century. Leaving behind the Wittelsbach fountain turn eastward into the Grosse Messergasse from which several narrow alleys lead steeply down to the Donau and to the *Rathaus*.

Some small but excellent restaurants are to be be found in the alleys and the town hall has its own fine restaurant, the Ratskeller. The fourteenth-century *Rathaus*. had to be demolished in 1811 and the present one with its mighty tower was only built in 1890.

With the Donau behind, a few minutes walk through Milchgasse leads to the former Jesuit church of St Michael with ornate interior decoration of the seventeenth century. The associated buildings now house the Leopoldinum grammar school and the state library. The old library with stucco decoration in the Italian style is worth seeing. Nearby Kloster Niedernburg dates from the eighth century. Its buildings now provide homes for two girls' schools under the auspices of the Englischen Fräulein and only the Church of the Holy Cross, originally built in the thirteenth century, is normally open to the public.

From here it is a pleasant short walk right out to the tip of the tongue of land between the two big rivers. A walk back beside the Inn leads to the picturesque Schaiblingsturm, a relic of old fortifications and a favourite subject for artists. High above the Donau on the north bank is the fortress Veste Oberhaus which today contains the town museum and art gallery. Here, with magnificent views, is a 200-bed youth hostel. The art gallery and museum are well worth a visit and from May to October there is a regular bus service (No 9) from the town centre, avoiding the stiff climb. By parking up here the motorist can avoid the problems of city centre congestion.

Music plays an important part in the rich cultural life of Passau. In addition to a major international festival from mid-June until the beginning of August there are concerts, operas, operettas, etc throughout the year. There is a consumers' fair in April and the *Maidult* at the beginning of May. On the first Sunday of the *Dult* there is a procession with about 4,000 participants in costume and some twenty bands from different parts of Bavaria and Austria. About the second week in September is the *Herbstdult* (Autumn Fair) while December sees the great Christmas fair, the *Christkindlmarkt*.

On the north bank of the Donau between Passau and the Austrian border is **Obernzell** where the fifteenth-century *Schloss* houses the ceramics department of the Bavarian National Museum as well as the *Heimatmuseum*. The Marktkirche is a baroque building (1745) with a carved wooden pulpit, while the fifteenth-century late Gothic parish church above the village has a pulpit of granite, a material obtained in the nearby hills. Many fairly easy walks can be started here including one into the Erlautal where there is a *Waldlehrpfad*. Boat hire, water-skiing and angling are among the river-based activities here. Around 370km (230 miles) in river distance from its entry into Bavaria at Neu-Ulm the Donau now disappears into Austria to flow eastwards for another 2,200km (1,375 miles) to the Black Sea.

Additional Information

Places to Visit

Abensberg
Aventinus-Museum
Karmelitenplatz 5
93326 Abensberg
☎ 09443-5921
Open: Wednesday, Friday,
Saturday and Sunday 2-4pm.

*Niederbayerischer Vogelpark (Lower
Bavarian Bird Park)*
93326 Abensberg
☎ 09443-1215
Open: April to October daily 10am-
5pm.
Children's play area, kiosk and
beer garden.

Burgau
Auto-Motorrad-Museum
Bleichstrasse 18
89331 Burgau
☎ 08222-1333
Open: daily 10am-5pm.

Eichstätt
Willibaldsburg
Burgstrasse
85071 Eichstätt
☎ 08421-2956
Open: Tuesday to Sunday, April to
September 9am-12noon, 1-5pm,
October to March 10am-12noon, 1-
4pm. Closed 1 January, Shrove
Tuesday, 1 November, 24, 25, 31
December.
Houses the Jura-Museum and the
Historisches Museum. Admission
charge includes both museums.
Café.

Ellingen
Residenz and Deutschordensmuseum
91792 Ellingen
☎ 09141-3327

Open: Tuesday to Sunday, April to
September 9am-12noon, 1-5pm,
October to March 10am-12noon, 2-
4pm. Closed 1 January, Shrove
Tuesday, 1 November, 24, 25, 31
December.

Gundelfingen
Automobil-Veteranan-Salon
Bächinger Strasse 68
89423 Gundelfingen
☎ 09073-2575
Open: Easter to mid-October 9am-
6pm.

Ingolstadt
Bayerisches Armeemuseum
Neues-Herzogs-Schloss
Paradeplatz 4
85049 Ingolstadt
☎ 0841-35067
Open: Tuesday to Sunday 8.45am-
4.30pm. Accompanied children
free.

Kelheim
Befreiungshalle
93309 Kelheim
☎ 09441-1584
Open: April to September 9am-
5pm, October to March 10am-4pm.
Closed 1 January, Shrove Tuesday,
1 November, 24, 25, 31 December.
Accompanied children free.

Landshut
Burg Trausnitz
84036 Landshut
☎ 0871-22638
Open: April to September daily
9am-12noon, 1-5pm, October to
March, Tuesday to Sunday 10am-
12noon, 1-4pm. Closed 1 January,
Shrove Tuesday, 1 November, 24,
25, 31 December.

Residenz and Art Gallery
In the Altstadt
Telephone number and opening
times as next above.

Ortenburg
Schloss-Museum
94496 Ortenburg
☎ 08542-7321 (Verkehrsamt)
Open: April to October daily
9.30am-5.30pm and by arrangement.

Regensburg
Museum der Stadt
Dachauplatz 2-4
93047 Regensburg
☎ 0941-5073443
Open: Tuesday to Saturday 10am-
4pm, Sunday 10am-1pm. Groups
limited to 35 persons.

Schlossmuseum
Emmeramsplatz
93047 Regensburg
☎ 0941-50480
Conducted tours Monday and
Wednesday to Saturday 2 and
3pm, Sunday 11 and 11.15am. Tour
groups limited to 40 persons.

Walhalla
93093 Donaustauf
☎ 09403-3909
Open: April to September daily
9am-5.45pm, October 9am-4.45pm,
November to March 10-11.45am, 1-
3.45pm. Closed Shrove Tuesday,
24, 25, 31 December. Concessions
for students and senior citizens.

In addition to those listed, there are
many more museums and galleries
in Regensburg — brochure from
Tourist Information Office.

Riedenburg
Bayerischer Landes-Jagdfalken-Hof
Schloss Rosenburg
93339 Riedenburg

☎ 09442-1843
Open: Tuesday to Sunday 9am-
5pm.
Free flying birds of prey at 3pm.
Refreshments.

Kristallmuseum
93339 Riedenburg
☎ 09442-1811
Open: April to October with
conducted tours from 10am daily.
Reductions for school parties, etc.

Schloss Prunn
93339 Riedenburg
☎ 09442-1765
Open: April to September daily
9am-12noon, 1-5pm, October to
March, Tuesday to Sunday 10am-
12noon, 1-4pm. Closed 1 January,
Shrove Tuesday, 1 November, 24,
25, 31 December. Conducted tours
only. Accompanied children free.
Restaurant.

Solnhofen
Bürgermeister-Müller-Museum
Bahnhofstrasse 8
91807 Solnhofen
☎ 09145-6777
Open: April to October daily 9am-
12noon, 1-5pm, November to
March, Sunday 1-4pm and by
arrangement.

Straubing
Gäubodenmuseum
Fraunhoferstrasse 9
94315 Straubing
☎ 09421-16326
Open: Tuesday to Sunday 10am-
4pm.

Tiergarten (Zoo)
Regensburger Strasse
94315 Straubing
☎ 09421-21277
1km W of town

Open: daily March to September
8.30am-7pm, October to February
9.30am-5pm. Children under 6 free.
Concessions for groups, senior
citizens, students etc.

Local Events and Festivals
Landshut
Fürstenhochzeit — June every 4
years (1997, 2001 etc)
Colourful historical pageant

Straubing
Gäubodenfest — 2 weeks in mid-
August

Agricultural show with fairground,
beer tents, etc

Agnes Bernauer Festspiele — every
4 years (1994, 1998, etc)

Steam Railway
Dollnstein-Rennertshofen
Museumsbahn Dollnstein
Postfach 101006
85051 Ingolstadt
☎ 0841-85749 or 61469
Operates 2 steam-hauled passenger
trains, usually two Sundays per
month May to September. Refreshments and facilities for disabled on
all trains. Cycles carried free.
Family tickets available.

Model Railway
Altmühltal Model Railway Club
Visitors are invited to view the
club's Märklin HO layout in the
school at Solnhofen 9am-12noon
Sundays (usually 2 per month) and
holiday Mondays, also7-9pm
alternate Fridays April to early
October. Actual dates from Herr
Frohrieb ☎ 09141-2422.

Tourist Information Centres
Fremdenverkehrsverband
   Ostbayern eV
Landshuter Strasse 13
93047 Regensburg
☎ 0941-560260
For general information about
Lower Bavaria.

For local detail, accommodation
lists etc write to 'Tourist Information' giving postcode and name of
town:

93326 Abensberg
93077 Bad Abbach
93333 Bad Gögging
92339 Beilngries
89331 Burgau
94469 Deggendorf
92345 Dietfurt
89407 Dillingen
86609 Donauwörth
85072 Eichstätt
89312 Günzburg
85049 Ingolstadt
93309 Kelheim
85125 Kinding
85110 Kipfenberg
84028 Landshut
86633 Neuburg an der Donau
94130 Obernzell
91788 Pappenheim
94032 Passau
93047 Regensburg
93339 Riedenburg
91807 Solnhofen
94315 Straubing
91757 Treuchtlingen
89073 Ulm
91717 Wassertrüdingen
86650 Wemding

8

FRANCONIAN SELECTION

In previous chapters, parts of Franconia (Franken) have been described but the central part of this largest constituent of Bavaria remains to be discovered.

Between Bayreuth and Bavaria's northern boundary lies the Frankenwald (Franconian Forest), an area of peace and beauty. Less than 20km (12 miles) north of Bayreuth and reached quickly on A9 to the Bad Berneck exit, then B303, is the outstanding Deutsches Dampflokomotiv Museum (Steam Locomotive Museum) at **Neuenmarkt** with dozens of engines from all over Germany, a must for every railway enthusiast. A little to the west, the Plassenburg in **Kulmbach** houses the Deutsches Zinnfiguren Museum, a collection of over 300,000 'tin' soldiers and other figures.

The B85 is a picturesque road to **Kronach** (population 12,000). Seek out the old upper town, with its 800-year-old castle, the birthplace of the famous painter Lukas Cranach, and many other historic sights. From Kronach, road and railway lead into the forest, dense between the small towns and villages. From **Pressig** an alternative westerly route closely follows the state boundary through splendid scenery. Around **Ludwigsstadt** the forest retreats a little, making way in summer for a colourful array of tents in this favourite camping and bathing area. The village of **Lauenstein** lies at the foot of the hill topped by the Mantelburg, an attractive castle taken over by the state and restored at considerable cost for the pleasure of today's sightseers. In the Burghotel guests can live for a little while in a genuine medieval atmosphere, surrounded by hunting trophies, ancient weapons, antique furniture and four-poster beds. However, central heating has been installed and the picturesque tiled stoves put into retirement. Lauenstein, with its Mantelburg landmark, is known as the 'Pearl of the Frankenwald'. The southern part of the Frankenwald is drained by the Weisser (white) Main and Roter (red) Main rivers, soon to merge and become the Main proper for the westward journey to the Rhein.

The city of **Coburg** (population 50,000) lies beneath its immense fortress, Veste Coburg, one of the largest castles ever built. The fortress was a bulwark against the incursions of the Slavs: today it is a bulwark of German culture and art, for the enormous building is a museum of massive proportions with collections of treasures of all kinds and works of the great masters of the past. The Coburgers are proud of their connection with the British royal family for Albert of Coburg was the consort of Queen Victoria. Her statue now stands in the town which also boasts the 'Edinburgh Palace' and the 'Windsor Castle' façade of the royal riding school. Even earlier is the 'English' Gothic of Schloss Ehrenburg, the imposing seat of the dukes of Coburg, with interior decoration from the seventeenth to nineteenth centuries. From the Schlossplatz in front of Ehrenburg, enter the *Hofgarten* for a pleasant walk up to the fortress above — a little over 1km. The town centre contains many buildings of interest in a compact area but with a maze of one-way streets motorists would be wise to park on the outskirts and walk the remaining short distance.

An excursion to **Neustadt bei Coburg**, 12km north-east, is recommended for a visit to the Trachtenpuppenmuseum with over a thousand dolls dressed in national costumes from all over the world. Neustadt, known as the 'doll town', is barely 5km from the world toy centre of Sonneberg in neighbouring Thuringia.

Many places along the Main valley are worth visiting: **Burgkunstadt** is a little town of old timbered houses, **Michelau**, the 'basket town' with the world's only basket museum, **Lichtenfels** another basket town with remains of fortifications from the fourteenth century and a pretty baroque *Rathaus* from 1743. The big attraction here is the pilgrimage church Vierzehnheiligen overlooking the valley from the south slope. Its history goes back to a shepherd who, in 1445–6, had visions of the Christ Child and the fourteen auxiliary saints or helpers to whom the faithful prayed for their earthly needs. Pilgrims soon started to visit the holy place where first a cross was erected, later a chapel and then a church. For the 300th anniversary of the vision it was decided to build a new church and one ot the most beautiful churches in Franconia was created here by Balthasar Neumann. The ceiling frescos are considered to be among the finest of the period.

Facing Vierzehnheiligen from the north bank of the Main is the former Benedictine abbey of **Banz**, built in 1710-19. The gatehouse wing in the main courtyard (1752) was by Balthasar Neumann. The

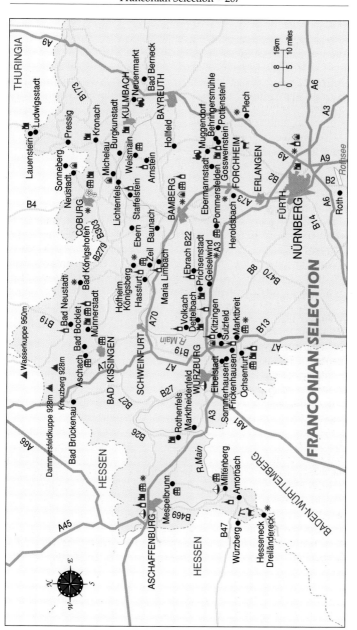

rich architectural style of the church is late baroque with the interior decoration in early rococo. The ceiling frescos are most striking and there are outstanding choir stalls, high altar, choir altar and pulpit. Banz is best approached from **Staffelstein** by a road to the right of the picturesque seventeenth-century *Rathaus*.

South of the River Main, the so-called Fränkische Schweiz (Franconian Switzerland) runs for some 60km (37 miles) south towards Nürnberg. South of Burgkunstadt (see above), a route through the rocky, romantic Kleinziegenfelder Tal enables the traveller to stop briefly in **Weismain** with its beautiful Renaissance *Rathaus*, or in **Arnstein** with the Catholic parish church of St Nikolaus (1732–4). The charms of the countryside have attracted many artists and people of leisure with a taste for good living. Fürst Pückler, creator of famous gardens and gourmet of repute, found 'trout, cherries and crayfish nowhere better than in **Muggendorf**', a delightful little town and health resort which can still provide a memorable meal. The charming valley of the River Wiesent with derelict water mills, narrow gorges, rocky cliffs topped by grim castles, caverns, towns and villages and fine old *Gasthöfe* is an experience in itself. The pilgrimage church of **Gössweinstein** was built by Neumann around 1730. Apart from the religious significance, the delightful stucco — now in new delicate colours — and the early rococo sculptures attract art lovers from all over the world.

The crenellated Burg Gössweinstein nearby is thought by some to have been the inspiration for the Gralsburg in Wagner's *Parsifal*. The castle is occupied, but from time to time, the Rittersaal (Knights' Hall) is thrown open for musical entertainment.

Pottenstein is another charming little town nestling under steep cliffs. An annual spectacle takes place on the festival of the Three Kings, 6 January, when there is a torchlight procession and the hills and cliffs all round are ablaze with bonfires and a sea of flickering light from thousands of torches. Close to Gössweinstein, the *Luftkurort* of **Behringersmühle** on the River Wiesent is beautifully situated among hills and woods at the convergence of four valleys.

An interesting 15km (9 mile) walk from here also takes in Gössweinstein and Pottenstein. From the Hotel Stern, walk along the Promenadenweg above the Wiesent (waymark red X) to the Gasthof Stempfermühle. In front of the *Gasthof* a well kept path with serpentine curves (waymark blue dot) goes off to the left and leads through woods with rocky outcrops to the car park at Gössweinstein. Two hundred metres along the main street is the great basilica. The Pottenstein road is then followed down to the end of the village to a filling station where the *Wanderweg* (vertical blue stripe) goes off to the left. After passing a *Waldcafé* continue through the hamlet of **Bösenbirkig** at the south end of which the path goes sharp left to quickly reach tiny **Hühnerloh**. Cross a road and enter the wood again. About 100m later, watch for the waymark where the path goes left into a small forest track and follow it until it crosses a little road. The path goes through fields for about 200m and then along the edge of a wood. A gentle climb leads to the hill, the Kreuzberg, with its Kreuzigungskapelle above Pottenstein. There is a wonderful view here into the Püttlachtal and down on to Pottenstein .

Behind the Catholic church there is a steep path (350 steps) up to the Teufelshöhle, splendid caves with stalactites and stalagmites, the biggest in the Fränkische Schweiz and well worth a visit. Leave the town on the Behringersmühle road (B470) and in about 250m turn left onto a beautiful path (red X), past the Bärenschlucht (ravine) with its camping place and in about 4km reach **Tüchersfeld**, sometimes called the 'Rock Village of the Fränkische Schweiz' with its impressive cliffs reminiscent of the Dolomites and houses perched in apparently precarious situations. Below the mill, cross the B470 and in about 150m bear right into the continuation of the *Wanderweg* following the red X back into Behringersmühle. The map for this area is the Fritsch edition, 1:50,000 *Innere Fränkische Schweiz*.

Between Behringersmühle and **Ebermannstadt** to the west, 16km of former Federal line has been taken over by a railway preservation society, making it possible once more to travel by train through part of the delightful Wiesenttal.

A large variety of animals and birds in natural surroundings can be found in the **Hundshaupten** *Wildgehege* 10km south of the B470 and midway between the A73 and A9 motorways. Close to the **Plech** exit on the A9 is the Fränkisches Wunderland, a leisure park with many different amusements for the family — fairy-tale themes, a miniature railway, Wild West scenes, a *Rodelbahn* and so on. Another similar place is the Familien-Freizeitpark Schloss Thurn at **Heroldsbach** near Forchheim westwards along the B470.

Near the south end of the Fränkische Schweiz is **Nürnberg**, the Franconian metropolis, with well over half a million inhabitants and the second city in Bavaria. The visitor would find no difficulty in spending many days sightseeing here, visiting the numerous museums, enjoying the gastronomic specialities of the area or just wandering through the old streets, now beautifully restored from the destruction of World War II. Only a small selection of Nürnberg's many attractions is mentioned here. Comprehensive lists of museums, etc are available from the Tourist Information Office.

The well known *Nürnberger Lebkuchen*, spicy little cakes or biscuits, come in many guises and are exported the world over in all sorts of attractive containers. The city has long been known as a toy-making centre and there is an annual fair. The Spielzeugmuseum (Toy Museum) is a wonderful experience, while the Verkehrsmuseum (Transport Museum) is Germany's foremost exhibition of transport — especially railway — and postal history. The first railway in Germany, between Nürnberg and Fürth, was opened in 1835 using the locomotive *Adler*, built by George Stephenson in Newcastle-upon-Tyne, England. The original engine no longer exists but the museum has an excellent replica. That railway may be travelled on in miniature Easter-October in the excellent zoo in Nürnberg.

Art lovers may visit the Albrecht Dürer House built in 1450–60 in the Gothic style where the artist lived during 1509–28. The National Museum exhibits German art and cultural history from prehistoric times to the present. Significant churches in Nürnberg include St Sebaldus (Protestant) (1230–40) restored after almost complete destruction as an object lesson on the futility of war. St Lorenz, also Protestant, was begun in the thirteenth century and like St Sebaldus, has many important art works . The Catholic Frauenkirche was built on the site of an old synagogue which had been destroyed along with the Jewish quarter in the fourteenth century. Kaiser Karl V made the present building his court church in 1355.

The *Christkindlmarkt*, founded in 1639, is Germany's oldest Christmas market. It begins on the Friday nearest to St Barbara's Day (4 December) and remains open until Christmas Eve. Every two years a 'Christ Child' is chosen to open the market by reciting, from the outside gallery of the Frauenkirche, a prologue accompanied by festive music and church bells. Nürnberg at this season, is very crowded.

To the south and south-west of Nürnberg within a distance of about 40km (25 miles) lies the Neue Fränkische Seenland, or New Franconian Lake District. Several large reservoirs have been created which, in addition to their primary purpose, provide extensive areas for swimming (with grassy slopes for sunbathing), sailing and surfing, while footpaths and cycle tracks (with cycle hire) encircle the lakes. The first-class facilities include restaurants, cafés, toilets, changing rooms, showers, etc. Nearest to Nürnberg is the Kleiner Rothsee only 2.4km long, and the Grosser Rothsee more than three times as big with an area of 170ha (420 acres). These are reached via B2 and the little town of **Roth**. Next are the two Brombachseen (via B2 and **Pleinfeld**) — the smaller has an area of 250ha (620 acres) and is encircled by an 8.5km long cycle track. The larger lake, currently under construction, will have an area of 950ha (2,355 acres). West of

The market place, Nürnberg, with the Frauenkirche

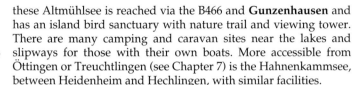

these Altmühlsee is reached via the B466 and **Gunzenhausen** and has an island bird sanctuary with nature trail and viewing tower. There are many camping and caravan sites near the lakes and slipways for those with their own boats. More accessible from Öttingen or Treuchtlingen (see Chapter 7) is the Hahnenkammsee, between Heidenheim and Hechlingen, with similar facilities.

North from Nürnberg, the A73 provides a speedy means of reaching **Bamberg** 63km (39 miles) away. Bamberg (population 80,000) escaped relatively unscathed from World War II and now has probably the finest concentration of historic buildings in original condition in Bavaria. One can wander happily through the streets and alleys but it is a pity to visit Bamberg without spending some time enjoying the various works of art and architecture. As in other towns, it is best on foot and a suitable circuit can be started at the Löwenbrücke (Lion Bridge) over the right arm of the River Regnitz. The motorist can park in the nearby Weidendamm *Parkplatz*: the rail traveller should walk west from the station to reach the bridge. From here Markusstrasse runs directly to the Markusbrücke over the left Regnitz arm in about 400m. From the bridge, to the left, is so-called Klein Venedig (Little Venice) with the colourful backs of old fishermen's houses on the water's edge, a favourite photographer's scene.

Over the bridge turn left into Sandstrasse and into the first alley on the right (Schrottenberggasse). In Ottoplatz, turn right again and keep bearing right up to the Michaelsberg. Continue forward along the left side of the church for a fine view over the Bamberg basin. Turn back to leave the Michaelsberg via Storchsgasse and then left down Jacobsberg when this is reached. Go through an arch and to the right in front of the archbishop's palace to explore a quiet medieval area of ivy-clad and timbered buildings, the canons' houses where time seems to have stood still. A gateway leads to the inner courtyard of the Alte Hofhaltung (Residenz) and out into a wide square with architecture hardly equalled in Europe. Here is the great cathedral of Emperor Heinrich II, with the new Residenz opposite.

Continue through the Judenstrasse at the end of which, on the right, is the charming patrician Böttingerhaus. The Palais Concordia is to the right in its town park laid out in the so-called 'English' style. The Alter Ebracher Hof is the former town residence of the bishops of Ebrach. Go left to the river at the Nonnenbrücke but turn left along the bank of the old King Ludwig I canal back towards the town centre. The Regnitz water still foams around the bottoms of old mills and, turning right to cross the river, is one of the most photographed buildings in northern Bavaria, the old town hall perched on a tiny island in the river, with bridges either side and the road passing through the middle of the building. To the left, 'Little Venice' can be seen from the opposite direction. Walk through Grüner Markt past the Maxplatz to the end of Kleberstrasse. Opposite is the information office. The Weidendamm *Parkplatz* is reached by turning left through Kleberstrasse. The 1½ hours or so needed for this walk do not allow time for visiting the cathedral or other notable buildings.

The thirteenth-century *Dom* owes its fame largely to its series of sculptures and its portals. It is a three-aisled basilica with four towers, a typical Romanesque building with choirs in the east and west. The most famous sculpture is the *Bamberger Reiter* (Bamberg Horseman). In front of the east choir the double sarcophagus of Emperor Heinrich and Empress Kunigunde (1499–1513) by Tilman Riemenscheider is in late Gothic style. The Bamberg altar (1520–5) in natural wood is by Veit Stoss. The church of St Michael on the Michaelsberg was built in 1121. The present west façade was erected in 1696 in front of the towers and in 1723 the wide steps and balustraded terrace were added. The vaulted ceiling is painted with the 'botanical garden', pictures of over 600 native and foreign plants, and is the outstanding feature of the church.

The Diocesan Museum at Domplatz 5 contains the many treasures of the cathedral and other relics of early Christianity. The collection of medieval textiles is of particular significance. The Karl-May Museum has a room representing the famous author's study which forms the basis of the little museum. In the Alte Hofhaltung at Domplatz 7, the impressive rooms of the Renaissance building are the home of the Historisches Museum which exhibits the history of Bamberg and its surroundings from the Stone Age to this century.

The Neue Residenz (1697–1703) was one of the first palaces built in Germany in the baroque style. In addition to having richly furnished rooms with valuable furniture it houses part of the Bavarian State Art Collection.

Bamberg, like that other Franconian city Rothenburg, is an essential element of the Bavarian experience and the first time visitor should plan his itinerary to include at least one of these places.

At **Pommersfelden**, 19km (12 miles) south of Bamberg, at the foot of the slopes of the Steigerwald stands the enormous palace known as Schloss Weissenstein. There is the story that Prince-Bishop Lothar Franz von Schönborn himself designed the spectacular entrance hall and staircase with its fine balustrades, lanterns supported by exquisite cherubs and so on. He then demanded that the architect compose the rest of the palace around his masterpiece. However, it is with music that Weissenstein has come to be mainly associated. Dr Karl Graf Schönborn founded his 'Bach weeks' here (later transferred to

Ansbach) and the establishment of the Collegium Musicum Schloss Pommersfelden ensured international recognition. Much of the *Schloss* is open to visitors. At the close of the academic year the splendid marble hall becomes the venue for public concerts when the students display their talents.

A walk of about 15km (9 miles) begins at the motorway service area *Rasthaus Steigerwald* on the A3 some 40km (25 miles) north-west of Nürnberg. Go north-eastwards from the service area and in about 500m the roofs of **Weingratsgreuth** village come into view. By the first houses follow the *Wanderweg* to the right (SE) towards the *Autobahn* but before reaching it turn sharp left onto a footpath northwards through a wood to **Horbach.** From here a minor road leads to nearby **Simmersdorf**; before this village turn right into a footpath to reach another minor road for the kilometre or so to **Mühlhausen.** The little River Reiche Ebrach is seen from time to time on the left. Go into the centre of Mühlhausen, crossing over the river, and turn right to leave it again (do not cross the railway) and after passing the last house, turn left into a footpath over meadows to Lempenmühle — a water mill. Here, the Reiche Ebrach is crossed again and the route continues east towards Schloss Weissenstein, soon seen in the distance and reached in about 7km from the start.

The Altmühlsee is popular for bathing and boating

After visiting the *Schloss* turn left along a footpath which more or less follows the park wall and then joins a minor road into **Limbach** in a very few minutes. Follow the road and leave the village mostly to the left; the road swings gently left when about level with the last houses but leave the road and follow a footpath straight ahead (S-SE) towards a wood. The wood goes right up to the *Autobahn* but the path curves to the right to take a westerly direction towards **Schirnsdorf**. About 500m after this village go left into a footpath through woods and meadows back to Weingratsgreuth and to the starting point.

Bamberg lies at one point of the rough triangle which encloses the Hassberge to the north-west, a small area of soft, peaceful hills. The other corners lie at Schweinfurt and Bad Königshofen. There is a whole string of little towns with unspoiled images of old Franconian half-timbered houses. The motorist could see some of the most attractive by making a tour from **Hassfurt** on the Main, north to **Königsberg, Hofheim** and **Bad Königshofen**, returning via **Ebern, Baunach** and **Zeil am Main**. Königsberg is particularly fine; Bad Königshofen is another new spa. In Hassfurt the principal, although not the only sight, is the late Gothic Catholic Ritterkapelle (Knights' Chapel) of St Maria built for the Franconian nobility at about the same time as the nearby parish church of St Kilian. The choir has a three-tiered frieze of 248 coats of arms of the knightly noblemen. The many fine works of art in St Kilian include a wooden figure of John the Baptist by Riemenscheider. Zeil am Main has many proud houses and the commanding sixteenth-century *Rathaus*, while nearby on the south side of the river the outstanding pilgrimage church Maria Limbach (1751–5) is well worth making a slight detour to see.

The Hassberge is, above all, an ideal rambling area with a remarkable network of paths, many of which are designed to lead the walker to the dozen or so historic ruined castles or the thirty-five *Schlösser*. The open-air enthusiast will be happy near the Ellertshäuser See, a little lake with provision for swimming, sailing, angling and other water activities. Not yet a victim of mass tourism, the Hassberge can be recommended as a district for those seeking a peaceful holiday location. As in the Fränkische Schweiz the altitude in the Hassberge rarely exceeds 500m (1,640ft), but in the north-west of Franconia, is the Bayerische Rhön whose more significant summits include the Dammersfeldkuppe and the Kreuzberg, both 928m (3,044ft). The many health resorts in the area include the spas of Bad Kissingen, Bad Bocklet, Bad Neustadt and Bad Brückenau.

The healing properties of the **Bad Kissingen** waters have been known at least since the ninth century but it was not until the sixteenth that it developed as a resort. The distinguished buildings of the *Kur* quarter were begun in 1834 and gradually extended along the River Saale, the final elements not being added until 1913.

The late sixteenth-century Altes Rathaus and the Neues Rathaus of 1709 are of interest. Kissingen (population 25,000) is a classic spa and has a casino, a theatre for opera or drama and many other entertainments. The visitor can take an excursion by genuine old post coach to Schloss Aschach. Passengers experience the unusual motion of this ancient vehicle and the accompanying sounds of hoofbeats and the rattle of harness as they roll along the avenues.

In **Aschach** there are some *Bildstöcke* (poles surmounted by a portrayal of the Virgin or a saint) said to be among the finest examples of this custom in Franconia. The arrival of the post coach at the *Schloss* is quite spectacular as it draws up before the external staircase of the castle to the sound of the post-horn. The *Schloss* contains a rich art collection — furniture, glass, paintings, carpets, ceramics and so on. A visit is recommended.

North-east of Bad Kissingen on the B19 is **Münnerstadt** with its well preserved medieval townscape, defensive walls and fine entrance towers from the mid-thirteenth century. Old half-timbered houses with pointed gables surround the Marktplatz with its late Gothic *Rathaus*. The little town has some significant historical gems, like the Catholic parish church of St Mary Magdalena which has the great Magdalenenaltar of 1492 by Riemenscheider and Veit Stoss, and excellent glass in the choir windows (about 1420–50). The rococo church (1752–4) of the former *Kloster* of the Augustinian hermits also has its treasures, in particular the altar and pulpit.

Nearby the popular resort of **Bad Neustadt** (population 13,500) has become an important north Franconian centre. Remains of the town's defensive walls can be seen and the former Carmelite *Klosterkirche*, St Petrus and Paulus (fourteenth century) near the *Rathaus* is worth seeing for its good interior fitments, especially the rococo pulpit from around 1750.

On the north-west fringe of the Rhön, close to the A7, is **Bad Brückenau**. It too has a long history as a spa and its waters are noted for the broad spectrum of complaints they benefit. A disastrous fire in 1876 almost completely destroyed the town which is thus poor in historic architecture. This is compensated for by the modern *Kur* developments started after 1900 and the resort today can offer its guests every comfort and convenience and a varied programme of leisure activities.

The principal resorts have been mentioned but for the foreign tourist the many smaller towns and villages have a lot to offer. In the

Rhön, as indeed in all Franconia, there are many walking possibilities. A comprehensive booklet *Wandern in Franken* is available from the main tourist office in Nürnberg. There is a corresponding publication for cyclists, *Radeln in Franken*.

There are many small places of interest along the B22 between Bamberg and Würzburg. **Ebrach** with its former Cistercian monastery church — one of the largest built by the order in Germany — and the *Kloster* building is most attractive. Excellent local dishes and fine wines are to be had in the small restaurant in the former station. **Prichsenstadt** lies just off the B22 on the B286 and presents a remarkably unspoiled medieval townscape with walls and towers. Further west on the B22 and now approaching Würzburg, **Dettelbach** is another little gem which should on no account be missed.

Close to the A8, midway between Erlangen and Würzburg, is the pleasure park Freizeit-Land Geiselwind, reached by the *Autobahn* exit **Geiselwind**. There are exotic birds, highland cattle, prehistoric monsters, a model exhibition, a model railway and a 'Wild West' train for children — just a few of the dozens of attractions here.

The Franconian vineyards are mostly to be found along the valley of the Main, and **Volkach**, some 20km east of Würzburg, is in the heart of them. The village is Bavaria's largest wine community and holds the principal wine festival in the state, in mid-August. This is when the Bavarian wine-queen for a year is chosen and crowned.

On the outskirts of the village, the little pilgrimage church of Maria im Weingarten rises from the vineyards, reached by a track marked by the Stations of the Cross. One of the treasures of this church is a famous limewood Madonna, again by Riemenscheider. This was taken hostage some years ago and only retrieved from the thieves by payment of a ransom of 100,000 Marks. Twenty kilometres down the Main, **Kitzingen**, with more than 18,000 inhabitants, is another place connected with the wine trade. Its landmark is the Falterturm, a tower with a crooked cupola. It now stands over a museum dedicated to the carnival tradition, only open at the weekend however.

The fifteenth-century Catholic parish church of St Johannes is a three-aisled hall church; the figure-decorated tabernacle, the beautiful choir-stalls and the late Gothic frescos are notable. The baroque seventeenth-century Protestant parish church should also be seen with, east of the river, the Kapelle Heiligkreuz (1741–5). A pleasant stroll is along the flower-bedecked promenade on the river bank. South-eastwards 8km (5 miles) along the B5 the charming vineyard village of **Iphofen** is well worth a visit.

Sulzfeld, about 5km from Kitzingen, on what for the moment is the west bank, is an unspoiled wine village where it seems as if almost every house is adorned with figures from the Bible. The church of St Sebastian, with its *Ölberg* (the scene on the Mount of Olives) outside, is worth the short climb. The wine festival here takes place the first weekend in August.

Downstream again, in a few kilometres is **Marktbreit** (population 3,500) on the other bank, one of the best examples of a romantic German town. In the Middle Ages there was a busy inland harbour and later it was an important European trading centre for coffee. The remains of the old commercial harbour, the warehouse and the treadwheel crane of 1773 are to be seen beside the river. The *Rathaus* dates from 1579 and is complemented by two fine patrician houses. The Hotel-Löwen (Lion) of 1450 has a splendid half-timbered façade and claims to be the second oldest *Gasthaus* in Bavaria. Afternoon coffee and cake in the Löwen can be highly recommended.

On the same bank, the lovely town of **Ochsenfurt**, with a population of around 13,000, has much for the visitor to see. Some of the narrow streets do not favour the motorist but there is ample free parking space a few minutes away beside the river. The general view of the town with its old walls, towers and timbered houses makes a

Iphofen

lasting impression. One of the towers, the Klingenturm is now a youth hostel. The Catholic church of St Andreas was built over a period from 1288 until the late fifteenth century. There is an extremely high nave and lavish tracery is a dominant feature of the interior; there is an excellent wooden figure of St Nikolaus.

The late Gothic *Rathaus* (1488–99) is one of the finest in Franconia. The clock tower with its comical figures has a mechanism dating from 1560 and is the unofficial emblem of the town. Ochsenfurt celebrates a number of local festivals including, from Easter Sunday until the following one, the *Frühlingsfest* (Spring Festival) on the Festplatz near the old Main bridge with fairground and firework displays and at Whitsun, the Sausage Festival — *Bratwurstfest* — when traditional Franconian costumes can be seen. On Whit Sunday every odd year there is *St Wolfgangs-Ritt* with a traditional procession of horses to St Wolfgangs-Kapelle. Usually on a mid-July weekend there is the street wine festival which is held mainly on the bank of the Main. During the first weekend in September, the town centre is closed to traffic for the roasting of an ox — it features on the town's coat of arms — and the *Altstadtfest* (Old Town Festival). The last September weekend sees a three-day autumn fair with a big programme of entertainments and the year ends with the Christmas celebrations when the old town is decorated and illuminated.

Across the river and a little way upstream is the exceedingly picturesque wine village of **Frickenhausen** with its encircling walls and four entrance towers. The late Gothic *Rathaus* has an original external staircase and there is a memorial to St Kilian nearby. The wine festival takes place the second weekend in August.

Downstream the river now heads north, but before reaching Würzburg, there are several more vineyard village resorts. **Sommerhausen** has its wine festival during the first week of June and a church festival with costume procession at the beginning of August. The village is sometimes compared with Rothenburg and with some justification. The fifteenth-century *Schloss* and two fountains known as 'Katharina' and 'Hansjörg' embellish the main street. **Eibelstadt** has similar festivals, wine mid-June and church the second weekend in August. The late baroque *Rathaus* (1706) presides over a town centre of great charm.

West of Würzburg is the area called Spessart and the visitor might well visit one or two places of interest here. The River Main still has a great influence on the landscape and a short distance upstream from **Marktheidenfeld** is **Rothenfels**, a small town with a long history. It was already documented in 1050 and by 1148 a castle had been built on the *roten Felsen* (red cliffs) above and still dominates the skyline today. It is now one of the largest youth hostels in Germany. Despite the traffic passing through, the town has retained its medieval character, with wrought-iron inn signs, narrow alleys and religious figures on some house fronts.

A pleasant walk of around 12.5km (8 miles) starts from the castle in a westerly direction through open country (waymark blue circle) to the Hainmarter, a modest ridge of 275m (900ft) where there is a wayside shrine and fine views up and down the River Main. The path curves to the right to run roughly north-west for nearly 2km through pretty woods. Descend into the Hafenlohrtal and on reaching the valley, turn left to cross the little River Hafenlohr and the main road and immediately turn right to resume the north-west direction up through the woods. Curving left, by the time Jagdschlösschen (Little Hunting Lodge) Karlshöhe is reached in about 2.5km from the river and road, the route is going due south. The lodge is in a woodland clearing and the forester's house here conceals a neat little *Gaststätte*. From here, walk south-east in a dead straight line for a good 3km until the marked path branches off to the left for the very steep descent back into the Hafenlohrtal.

On the main road is the Hotel Sankt Hubertus, the famous 'Wirtshaus im Spessart' known through the story and film of that name, and another film *Das Spukschloss* (Haunted Castle) *im Spessart*. This hostelry is highly recommended for a break as the walk nears its end; it is almost a little museum with historical objects the landlord has gathered together. The wayside shrine of St Hubertus outside the door is more than 300 years old and the doorway itself deserves special note. The objects of interest are listed on the menu which becomes a sort of visitor's guide to the Wirtshaus. From the hotel continue half-left over the river and steeply up through the woods north-easterly to open ground and directly back to Rothenfels.

The B8 westwards from Marktheidenfeld is a picturesque road and the parallel A3 has some striking views. About 60km (37 miles) from Würzburg (Weibersbrunn exit) is the much-visited Wasserschloss **Mespelbrunn** (fifteenth century). In its pretty wooded surroundings it is just made for the photographer. The Rittersaal (Knights' Hall) reached from the small courtyard is the principal room on the ground floor. Above, the Gobelinensaal contains a famous Gobelin tapestry from 1564. The Chinese salon and other rooms with interesting furnishings are open to view.

South on another great bend in the Main, the little town of **Miltenberg** is one of the gems of Bavaria and another 'must' for the visitor. That it is one of the most photographed towns in Germany speaks for itself. The superb Marktplatz is often thronged with sightseers but there are many other less busy attractive corners. The fine half-timbered buildings, which include the famous Gasthaus zum Riesen (The Giant) claiming to be one of the oldest hostelries in Germany, having been in use as early as 1504. From the Riesen through the long main street to the Marktplatz is a pedestrian zone. Car parking is available along the Main river front which is a hive of activity with steamers and small pleasure craft.

Ten kilometres south on the B469, little **Amorbach** is an essentially baroque town, the outstanding sight in which is the former Benedictine abbey church of St Maria, founded by Abbot St Amor in 734. In 1742 the old basilica was demolished except for the twelfth-century towers, and baroque rebuilding was completed in 1747. Secularisation in 1803 took it out of the hands of the Roman Catholic church and it is now the Protestant parish church. Rococo decorations on walls and ceiling are by the Wessobrunn school. Of particular note are the wrought-iron railings between the nave and the transept and the organ built in 1774–82. The Catholic parish church of St Gangolf (1752–4) is also very fine and it too has a lovely organ on which recitals are given from time to time. Amorbach also has connections with British royalty. After the death of her husband in 1814, Marie Louise Victoria (daughter of Francis, Duke of Saxe-Coburg-Saalfeld) travelled to England in 1817 to marry Edward, Duke of Kent and thus became Duchess of Kent. Their daughter was also given the name Victoria and became Queen of England in 1837.

A short excursion could be made westwards from Amorbach to the village of **Würzberg** (not to be confused with Würzburg) in the Odenwald, right on the Bavarian border and on the line of the Roman defensive wall, the Limes, mentioned earlier.

The Gasthaus zum Adler (*Ruhetag* Tuesday) is recommended for a meal and from here, a short way into the forest, are the restored remains of a Roman bath and other relics. The forest road leads through a wild boar park until, near the village of **Hesseneck**, an insignificant monument among the trees marks another 'three countries corner' where the former independent Kingdom of Bavaria and the Grand Duchies of Baden and Hessen met.

From Miltenberg, the Main turns northwards towards **Aschaffenburg** (population 60,000) where the red sandstone façade of the Johannisburg (1605–14) dominates the scene. It can be reached along the tree-lined path of the broad old fortification wall; the yacht harbour below adds a touch of gaiety to the scene.

Three times a day the carillon from the castle tower sends a joyful baroque sound over the town. The *Schloss* houses a fine collection of works of art including the town collection of paintings. Just beyond, the yellow profile of the Pompejanum enhances the skyline. The Pompejanum was another romantic idea of King Ludwig I who had it erected in 1840 as a copy of the villa of Castor and Pollux excavated in Pompeii. The building has friezes of classical symmetry and Mediterranean-style gardens; ivy-clad conifers, fountains and statues in rose beds ornament the vineyard sloping down to the river.

The modern *Rathaus* is in contrast to a few veteran half-timbered buildings. Here in the heart of the town is the 1,000-year-old Stiftskirche St Peter and Alexander with Norman cloisters. Inside there is the famous and startling painting *Beweinung Christi* by Matthias Grünewald. Three kilometres away across the river is Schönbusch with classically landscaped gardens, a *Schloss*, temples and lakes. The Hotel Post was a royal Bavarian 'Post Station' used by the princes of Thurn and Taxis for their postal service mentioned earlier.

The Gasthaus zum Riesen in Miltenberg claims to be one of the oldest inns in Germany

Aschaffenburg is the terminal for river cruises between here and ⚓ Nürnberg and occasionally to Mainz. Usually of 9–11 days duration some are purely pleasure cruises while others are study tours with a theme such as 'Franconia's Hidden Treasures' or 'On the Trail of Tilman Riemenschneider'. The cruise prices include travel, accommodation in good hotels, meals and excursions. Those who have enjoyed the better-known Rhein cruises will almost certainly enjoy these on the Main equally well, with the beautiful scenery and visits to historic towns. The completion of the Rhein-Main-Donau-Kanal now makes possible voyages to Passau, Linz and Wien (Vienna).

Additional Information

Places to Visit

Aschaffenburg
Schloss Johannisburg
Open: Tuesday to Sunday, April to September 9-11.30am, 1-4.30pm, October to March 10-11.30am, 1-3.30pm. Closed 1 January, Shrove Tuesday, 1 November, 24, 25, 31 December. Wine bar.

Schloss Schönbusch
Open: Tuesday to Sunday, April to September, 9.30am-12.30pm, 2-4.30pm. Restaurant.

Bamberg
Diözesanmuseum
Domplatz 5
96049 Bamberg
☎ 0951-5021
Open: Easter to October, Monday to Friday 10am-12noon, 2.30-6pm, Saturday 9am-1pm, Sunday 10am-1pm. Accompanied children free.

Neue Residenz and Art Gallery
Open: daily 9am-12noon, 1.30-5pm (4pm October to March). Café in rose garden (closed in winter). Closed 1 January, Shrove Tuesday, 1 November, 24, 25, 31 December.

Coburg
Schloss Ehrenburg
Open: Tuesday to Sunday 10am-12noon, 1-5.30pm (4.30pm in winter). Closed 1 January, Shrove Tuesday, 1 November, 24, 25, 31 December.

Veste Coburg
☎ 09561-95055
Open: April to October daily 9.30am-1pm, 2-5pm. November to March Tuesday to Sunday 2-5pm. Museum and Art Gallery. Restaurant, inn and café.

Trachtenpuppen-Museum
Hindenburgplatz
96465 Neustadt bei Coburg
☎ 09568-5600
Open: 15 March to 15 October, Tuesday to Sunday 9am-6pm.

Egglofstein
Wildgehege Hundshaupten
91349 Egglofstein (Fränkische Schweiz)
☎ 09197-241
Open: April to October daily 9am-5pm, November to March, Saturday, Sunday and holidays 11am-3pm. Children under 5 free. Facilities for disabled. Refreshments.

Kulmbach

Deutsches Zinnfigurenmuseum
Plassenburg
95326 Kulmbach
☎ 09221-5550
Open: Tuesday to Sunday, 10am-4pm (3.30pm October to March).

Plassenburg
Open: Tuesday to Sunday 10am-5pm (3pm in winter). Closed 1 January, Shrove Tuesday, 1 November, 24, 25, 31 December. Paintings and hunt weapons. Inn (closed December to February).

Michelau

Deutsches Korbmuseum
Bismarckstrasse 4
96247 Michelau
☎ 09571-8046 or 88246
Open: Monday to Friday 9am-12noon, 1-4pm. Saturday and Sunday by arrangement.

Lauenstein

Burg
Open: Tuesday to Sunday, April to September 9am-12noon, 1-5pm. October to March 10am-12noon, 1-3.30pm. Closed 1 January, Shrove Tuesday, 1 November, 24, 25, 31 December. Burghotel with accommodation.

Mespelbrunn

Wasserschloss
Open: Monday to Saturday 9am-12noon, 1-5pm, Sunday 9am-5pm. Restaurant nearby.

Nürnberg

Spielzeugmuseum
Karlstrasse 13-15
90403 Nürnberg
☎ 0911-2313164
Open: Tuesday to Sunday 10am-5pm (9pm Wednesday).

Verkehrsmuseum
Lessingstrasse 6
90443 Nürnberg
☎ 0911-2192428
Open: daily 9.30am-5pm (4pm October to March). Holiday arrangements publicised locally.

There are many more museums in Nürnberg — brochure from Tourist Information Office.

Nürnberger Tiergarten
90480 Nürnberg
☎ 0911-571348
4km E of city centre
Open: daily March to October 8am-sunset, November to February 9am-sunset. Additional charge for dolphinarium. Restaurant and bars.

Leisure Centres

Geiselwind

Freizeit-Land
96160 Geiselwind
☎ 09556-234 or 357
Open: daily from around Easter to mid-September 9am-6pm then weather permitting Saturday, Sunday and holidays until end October. Café, restaurant, bars, etc.

Heroldsbach

Familien-Freizeitpark
Schloss Thurn
91336 Heroldsbach bei Forchheim
☎ 09190-555
Open: daily April to October 9am-5pm. Restaurant, wine-tasting.

Plech

Fränkisches Wunderland
Freizeitpark
91287 Plech
☎ 09244-451
Open: daily Easter to October 9am-6pm. Café.

Local Festival

Pottenstein

6 January — Festival of The Three
Kings
Unusual spectacle with torchlight
procession and surrounding hills
ablaze with bonfires and lights.

Long Distance Paths

*Entlang Der Fränkischen Saale und
Sinn* (112km/70 miles)
Circular route Bad Kissingen,
Hammelburg, Bad Bocklet, Bad
Kissingen

Quer durch die Rhön (225km/141
miles)
Circular route Fladungen, Bad
Neustadt, Bad Bocklet, Bad
Kissingen, Fladungen. *Wandern
ohne Gepäck* (Hiking without
luggage) arrangements possible.

Details for both above and other
walks available from
Tourist Information Rhön,
Landratsamt,
97616 Bad Neustadt.

Steam and Tourist Railways

Ebermannstadt-Behringersmühle
Dampfbahn Fränkische Schweiz eV
Postfach 1
91320 Ebermannstadt
☎ 09131-65873
Operates steam passenger trains
Easter to September usually on two
Sundays each month. Connections
from Forchheim by DB bus.
Reductions for families and those
staying locally (with *Kurkarte*)

Neuenmarkt
Deutsches Dampflokomotiv-Museum
Zweckverband DDM
95339 Neuenmarkt
☎ 09227-5700

Open: May to October Tuesday to
Friday 9am-12noon, 1-5pm,
Saturday and Sunday 10am-5pm,
November to April Tuesday,
Friday, Saturday and Sunday
10am-12noon, 1-4pm.
Narrow-gauge railway in operation
May to October with steam and
diesel traction.

Nürnberg
In the Tiergarten (Zoo)
Easter to October. Miniature
passenger-carrying replica of first
German railway, which ran
between Nürnberg and Fürth.

*In the Verkehrsmuseum (Transport
Museum)*
Extensive display of rail vehicles,
etc. Model railway.

*In the Spielzeugmuseum (Toy
museum)*
Large model railway layout.

Tourist Information Centres

Fremdenverkehrsverband-Franken
Am Plärrer 14
90408 Nürnberg
☎ 0911-264202
General information about
Franconia.

For local detail, accommodation
lists, etc write to 'Tourist Information' giving postcode and name of
town:

63196 Amorbach
63739 Aschaffenburg
97769 Bad Brückenau
97688 Bad Kissingen
97631 Bad Königshofen
97616 Bad Neustadt
96047 Bamberg
96450 Coburg
91327 Gössweinstein

91703 Gunzenhausen (For Neues
   Fränkische Seenland)
97437 Hassfurt
97318 Kitzingen
95326 Kulmbach
97340 Marktbreit
63875 Mespelbrunn

63897 Miltenberg
97702 Münnerstadt
95339 Neuenmarkt
90403 Nürnberg
97199 Ochsenfurt
91278 Pottenstein
97332 Volkach

Bavaria Fact File

Note: The postcode for German addresses appears immediately before the place name, eg 93059 Regensburg. To telephone Bavaria from the UK, dial 010-49- then omit the first '0' of the phone code.

Accommodation

Accommodation is available throughout Bavaria in hotels, inns, *pensions,* private houses, farmhouses, holiday flats or houses, youth hostels and camp sites. Accommodation lists for the principal resorts are obtainable from German National Tourist Offices (GNTO) overseas but often exclude private houses, farms, holiday flats and camp sites. More detailed lists which include these may be requested from the local tourist information office.

Once there, accommodation in private houses is often indicated by a sign *Zimmer frei* (rooms available). A holiday flat to let can be recognised by a notice *Ferienwohnung zu vermieten.* Inns and *pensions* may display a sign *Fremdenzimmer* to show that they have rooms for casual guests. A comprehensive book *Urlaub auf dem Bauernhof* (Holidays on the Farm) should be available from GNTOs or in case of difficulty write to local offices. Some of the 'farms' are really riding schools and others cater for unaccompanied children, usually from 10 years upwards.

Self-catering accommodation is widely available in farmhouses and elsewhere. There are numerous camping and caravan sites. Advance booking is advisable in the summer months and this also applies to the many youth hostels. Here is a list of useful terms.

Aufenthaltsraum — lounge; sitting-room
Bad — bath
Bauernhof — farm
Doppelzimmer (Dz) — double room
Dusche — shower
Einzelhof — isolated farm, ie not in a village
Einzelzimmer (Ez) — single room
Endreinigung — cleaning after departure of visitor from self-catering accommodation
Feriendorf — holiday village, usually with purpose-built bungalows
Ferienhaus/Ferienwohnung (Fewo) — holiday house or flat

Fernseher — television
Frühstück — breakfast
Gasthaus — restaurant, inn, tavern
Gasthof — hotel or inn
Halbpension (HP) — half-board
Hotel-garni — hotel which does not serve meals (except breakfast)
Kinderermässigung — reductions for children
Mehrbettzimmer (Mz) — family room
Nebenkosten — extras
Pension — boarding house; board and lodging
Ruhige Lage — peaceful situation
Strom — electricity
Übernachtung mit Frühstück (ÜmF) — bed and breakfast
Unterkunftsverzeichnis — Accommodation list
Vollpension (VP) — full-board
Vor- und Nachsaison (VN) — outside the main holiday season
Wirtshaus — inn or public house
Zentralheizung — central heating
Zimmer frei/besetzt — Vacancies/No vacancies

The German Hotel Reservation System (ADZ) is a department of the German National Tourist Board through which accommodation can be booked in all hotels and boarding houses. Contact:
DZT-Serviceabteilung ADZ
Corneliusstrasse 34, 60325 Frankfurt
☎ (069) 740767

Banks & Post Offices

Banks are usually open weekdays 8.30am-1pm and from 2.30-4pm (Thursday to 5.30pm). They are closed at weekends.

The Deutsche Verkehrsbank has branches in railway stations of most main cities and are sometimes open all week and until quite late in the evening.

Post Offices (die Post) are usually open Monday to Friday 8am-6pm, Saturdays 8am-12noon. At railway stations in larger cities they are open during the week until late in the evening. Post offices can also change currency.

Business Hours

Shop opening times vary but in general they are open between

9am-6.30pm during the week, Saturdays until 2pm and they are closed Sundays. Bakeries are usually open at least by 7am.

On the first Saturday of every month (Langer Samstag) and for 4 weeks before Christmas, shops may remain open until 6pm.

Museums and historic monuments are usually closed Mondays and admission charges for museums vary greatly. For the most part village churches are open during the day, if locked then check the notice board for the address of the Küster or whoever else might hold the key (Schlüssel). Large churches, cathedrals, and monasteries may have set opening times and if they are not pinned up by the main entrance then inquire at the Verkehrsamt. Visitors should refrain from taking photos during services; especially with a flash. At some of the more important places there are often booklets or leaflets available in English.

Chemists

Open during normal business hours. Usually clearly visible at the shop front are details of which chemist is on night or Sunday duty (Apothekennotdienst or simply Notdienst). This information is also found in the local newspapers.

Medicines on doctor's prescription are only available from the chemist. No prescription is necessary for aspirins and other mild medication. A Drogerie (Drug Store) sells things like insect repellants, vitamin tablets etc.

There are several international pharmacies in München including Bahnhof-Apotheke, Bahnhofplatz 2; Internationale Lerchen-Apotheke, Schleissheimer Strasse 201 (including homeopathic preparations); Internationale Ludwigs-Apotheke, Neuhauser Strasse 8.

Climate

In an area as large as Bavaria, there are considerable variations of climate; the summers are usually warm or very warm and the winters can be severe. In the Alpine regions of the south, snow may persist for about 6 months of the year and in the east and north-east, even though the snow may not last as long, temperatures can remain low for many months with markedly longer winters and shorter summers in consequence. As one moves west and north-west the severest winter conditions are likely to be tempered a little by milder air coming in from the Atlantic and the vineyards

Average monthly rainfall

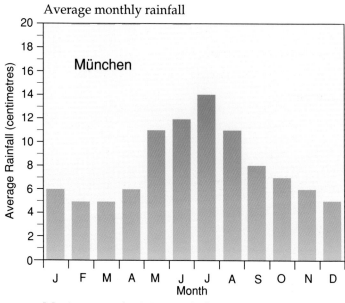

München

Maximum and minimum daily temperatures

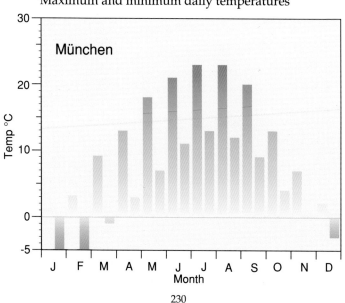

München

which flourish along the River Main are further evidence of climatic variety.

Consulates & Embassies

The main German consulates and embassies abroad are:

Australia
German Embassy
119 Empire Circuit
Yarraluml ACT 2600, Canberra
☎ 062-701911

Canada
German Embassy
1 Waverley Street
Ottawa, Ontario K2P 0T8
☎ 613-2321101

German Consul General
77 Admiral Road
Toronto, Ontario M5R 2L4
☎ 416-9252813

New Zealand
German Embassy
90-92 Hobson Street
Thornton, Wellington
☎ 850289

UK
German Embassy
23 Belgrave Square
London SW1 X8PZ
☎ 071-2355033

German Consul General
16 Eglinton Crescent
Edinburgh EH12 5D9
☎ 031-3372323

USA
German Embassy
4645 Reservoir Road NW
Washington DC
☎ 202-2984000

German Consul General
460 Park Avenue
New York NY
☎ 212-3088700

Main foreign embassies in Germany and consulates in Bavaria:

Australian Embassy
2 Godesberger Allee 107
53175 Bonn
☎ 0228-81030

Canadian Embassy
Friedrich-Wilhelm-Strasse 18
53113 Bonn
☎ 0228-231061

Canadian Consulate
Tal 29
80331 München
☎ 089-222661

New Zealand Embassy
Bonn Zentrum
53113 Bonn
☎ 0228-214021

British Embassy
Friedrich-Ebert-Allee 77
53113 Bonn
☎ 0228-234061

British Consul General
Bürkleinstrasse 10
80538 München
☎ 089-211090

United States Embassy	US Consul-General
Deichmanns Aue 2	Königinstrasse 5
53179 Bonn	80539 München
☎ 0228-3391	☎ 089-28880

Other embassies are listed in the telephone book under 'Botschaften'.

Credit Cards & Currency

The German unit of currency is the Deutsche Mark (DM). 100 Pfennigs (Pf) = 1DM. It is freely convertible ie, it can be exchanged for any foreign currency at any time at the going rate. You can bring as much currency as you wish into Germany.

The Deutsche Mark comes in **notes** of DM10, 20, 50, 100, 200, 500 and 1,000; **coins** of 1, 2, 5, 10 and 50 Pfennige, 1, 2 and 5 Marks.

Major credit cards (Visa, Mastercard, American Express, etc) and UK debit cards are widely accepted especially in large cities and major tourist centres, in hotels and at most filling stations on main roads. Many cashpoints have a button for display of instructions in English. British EC (Eurocheque) cards cannot be used in Greman EC cashpoints.

All banks exchange traveller's cheques. If the cheques are in Deutschmarks the full face value will be given. If they are in a foreign currency the bank will make a service charge of around 2 per cent. Larger banks will also give cash advances against major credit cards, usually subject to a DM100 minimum.

Eurocheques, together with a cheque card, are used like ordinary domestic cheques and must be made out in the local currency. Eurocheques can be used for all business transactions but petrol stations make a small additional charge. These cheques can only be cashed up to a value of 400DM per transaction. Scottish bank notes are not accepted for exchange nor are foreign coins.

Bureaux de change: at airports, main railway stations and border crossings. Open: usually 6am-10pm.

Customs Regulations

There are no restrictions on the import/export of German or any other currency. Goods, including foodstuffs, for personal use during a visit may be imported but there are restrictions on he amount of tobacco, spirits, coffee, tea and perfumes which may be imported duty free from outside the European Union (EU). The following is a broad guide to duty free allowances for adults:

Tobacco: 200 cigarettes, 250g tobacco. Spirits: 1 litre 22‰ or 2 litres less than 22‰ or 3 litres liquors, fortified wine, etc. Coffee: 250g beans or 100g instant. Tea: 100g leaf or 40g instant. Perfume/ toilet water: 50g perfume and 0.251 toilet water.

For practical purposes there are no restrictions on what citizens of the EU may export from Germany for personal use but if in doubt, inquire at 'home' airports or seaports. Citizens of other countries should consult the domestic regulations as to what they are allowed to import. The import/export of drugs (other than for personal medical purposes) is prohibited everywhere.

Cycling & Cycle Hire

From April to October cycles may be hired at more than eighty railway stations of the DB or Münchner S-bahn; cyclists arriving by train pay only half the normal charge. Local tourist information offices can provide addresses of private hirers. Write to main tourist offices for cycling suggestions in the areas they cover. Organisations offering *Radeln ohne Gepäck* (cycling without luggage) holidays include Arbeitsgemeinschaft Fernwanderwege im Voralpenland, Von-Kühlmann-Strasse 15, 86899 Landsberg (particularly the area covered by König-Ludwig-Weg, Lech-Höhenweg and Prälatenweg — see 'Long Distance Paths'), the Fremdenverkehrsverband at the same address (Ammersee and Lech valley) and 'Leo'Aktiv Reisen GmbH, Söckinger Strasse 1, 82319 Starnberg (Upper Bavaria and Allgäu).

In München guided tours of the city by bicycle are provided by:
City Hopper Touren, Stefanie Pokorny
Hohenzollernstrasse 95, 80796 München
☎ 089-2721131
Daily tours (weather permitting) by arrangement

Radius Touristik
Arnulfstrasse 3, (In Hauptbahnhof near platform 31)
80335 München
☎ 089-596113
Open: daily May to September 10am-6pm. Cycle tours on Saturdays May to September include guided tour of Schloss Nymphenburg. Also tours on foot and by tram Monday, Thursday and Saturday. Cycles for hire — 100 machines at the Hauptbahnhof and 50 more at the Englischer Garten (Königinstrasse entrance)

Cycles may be taken by train, other than IC, EC and ICE services. A ticket (*Fahrrad-Karte*) must be purchased. Owner responsible for taking machine to luggage van (*Gepäckwagen*).

Documents

Nationals of the UK and other EU countries require no visa but a valid passport. Holders of Australian, USA, Canadian and New Zealand passports do not need a visa provided they do not take up employment and their stay does not exceed 3 months.

Electricity

Electricity operates at 220 volts AC 50 Hertz. Round ended, two pronged continental adaptors are needed for UK/USA appliances. Note that the adaptor should be constructed so as to fit into recessed sockets.

Facilities for the Disabled

Facilities for the disabled are fairly good in Germany. Facilities are usually indicated by the blue pictogram of a person in a wheelchair. Most motorway service stops have toilet facilities for the handicapped and there are usually reserved parking places for people in wheelchairs in multi-storey car parks and elsewhere. Most important museums and public buildings are accessible for the handicapped. Town guides for the handicapped are available (free) at tourist offices in major cities and are mostly bilingual.

Helpful information may also be forthcoming from:
Zentrale Verkaufsleitung der DB
(Kontaktstelle für Behindertenfragen)
Rhabanusstrasse 3, 55118 Mainz
☎ 06131-155216
Information about German Federal Railways' facilities for handicapped. The *Reiseführer für unsere behinderten Fahrgäste* (Guide for disabled passengers) partly in English is available from stations, DB Agencies and DER offices.

Gesellschaft für Nebenbetriebe (GfN) der Bundesautobahn
Poppelsdorfer Allee 24, 53115 Bonn ☎ 0228-7090
For the pamphlet *Autobahn-Service für Behinderte* (Motorway Service for the disabled). Also available at *Autobahn* service areas.

In München:
Infozentrale für Behinderte (Information Centre for the disabled).
☎ 089-21171

Language

Although English is quite widely spoken it is a good idea to get a good phrase book such as *Berlitz Language Guide: German for Travellers* or *Language Guide Germany* by Polyglott. Even mastery of the very simplest phrases produces a positive response. Note that 'ß' is sometimes used in German to represent a double 's'. Double 's' is used in this book. What follows is a list of words frequently used in the text and encountered when touring.

Abtei — abbey
Autobahn (A-) — motorway
Bad (spa) — health resort with medical facilities/treatment
Bundesstrasse (B-) — Federal road
Burg — castle or fortress
Deutsche Bundesbahn (DB) — Federal railway
Dult — seasonal fair/market
Dom — cathedral
Fasching, Fastnacht, Fasnacht etc — carnival time prior to Lent
Freibad (beheizt) — Open air swimming pool (heated)
Gaststätte — restaurant
Hallenbad — indoor swimming pool
Hallenwellenbad — indoor swimming pool with artificial waves
Hauptbahnhof — principal railway station
Heimatabend — traditional folk evening
Heimatmuseum — local museum
Hof — courtyard or sometimes superior hotel; often compounded
     with other words to mean court or royal, eg *Hofgarten*
Kapelle— chapel
Kirche — church
Kloster — monastery, nunnery, convent, etc. plural *Klöster*
Kurort/Luftkurort — health resorts with medical facilities/treat-
     ment
Münster — minster
Platz — square. Thus *Marktplatz, Stadtplatz*, etc.
Rathaus — town hall
Ruhetag — rest day for restaurant, etc.
Schloss — palace or residential castle, plural *Schlösser*

See — lake
Strasse — road / street
Tal — valley. Usually combined with river name, eg Inntal
Trimm-Dich or *Sport-pfad* — keep-fit circuit, usually in the woods
Wanderparkplatz — car park with access to walking area
Wanderweg — rambling route
Wallfahrtskirche — pilgrimage church
Wellenfreibad — open-air swimming pool with waves
Wildgehege — enclosure for deer, boars, etc

Measurements

The metric system is used in Germany. The following conversions may be helpful to the foreign tourist

1 foot (12 inches) = 0.305 metre
1 yard (3 feet) = 0.914 metre
1 mile (1760 yards) = 1.609 kilometres
1 centimetre (10mm) = 0.394 inch
1 metre (1000mm) = 1.094 yards
1 kilometre (1000m) = 0.621 mile
1 acre (4840sq yd) = 0.405 hectare
1 sq mile (640 acres) = 259 hectares
1 hectare = 2.471 acres
1 sq kilometre = 0.386sq mile
1 pint (British) = 0.568 litre
1 pint (American) = 0.473 litre
1 gallon (British) = 4.546 litres
1 gallon (American) = 3.785 litres
1 ton (British) = 1.016 tonnes
1 ton (American) = 0.907 tonnes
1 kilogram = 2.205 pounds
1 tonne = 0.984 ton (British)

Personal Insurance & Medical Cover

Visitors from the UK are covered by reciprocal agreements when in Germany. They require an E111 form, obtainable from post offices or DSS office. If medical treatment is required Form E111 must be validated at the local AOK (*Allgemeine Ortskrankenkasse*); the address is in the telephone book. Nationals of other countries should have adequate medical cover before departing.

Doctors' (*Arzt*) and dentists' (*Zahnarzt*) hours are normally 10am-12noon and 4-6pm, except Wednesdays, Saturdays and Sundays. In some cases they may be open earlier and longer, depending on the doctor. To call an ambulance dial 110. For the ADAC Ambulance Service Munich and Telephone Doctor (*Telefonarzt*) ☎ (089) 76762244. This service is offered daily 8am-8pm and during the main holiday season 7am-11pm. The Telephone Doctor gives advice on medicaments for less serious problems.

Photography

All the main brands of film (Agfa, Fuji, Kodak) are readily available. Prices for all brands of film are reasonable but the cheapest name-brand is Agfa. Shops belonging to the chains of Porst and Quelle sell even cheaper 'no-name' film. Look out for multi-buy bargains everywhere. Film for slides (*Dias*) does not always include processing in the price, so check the carton details.

The best time of the day for photos is the early morning or late afternoon. In summer the light can be very hazy, some of the clearest weather being in autumn and spring.

Public Holidays

1 January *Neujahr* (New Year's Day)
6 January *Heilige Drei Könige* (Epiphany)
Karfreitag (Good Friday)
Faschingsdienstag (Shrove Tuesday) (Many museums and public buildings closed.)
Ostermontag (Easter Monday)
1 May *Tag der Arbeit* (May Day, Labour Day)
Pfingstmontag (Whit Monday)
Fronleichnam (Corpus Christi. In areas with mainly Catholic population.)
15 August *Mariae Himmelfahrt* (Assumption of Mary. In areas with mainly Catholic population.)
3 October *Tag der deutschen Einheit* (Day of German Unity)
1 November *Allerheiligen* (All Saints Day)
Buss- und Bettag (Repentence Day. In areas with mainly Protestant population)
Weihnachten (Christmas)
31 December *Sylvester* (New Year's Eve. Most museums and public buildings closed. Many businesses close around mid-day.)

Public Transport

Rail

Rail services are operated mainly by the Federal Railway, Deutsche Bundesbahn (DB). Leaflets giving details of local services available at stations, also free booklet timetables *Städteverbindungen* for journeys between main centres. Tickets for journeys up to 100km should be obtained from automatic machines where provided; these accept coins, also notes of DM 10 and 20 and give change if exact fare is not inserted. Children 4-11 pay half fare. Numerous 'Saver' and 'Super-Saver' fares are also available. For foreign visitors planning to use rail travel for their holiday, there is the choice of the German Rail Pass covering the whole country or a Regional Pass covering specified areas. Both can only be purchased in the visitor's home country and the Regional Passes only in Great Britain and Ireland. German Rail Pass holders may also use the coaches of DB subsidiary Deutsche Touring GmbH (DTG) which has a dozen or so tourist routes including the Romantische Strasse. Two Regional Passes cover virtually the whole of Bavaria, number 113 Nürnberg-Franconia-Bavarian Forest and number 114 München-Bavarian Alps.

General rail travel information can be obtained locally from DB stations and agencies.

For information about German Rail and Regional Passes. No personal callers:
German Rail
Suite 118, Hudson Place
Victoria Station
London SW1V 1JL

For coach service details and bookings:
Deutsche Touring GmbH
Am Römerhof 17
60486 Frankfurt
☎ 069-7903248

Europabus DTG
Arnulfstrasse 3 (Hauptbahnhof)
80335 München
☎ 089-591824

For sale of German Rail, Regional Passes and other tickets:

DER Travel Service
German Rail Sales
16 Conduit Street
London W1R 9TD
☎ 071-499-0577/8

Eurotrain
34 Lower Abbey Street
Dublin 1
☎ 01-787382
Also main travel agencies in the UK and Ireland.

Information about public transport in and around München:
Münchner Verkehr- und Tarifverband (MVV)
Thierschstrasse 2
80358 München
☎ 089-238030

Visitors arriving/departing by air can use the S-bahn service between München city centre and Franz-Josef-Strauss airport — trains every 20 minutes from about 4am until 12.30am. There is also a bus link from Kiefersgarten underground station (line 6) in the northern part of the city. First bus from city 4am, from airport 7am then every 40 minutes until 7pm outwards, 8.20pm inwards.

River and Lake Boat Services
On the Rivers Altmühl and Donau (see Chapter 7), Kelheim-Weltenburg, April to October; Kelheim-Riedenburg, Dietfurt, Beilngries and Berching, May to early October; Regensburg-Walhalla, June to September; Regensburg-Straubing, some Sundays in August; Deggendorf-Passau-Obernzell, mid-May to September; Passau-Linz (Austria), mid-April to about mid-October.

On the River Main (see Chapter 8), Aschaffenburg-Bamberg etc, high season and charter sailings.

State-owned vessels sail on the Bavarian lakes of Königsee and Tegernsee, year-round, weather permitting; on Ammersee and Starnberger See, April to October (see Chapters 2 and 3). There are privately-owned vessels on the Chiemsee (see Chapter 5), year round, weather permitting and on a number of the smaller lakes in the summer months. For further information:

'Tourist Information'
93309 Kelheim
☎ 09441-701234

Staatliche Schiffahrt
Seestrasse 70
83684 Tegernsee
☎ 08022-4760
or
Seestrasse 56
83471 Königssee
☎ 08652-4026

or
Dampfschiffstrasse 5
82319 Starnberg
☎ 08151-12023
or
79252 Stegen/Ammersee
☎ 08143-229

Donauschiffahrt
Wurm und Köck
Höllgasse 26
94032 Passau
☎ 0851-929292

Fränkische Personenschiffahrt
Kranenkai 1
97070 Würzburg
☎ 0931-55356

Chiemsee-Schiffahrt Ludwig
Fessler
83209 Prien
☎ 08051-1510

Telephones

In the main post offices you can use the direct phone service. Ask at the counter marked Ferngespräche for a phone booth. You pay at the counter when you have finished your phone call. This is much more convenient than queuing for a pay phone and saves having to find change.

International calls can be made from post offices and phone booths with a phone marked 'Auslandsgespräche'.

Coins that can be used for international calls are: 10 Pfennig (minimum 30Pfg), 1DM, 5DM. A much more comfortable way of telephoning is with a Telefonkarte. These cards are available at post offices and obviously solve the problem of small change. Telephone booths which accept these cards are usually marked 'Kartentelefon' — they are becoming more widespread but may not yet exist in smaller towns or villages.

Instructions on how to use payphones are written in English in phone booths for international calls.

Telephone call rates are cheaper after 8pm and at weekends. This does not apply to calls outside Germany.

When dialling from Germany remember after dialling the national code to omit the first zero of the number you are ringing.

International directory inquiries 0 01 18 (Also for language difficulties in finding a number in an emergency.) National directory inquiries 11 88 or 0 11 88

Emergency Numbers
Police and accidents 110
Fire brigade 112

Main international direct dialling codes:

Australia 00 61
Britain 0044
Irish Republic 00 353
New Zealand 00 64
USA and Canada 00 1

Theft

In the event of property, money, credit cards, etc being stolen or lost, the first priority is to inform the police. If appropriate the hotel staff may be prepared to do this for you. Observe the instructions regarding loss which are provided with traveller's cheques and credit cards. If travel insurance has been taken out, advise the company direct or its representative in Germany.

Tourist Offices

The main German National Tourist Offices are:

Australia
Lufthansa House
12th Floor
143 Macquarie Street
Sydney 2000
☎ (02) 221-1008

Canada
175 Bloor Street East
North Tower, 6th Floor
Toronto, Ontario M4 W3R8
☎ (416) 968-1570

Germany
Deutsche Zentrale für
  Tourismus eV (DZT)
Beethovenstrasse 69
60325 Frankfurt
☎ (069) 7572-0
(general information)

UK
Nightingale House
65 Curzon Street
London W1Y 7PE
☎ (071) 4953990/1

USA
444 South Flower Street
Suite 2230
Los Angeles CA 90071
☎ (213) 688-73 32

747 Third Avenue
33rd Floor
New York
NY 10017
☎ (212) 308-3300

Travel

Air

All major international airlines have direct flights to Frankfurt and many, also to München. There is also a major airport at Nürnberg. There are more than 60 direct flights from the UK to München each week and a daily service from London (Heathrow) to Nürnberg. There are regular domestic flights between all German airports. In München the S-bahn provides a direct link between the city centre and the airport (*Flughafen*). In Nürnberg service bus number 32 connects the airport to the city (Fritz-Munkert-Platz), then tram number 2 to Hauptbahnhof. There is also a direct bus between the station and the airport every two hours.

Sea

Motorists travelling from Scotland or northern England may find the North Sea Ferries services from Hull to Rotterdam or Zeebrugge (14 hours) a convenient connection. On the east coast there are the shorter Felixstowe to Zeebrugge and Harwich to the Hook of Holland routes (7-8 hours), operated by P&O Ferries and Sealink Stena Line respectively. South of the Thames crossings can be made from Ramsgate to Ostend with Belgium Railways Maritime and there are day and night crossings from Dover to Zeebrugge with P&O Ferries taking about 4 hours. Finally there are many sailings on the short sea route from Dover to Calais with P&O Ferries and Sealink Stena Line.

The majority of rail travellers will go via London and cross from Harwich to the Hook of Holland or from Ramsgate to Ostend.

The European ports have good motorway connections to Bavaria. After crossing the low countries, join the German *Autobahn* network at Aachen and follow A4 eastwards towards Köln (Cologne). If destined for northern or eastern Bavaria, continue to junction with A3 and follow this motorway past Frankfurt and all the way to Würzburg, Nürnberg, Regensburg and Passau. If München and southern Bavaria are the goal, leave A4 at Kerpen, 40km (25 miles) from Aachen and join the A61 via Koblenz and Ludwigshafen to the Hockenheim triangle, there to join A6 to Heilbronn, then A81 to Stuttgart and A8 to München. (This route is usually preferable to that from Hockenheim to Karlsruhe via A5 but observe illuminated road-side signs giving guidance as to the best alternative).

Some distances are:
Dunkirk to Frankfurt am Main 578km (359 miles)
Dunkirk to München 969km (602 miles)

P&O European Ferries
Russell Street
Dover CT16 1QB
☎ (0304) 203388

Car Ferry Terminal
The Docks
Felixstowe IP11 8TB
☎ (0394) 604802

The Continental Ferry Port
Mile End
Portsmouth PO2 8QW
☎ (0705) 827677

Graf-Adolf-Strasse 41
40210 Düsseldorf
☎ (0211) 387060

Sally Line
Argyle Centre, York Street
Ramsgate CT11 9DS
☎ (0843) 595566

Münchener Strasse 48
D-60329 Frankfurt 1
☎ (069) 250197 or 236798

Motoring

At the Filling Station (Tankstelle)
Unleaded (*bleifrei*) petrol is now the norm in Germany. There are two grades, 'Benzin' (normal) and 'Super' while a third grade, 'Super-Plus', is gradually being introduced. Leaded petrol is also available everywhere.

Vehicle Lights
Left-dipping headlights must be adjusted to dip to the right. Cars may not be driven on sidelights and headlights must be used, even during daylight hours, if visibility is impaired by fog, snow, rain, etc. Rear fog lights may be used if visibility is less than 50m (160ft) but not in built-up areas.

Documentation
There are no special requirements for private cars. The Vehicle Registration Document should be carried and although not obligatory for citizens of the EU, the possession of an insurance 'Green Card' may well help to avoid complications in the event of an accident.

On the Road
All traffic drives on the right-hand side of the road. General speed restrictions are 50km per hour (31mph) in built-up areas; 100kph (62mph) on ordinary roads outside built-up areas; 130kph (81mph) (recommended) on *Autobahnen*. These speeds are not indicated by signs but variations from them are shown in km per hour. The rectangular yellow sign bearing the place name denotes the entrance to a built-up area and the similar sign with a diagonal stripe indicates the exit from this. Place names on a green sign do not constitute a speed restriction.

Other than on minor roads in rural areas and in residential streets in built-up areas, priority is indicated on signs approaching a junction. Special care is needed in residential areas as many previous priority signs have been removed and 'priority from the right' applies. Traffic on a *Bundesstrasse* (state main road) always has priority. *Bundesstrassen* are recognised by a small rectangular yellow plate bearing the road number. Priority is shown elsewhere by a yellow square with white border set on its corner while the same sign with diagonal black line indicates the end of priority. Standard 'Give Way' or 'Stop' signs will be found on converging roads.

Parking is forbidden on main roads or those with fast moving traffic, on or near tram lines, near bus or tram stops, traffic lights, taxi ranks and intersections. It is also forbidden to park on the 'wrong' side of the road, except in one-way streets.

The German police are very strict on tyre condition and a vehicle found with less than 2mm tread depth over the whole surface will not be allowed to proceed until the tyres have been replaced.

Warning triangles are compulsory and must be placed 100m behind a broken-down vehicle (200m on an *Autobahn*).

The German motoring association is ADAC (*Allgemeiner Deutscher Automobil-Club*) and members of associated organisations will be given advice or assistance should the need arise. ADAC operates a road patrol service with yellow patrol vehicles recognised by the word *Strassenwacht* on the front. The organisation has a central telephone information office in München:
ADAC-Informationszentrale, ☎ 089 505061
and travel centres (ADAC-Reise Center) operated by agents at:
Ridlersrasse 35 (☎ 089 5195331),
Sendlinger-Tor-Platz 9 (☎ 089 595450),
Frankfurter Ring 30 (☎ 089 3597891)
Elsässer-/Ecke Orleansstrasse (Ostbahnhof) (☎ 089 4488715).

Motorway telephones are clearly indicated and may be used by the motorist in distress to communicate with the police who will, if appropriate, inform the ADAC patrol. Emergency telephones are now gradually being installed on other main roads.

Traffic signs, in general, conform to international standards but the meanings of the following signs should be memorised:

Ausfahrt — Exit from motorway or dual carriageway
Bankett nicht befahrbar — Soft verges
Einbahnstrasse —One-way street
Einordnen — Get in lane
Freie Fahrt — End of restrictions, usually after passing roadworks
Gegenverkehr — Oncoming traffic
Glatteisgefahr — Danger of icy road
Langsam fahren — Drive slowly
Rollsplit — Loose chippings

Umleitung (on yellow arrow) — Traffic diversion
Links/Rechts fahren — Drive on the left/right

Accidents

All accidents must be reported to the police, even if no personal injuries. If another vehicle involved, complete European Accident Statement (provided by Insurance Company issuing Green Card) in conjunction with other driver. Obtain names and addresses of witnesses. Make a note of police and motoring organisation representatives who attend at the scene.

Car Hire (Autovermietung)

The principal international car hire firms have offices at airports and at many of the bigger railway stations. There are various lower and upper age limits for hirers but, in general, the lower limit is 21 years. In München there are also many independent rental firms and Unix-Rent, Autovermietung, Pasing GmbH, Gotthardstrasse 38, 80686 München (☎ 089-5500177) offers a chauffeur-driven service. It is wise to ensure that the rental contract includes Collision Damage Waiver (CDW).

Autoreisezug (Motorail)

German Federal Rail's service links up with the European network. By night passengers travel in sleeping-cars or couchettes and by day in first class carriages. Cars are carried on the same train. An overall charge is made for car and driver, with reduced rates for accompanying passengers. See also 'Public Transport'.

Current information about Motorail services and rail travel generally can be obtained from:

Germany
Deutsches Reisebüro GmbH
Eschersheimer Landstrasse 25-27
60322 Frankfurt
☎ (069) 1566-289/345

UK
DER Travel Service
18 Conduit Street
London W1R 9TD
☎ 071 499 0577/8

USA
DER Travel Service Inc
230 Park Avenue, Suite 1511
New York

New World Travel Inc
747 Third Avenue, 18th Floor
New York
NY 10017

Canada
DER Travel Service Ltd
1290 Bay Street
Toronto , Ontario M5R2C3

Youth Hostels

German youth hostels have a
high reputation and there are
many in Bavaria. A complete
list of hostels in Germany can

be obtained by sending eight International Reply Coupons or
DM6.50 to Deutsches Jugendherbergswerk, Hauptverband,
Bismarckstrasse 8, 32756 Detmold. Details of all European hostels,
including Germany, are included in *Hostelling International: Budget
Accommodation* Vol 1, published by the International Youth Hostel
Federation and available through all good bookshops. US visitors
should contact American Youth Hostels Inc, 1332 'I' Street NW,
Washington, DC 20005, ☎ (202) 783 61 61.

Hostels in Germany can be recognised by a green triangle with
the letters DJH (Deutsche Jugendherberge). DJH has two conventional hostels in München with 645 beds together with a Youth
Guest House (344 beds) for bed and breakfast at Miesingstrasse 4,
81379 München, ☎ 089-7236560. There are three other hostels
within 35km of München. In the capital, further accommodation
is available for young people at:

Haus International/Jugend-Gästehaus
Elisabethstrasse 87
80797 München
☎ 089-120060
Underground line 8 to Hohenzollernplatz. 480 beds.

Christlicher Verein junger Männer (CVJM) /Jugend-Gästehaus
Landwehrstrasse 13
80336 München
☎ 089-5521410
Underground lines 1, 3, 6 or 8 to Sendlinger Tor or 5 minutes on
foot from the *Hauptbahnhof*. 80 beds. Similar to YMCA but
women can also be accommodated. Reductions for groups.

Jugendhotel für weibliche Jugendliche
Goethestrasse 9
80336 München
☎ 089-555891.
At the *Hauptbahnhof*. 26 beds. Women only up to 25 years.

Sportschule Grünwald
Ebertstrasse 1
82031 Grünwald
☎ 089-641440.
Tram line 25, about 50 minutes journey from *Hauptbahnhof*. Only
for pre-arranged groups.

In the *Oberpfälzerwald* in addition to youth hostels there are:

Tagungshaus Stützelvilla
Bahnhofstrasse 29
92670 Windischeschenbach
200m from station. Information and booking: Kreisjugendring,
Landratsamt, 92660 Neustadt a.d.Waldnaab., ☎ 09602-79268.
50 beds. Suitable for school parties, holiday groups, conferences,
etc.

Pfreimdtalhütte des Oberpfälzer Waldvereins
Augustin Waldtraud
Tanzmühle 2
92723 Tännesberg
☎ 09655-313
One family room (6 beds) and two 8-bed rooms for youth groups.
Specially suitable as a base for rambling parties.

INDEX

A Note to the Reader

Thank you for buying this book, we hope it has helped you to enjoy your visit to Bavaria. We have worked hard to produce a guidebook which is as accurate as possible. With this in mind, any comments, suggestions or useful information you may have would be appreciated.

Please send your letters to:
The Editor
Moorland Publishing Co Ltd
Moor Farm Road West
Ashbourne
Derbyshire
DE6 1HD

MPC The Travel Specialists

MPC Visitor's Guides To
GERMANY
& Surrounding Countries

MPC Visitors Guides to:

Austria
Austria: Tyrol & Vorarlberg
Belgium & Luxembourg*
Czechoslovakia
France (and many regional
  guides)
Denmark
Holland

Northern Italy
Germany:
  Northern Germany
  Southern Germany
Bavaria
Black Forest
Rhine & Mosel
*available 1995

MPC *Visitor's Guides* bring important practical details to your fingertips. Most of them are based upon itineraries, recognising that you may wish to tour around and take in the major places of interest.

Our unique system of symbols readily identify particular features in the text and on the maps. Each chapter finishes with lists of addresses and phone numbers we think may be of help to you. Additionally our Fact File highlights the essential information you need to know about accommodation, currency and credit cards, travel etc.

Our production team works hard to produce user-friendly guides with you in mind. We hope this helps to make your visit more rewarding.

Visitor's Guides are produced in three categories:

Country Traveller covering particular countries and printed in full colour in a larger format.

Regional Traveller Printed in a handy pocket size and in full colour. These books cover particular areas or states within a country.

Holiday Islands Detailed information on far away islands where dreams are made! They are in the same format as the *Regional Traveller* and ideal for packing in your travel bags.

Visitor's Guides

Itinerary based guides for independent travellers

MPC

America:
American South West
California
Florida
Orlando & Central
    Florida
USA

Austria:
Austria
Austria: Tyrol &
    Vorarlberg

Britain:
Cornwall & Isles of
    Scilly
Cotswolds
Devon
East Anglia
Hampshire & Isle of
    Wight
Kent
Lake District
Scotland: Lowlands
Somerset, Dorset &
    Wiltshire
North Wales &
    Snowdonia
North York Moors,
    York & Coast
Northern Ireland
Northumbria
Peak District
Treasure Houses of
    England
Yorkshire Dales &
    North Pennines

Canada
Czechoslovakia

Denmark
Egypt

France:
Champagne &
    Alsace-Lorraine
France
Alps & Jura
Brittany
Burgundy &
    Beaujolais
Dordogne
Loire
Massif Central
Normandy
Normandy Landing
    Beaches
Provence & Côte
    d'Azur

Germany:
Bavaria
Black Forest
Northern Germany
Rhine & Mosel
Southern Germany

Greece:
Greece (mainland)
Athens &
    Peloponnese

Holland
Hungary
Iceland & Greenland

India:
Delhi, Agra & Rajasthan
Goa

Ireland

Islands:
Corsica
Crete
Cyprus
Gran Canaria
Guernsey,
    Alderney & Sark
Jersey
Madeira
Mallorca, Menorca,
    Ibiza &
    Formentera
Malta & Gozo
Mauritius, Rodrigues
    & Reunion
Rhodes
Sardinia
Seychelles
Tenerife

Italy:
Florence & Tuscany
Italian Lakes
Northern Italy
Southern Italy

Norway
Peru
Portugal

Spain:
Costa Brava
    & Costa Blanca
Northern & Central
    Spain
Southern Spain
    & Costa del Sol

Sweden
Switzerland
Turkey

MPC Visitor's Guides are available through all good bookshops. Free
catalogue available upon request from Moorland Publishing Co Ltd, Moor
Farm Rd, Ashbourne, Derbyshire DE6 1HD, England ☎ 01335 344486.

Mail Order In case of local difficulty, you may order direct (quoting your
Visa/Access number) from Grantham Book Services on ☎ 01476 67421.
Ask for the cash sales department. There is a small charge for postage and
packing.